Philosophers in Depth

Series Editors: **Stephen Boulter** and **Constantine Sandis**

Philosophers in Depth is a series of themed edited collections focusing on particular aspects of the thought of major figures from the history of philosophy. The volumes showcase a combination of newly commissioned and previously published work with the aim of deepening our understanding of the topics covered. Each book stands alone, but taken together the series will amount to a vast collection of critical essays covering the history of philosophy, exploring issues that are central to the ideas of individual philosophers. This project was launched with the financial support of the Institute for Historical and Cultural Research at Oxford Brookes University, for which we are very grateful.

Constantine Sandis and Stephen Boulter
Oxford

Titles include:

Leonard Kahn (*editor*)
MILL ON JUSTICE

Arto Laitinen and Constantine Sandis (*editors*)
HEGEL ON ACTION

Katherine Morris (*editor*)
SARTRE ON THE BODY

Charles R. Pigden (*editor*)
HUME ON MOTIVATION AND VIRTUE

Sabine Roeser
REID ON ETHICS

Daniel Whiting (*editor*)
THE LATER WITTGENSTEIN ON LANGUAGE

Forthcoming titles:

Alison Denham (*editor*)
PLATO ON ART

Pierre Destree (*editor*)
ARISTOTLE ON AESTHETICS

Philip Goff (*editor*)
SPINOZA ON MONISM

Henrik Rydenfelt and Sami Pihlström (*editors*)
JAMES ON RELIGION

AF631508

Philosophers in Depth
Series Standing Order ISBN 978–0–230–55411–5 Hardback
978–0–230–55412–2 Paperback
(*outside North America only*)

You can receive future titles in this series as they are published by placing a standing order. Please contact your bookseller or, in case of difficulty, write to us at the address below with your name and address, the title of the series and one of the ISBN is quoted above.

Customer Services Department, Macmillan Distribution Ltd, Houndmills, Basingstoke, Hampshire RG21 6XS, England

---

Also by Leonard Kahn

MORALITY AND MOTIVATION

J.S. MILL'S 'ON LIBERTY' AND OTHER ESSAYS (*editor*)

Mill on Justice

Edited by

Leonard Kahn
United States Air Force Academy, Colorado, USA

palgrave
macmillan

© Leonard Kahn 2012
Chapters © their individual authors 2012
Softcover reprint of the hardcover 1st edition 2012 978-0-230-57698-8

All rights reserved. No reproduction, copy or transmission of this publication may be made without written permission.

No portion of this publication may be reproduced, copied or transmitted save with written permission or in accordance with the provisions of the Copyright, Designs and Patents Act 1988, or under the terms of any licence permitting limited copying issued by the Copyright Licensing Agency, Saffron House, 6–10 Kirby Street, London EC1N 8TS.

Any person who does any unauthorized act in relation to this publication may be liable to criminal prosecution and civil claims for damages.

The authors have asserted their rights to be identified as the authors of this work in accordance with the Copyright, Designs and Patents Act 1988.

First published 2012 by
PALGRAVE MACMILLAN

Palgrave Macmillan in the UK is an imprint of Macmillan Publishers Limited, registered in England, company number 785998, of Houndmills, Basingstoke, Hampshire RG21 6XS.

Palgrave Macmillan in the US is a division of St Martin's Press LLC, 175 Fifth Avenue, New York, NY 10010.

Palgrave Macmillan is the global academic imprint of the above companies and has companies and representatives throughout the world.

Palgrave® and Macmillan® are registered trademarks in the United States, the United Kingdom, Europe and other countries.

ISBN 978-1-349-36681-1   ISBN 978-0-230-35497-5 (eBook)
DOI 10.1057/9780230354975

This book is printed on paper suitable for recycling and made from fully managed and sustained forest sources. Logging, pulping and manufacturing processes are expected to conform to the environmental regulations of the country of origin.

A catalogue record for this book is available from the British Library.

Library of Congress Cataloging-in-Publication Data

Mill on justice / edited by Leonard Kahn.
p. cm.
Includes index.
Summary: "John Stuart Mill was one of the most important figures in political philosophy but little has been published on his ideas on justice. This impressive collection by renowned Mill scholars addresses this gap in Mill studies and theories of justice" – Provided by publisher.
1. Justice. 2. Justice (Philosophy) 3. Mill, John Stuart, 1806– 1873 – Political and social views. I. Kahn, Leonard.

JC578.M49 2011
320.01′1—dc23   2011043421

10 9 8 7 6 5 4 3 2 1
21 20 19 18 17 16 15 14 13 12

Transferred to Digital Printing in 2012

To MLK and KJK

Contents

Acknowledgments

I am very grateful for the help of many people, some of whom I will, no doubt, forget to thank here. I apologize to them for my poor memory. As for those whom I do remember, I begin with the series editors of the *Philosophers in Depth* series, Stephen Boulter and Constantine Sandis, for their initial invitation to edit this volume. I must also mention Melanie Blair and especially Priyanka Gibbons at Palgrave Macmillan for their continued support and patience with me as this book sailed past one deadline after another. It almost goes without saying that I greatly appreciate those who contributed to this volume. Moreover, I am in the debt of David L. Brooks, who first introduced me to Mill's work, and to many philosophers over the last decade who have taken the time to discuss Mill's ideas with me, though here I must single out Roger Crisp, Carl Ficarrotta, Brad Hooker, Geoffrey Sayre-McCord, Nicholas Sturgeon, and Derek Parfit for their insightful contributions. My students at the U.S. Air Force Academy, both in my course on ethical theory and in my seminar on Mill's moral and political philosophy, have pushed me to clarify my interpretation of Mill and show why it is relevant; for this I am most thankful. Finally – and as always – I am grateful to Kimberly, without whom none of this would be possible.

Contributors

David O. Brink is Professor of Philosophy at the University of California, San Diego. He is also Director of the Institute for Law and Philosophy at the University of San Diego Law School and Editor of the journal *Legal Theory*. He is the author of *Perfectionism and the Common Good: Themes in the Philosophy of T.H. Green* (2003) and *Moral Realism and the Foundations of Ethics* (1989) as well as the editor of T.H. Green's *Prolegomena to Ethics* (2003). He has published articles in journals such as *Philosophical Review*, *Philosophy and Public Affairs*, and the *Journal of Philosophy*.

D. G. Brown was Professor Emeritus in the Philosophy Department at the University of British Columbia between 1955 and 1985 and a former Fellow of Magdalen College, Oxford (1952–5). He has published a number of papers on Mill, including 'Mill on Liberty and Morality,' *Philosophical Review* (1972) and 'Millian Liberalism and Colonial Oppression,' *Canadian Journal of Philosophy*, Supp. Vol. (1999). His current interests are in moral theory and practical reason.

Leonard Kahn earned his doctorate at Oxford University and is currently Assistant Professor of Philosophy at the United States Air Force Academy. He is currently working on a book titled *Morality and Motivation* as well as a number of papers on ethical theory, applied ethics, and political philosophy. He is also the editor of *'On Liberty' and Other Essays by John Stuart Mill*.

Dale E. Miller is Associate Professor in the Department of Philosophy and Religious Studies at Old Dominion University. He is the author of *J. S. Mill: Moral, Social and Political Thought* (2010) and coeditor of *John Stuart Mill and the Art of Life* (with Ben Eggleston and David Weinstein, 2010) and *Morality, Rules, and Consequences: A Critical Reader* (with Brad Hooker and Elinor Mason, 2000). His work has been widely published in journals such as *Ratio*, *Utilitas*, and *History of Political Thought*.

Jonathan Riley is Professor of Philosophy and Political Economy at Tulane University, New Orleans, LA. He has contributed more than 50 articles to edited volumes and journals such as *Ethics*, *American Political Science Review*, *Political Theory*, *Social Philosophy and Policy*, and *Utilitas*. His most recent book is *Mill's Radical Liberalism*. He is currently completing two new book manuscripts, one on Mill's utilitarianism and the other on the historical development of liberal moral and political philosophy after Mill. He is also a founding editor of the journal *Politics, Philosophy and Economics*.

William H. Shaw is Professor of Philosophy at San Jose State University. In addition to essays in a variety of professional journals, Shaw has edited or coedited six books and is the author of *Marx's Theory of History* (1978), *Moore on Right and Wrong: The Normative Ethics of G. E. Moore* (1995), *Contemporary Ethics: Taking Account of Utilitarianism* (1999), *Business Ethics* (6th ed., 2008), and *Moral Issues in Business* (with Vincent Barry, 11th ed., 2010).

Chin Liew Ten is Professor of Philosophy at the National University of Singapore. He is the author of *Mill on Liberty* (1980), *Crime, Guilt, and Punishment* (1987), *Mill's Moral, Political, and Legal Philosophy* (1999), *Was Mill a Liberal?* (2004), and *Theories of Rights* (2006). He is a Fellow of the Australian Academy of the Humanities of the Academy of Social Sciences in Australia. Ten serves on editorial boards on the *Australasian Journal of Philosophy, Utilitas*, the *Journal of Political Philosophy, Bioethics*, and the *Journal of Moral Philosophy*.

Henry West is Professor of Philosophy at Macalster College, Minnesota, USA. He is the author of *An Introduction to Mill's Utilitarian Ethics* (2004) and *Mill's Utilitarianism: A Reader's Guide* (2007), and the editor of *The Blackwell Guide to Mill's Utilitarianism* (2006). West's work has been published in journals such as *Mind, Ethics, Philosophical Review* and *Philosophy*.

Fred Wilson is Professor Emeritus at the University of Toronto, where he taught for 38 years. He has written widely on ontology, the philosophy of science, and the history of philosophy, including on authors such as Aristotle, Descartes, Newton, Hume, Mill, Spencer, F. H. Bradley, Bertrand Russell, and Gustav Bergmann. His work has been published in the *Journal of Philosophy, Mind, Philosophical Studies, Synthese, Journal of Business Ethics*, and *Philosophy of Science*. He has published books on the philosophy of science, and on Hume and Mill. His most recent volume is *The External World and Our Knowledge of It: Hume's Critical Realism, an Exposition and a Defense* (2008). In 1994 he was elected a Fellow of the Royal Society of Canada.

A Note on the Text

All references to work by John Stuart Mill are to the respective volumes of his collected works. For example, the first sentence of Chapter I of Mill's *Utilitarianism* is referenced as CW X, p. 205 since it is on page 205 of volume X of the collected works. Likewise the last sentence of Chapter V is referenced as CW X, p. 259.

Introduction: Mill on Justice

Leonard Kahn

1 The purpose of this volume

The concept of justice has recently been – and continues to be – one of the most vibrant and fruitful sources of work in ethics, political philosophy, and the philosophy of law. While the resurgence of interest in justice can be traced to John Rawls's *A Theory of Justice* (1971), the topic has taken on a life of its own. Of course, while Rawls (1993) and others (e.g., Nagel, 1991; Scanlon, 1998; and Daniels, 2007) continue to develop his versions of liberal egalitarianism and contractualism, many other theories of justice have flourished in this environment. These include right libertarian theories (e.g., Nozick, 1974), left libertarian theories (Otsuka, 2003), communitarian theories (e.g., Sandel, 1982 and 2009), and Marxist theories (e.g., Cohen 1995 and 2008), as well as alternative forums of social contract theory (e.g., Gauthier 1986; Skyrms, 1996; Binmore, 2005; and Parfit, 2011). While many of the developments of, and responses to, Rawls have focused on distributive justice, it is worth recalling that his theory was itself an attempt to find a replacement for utilitarianism (Rawls, 1971, pp. 19–24). Despite this fact, utilitarians, as well as consequentialists in general, have largely, though not entirely, stayed at the outskirts of work on justice.[1] This is unfortunate, not only because utilitarianism has much to say that is immediately relevant to Rawls and company but also because in some cases utilitarians offer a broader conception of justice which has much of value to offer moral philosophers of all stripes, if in some cases simply by way of sharpened challenges.

As all of the contributors to this volume would agree, the careful study of John Stuart Mill's theory of justice offers a step in the right direction. While there is much disagreement about the details of Mill's theory, on any reasonable interpretation it is sophisticated and illuminating. More controversially, many continue to find it a live option. In section 2 of this introduction, I provide a brief outline of Mill's account of justice, situating it in the context of his account of the other central moral concepts. In section 3, I consider some – but only some – of the interpretative and philosophical points regarding Mill's theory of justice in general and his theory of moral concepts in general made by the authors in the first section of this book. In section 4, I turn to the contributions which focus on comparisons between Mill's theory of justice and the theories of others made in the second section of the book.

2 Mill's moral concepts

The first part of this collection focuses on Mill's account of moral concepts – especially his view of moral rightness and wrongness, moral obligations or duties, moral rights, and, of course, justice, as well as the close relationship among them. In order better to understand the contributions in this part, it will be useful to say a word or two about these concepts.

Let us begin with moral rightness and moral wrongness. As Mill himself put the matter when stating his famous Principle of Utility,

> [A]ctions are right in proportion as they tend to promote happiness, wrong as they tend to produce the reverse of happiness. (CW X, 210)

But what exactly did Mill mean by this? Many interpreters of Mill, following J.O. Urmson (1953), have tried to answer this question by assimilating the Principle of Utility to either or the other of two versions of utilitarianism whose status has been widely debated since the middle of the twentieth century. In his chapter in this volume, David Brink helpfully presents these two versions of utilitarianism as follows:

> **Act Utilitarianism**: An act is right insofar as its consequences for the general happiness are at least as good as any alternative available to the agent.
>
> **Rule Utilitarianism**: An act is right insofar as it conforms to a rule whose acceptance value for the general happiness is at least as great as any alternative rule available to the agent. (1953, p. 104)[2]

As Roger Crisp (1997, p. 67) notes, the Principle of Utility initially lends itself more naturally to an act utilitarian, rather than a rule utilitarian, reading. That said, it is probably best to place heavy emphasis on the word 'initially' and see the Principle of Utility as Mill's *first* word on the moral rightness and wrongness of actions, not his *last* word. To begin with, the Principle of Utility is about the relation between, on one side, rightness and wrongness and, on the other side, the *tendency* to produce happiness and unhappiness. It would be too hasty to conclude that Mill thought that this relation is as simple and as straightforward as one might think. Another good reason for caution is Mill's claim that

> We do not call anything wrong, unless we mean to imply that a person ought to be punished in some way or other for doing it; if not by law, by the opinion of his fellow creatures; if not by opinion, by the reproaches of his own conscience. (CW X, p. 246)

Mill offers us a necessary condition for the application of the concept of moral wrongness of an action which is not directly a function of the amount of utility that the action produces, as the simple reading of the Principle of Utility seems to require. With a bit more formality, we state Mill's claim as

[1] X acts morally wrongly by doing F only if X's doing F warrants punishing X.

Later in this chapter, I shall return to the question of Mill's understanding of the moral rightness and wrongness of actions. However, before doing so it will be useful to have more of Mill's thinking before us.

A reasonable move in the direction of a better understanding of Mill's thinking involves an investigation of Mill's treatment of the concept of moral obligation. Mill makes an important distinction among two kinds of obligation. In particular, he appeals to a distinction among deontic concepts made in the case of rights by Grotius ([1625] 1955), in the case of duties by Pufendorf ([1673] 1991), and in terms of duties by Kant ([1785] 1998) and ([1797] 1996). Though this distinction undergoes subtle changes in the hands of each of these thinkers, all seem to agree that it concerns the stringency and specificity of the concept, with the perfect version of the concept being more stringent and specific than the imperfect version. More specifically, Mill distinguishes between perfect and imperfect obligations as follows. Suppose X violates some moral obligation by doing F:

[2a] X violates a moral obligation by doing F that is specifiable in some way at some particular time and place if and only if X violates a perfect moral obligation by doing F.

In contrast,

> [2b] X violates a moral obligation by doing F that is not specifiable in some way at some particular time and place if and only if X violates an imperfect moral obligation by doing F.

We can further flesh out Mill's understanding by invoking the notion of choice. A perfect moral obligation is one in which the agent has no real choice about the manner, etc., of doing it, while an imperfect moral obligation is one in which the agent does have at least some choice.

Mill's distinction between perfect and imperfect obligations is meant to link up with his conception both of moral rights and of justice. He puts the matter this way:

> Now it is known that ethical writers divide moral duties into two classes, denoted by the ill-chosen expressions, duties of perfect and of imperfect obligation; the latter being those in which, though the act is obligatory, the particular occasions of performing it are left to our choice, as in the case of charity or beneficence, which we are indeed bound to practise, but not towards any definite person, nor at any prescribed time. In the more precise language of philosophic jurists, duties of perfect obligation are those duties in virtue of which a correlative right resides in some person or persons; duties of imperfect obligation are those moral obligations which do not give birth to any right. I think it will be found that this distinction exactly coincides with that which exists between justice and the other obligations of morality. (CW X, p. 247)

So, on the one hand, Mill affirms a link between perfect moral obligations both to moral rights and to justice, and, on the other hand, he denies this link between imperfect moral obligations and both moral rights and justice.

If moral obligations are to be understood, at least in part, by reference to moral rights and to justice, then, of course, we need an understanding of these concepts as well. Mill tells us that a right is 'a valid claim on society to protect him in the possession of it' (CW X, p. 225), i.e., that 'which society ought to defend ... the possession of' (CW X, p. 226). A little more formally,

> [3] X violates Y's moral right to G by doing F if and only if
> [i] X violates Y's claim to G, and
> [ii] society ought to protect Y's claim of G.

Mill's understanding of justice is considerably less easy to paraphrase in this manner. He initially identifies six 'spheres' in which we speak of justice and injustice: legal rights, moral rights, desert, contracts, impartiality, and fairness. But what, if anything, unifies these spheres? Mill speculates on the basis of etymology that originally what unified them was our understanding of what law actually permits and forbids. Yet, Mill contends, this is far from the end of the story. Our thinking about what the law *does* permit or forbid developed into thinking about what the law *ought to* permit and forbid. As a result of this, we eventually came to have 'a sentiment of justice' which contains 'two essential ingredients' – namely, 'the desire to punish a person who has done harm, and the knowledge or belief that there is some definite individual or individuals to whom harm has been done' (CW X, p. 248).

Though Mill thinks that every case of injustice is a case of a harm done to an individual, he does not think that every case in which a harm is done is a case of injustice. Rather, Mill insists that in case of justice the harm to some definite individual (or individuals) must be the violation of that individual's right (or individuals' rights). So, from this claim and [3], Mill can infer both

> [4] X acts unjustly by doing F if and only if X's doing F violates Y's moral right to G,
>
> and
>
> [5] X acts unjustly by doing F if and only if by doing F
> [i] X violates Y's claim to G, and
> [ii] society ought to protect Y's claim of G.

Mill's insistence that there must be 'some definite individual or individuals to whom harm has been done' is vital for seeing the connection between, on the one hand, rights and justice and, on the other, perfect obligations. One cannot violate the rights of another without doing so in a way that is specifiable and that is at a particular time and place. If I violate your moral right to your life, to your property, or to anything else, I do so in a certain way, at a certain time and place. And, trivially, if I fail to violate any of your moral rights, I cannot have done so in any specific manner whatsoever. More formally,

> [6] X violates Y's moral rights by doing F if and only if X violates a moral obligation to do F that is specifiable in some way at some particular time and place.

From [2a] and [6], it follows that

> [7a] X violates Y's moral rights by doing F if and only if X violates a perfect moral obligation not to do F.

And, [2b] and [6] support that

> [7b] If X violates an imperfect moral obligation not to do F, then X does not violate Y's moral rights by doing so.

Moreover, from [6] and [7a], it follows that

> [8] X acts unjustly by doing F if and only if X violates a perfect moral obligation to do F.

Finally, [3] and [7a] justify the inference that

> [9] X violates a perfect moral obligation by doing F if and only if by doing F
> [i] X violates Y's claim to G, and
> [ii] society ought to protect Y's claim of G.

In short, Mill provides us with a subtle and sophisticated story about the connections among perfect and imperfect obligations, rights, justice, and what claims society ought and ought not to protect.

3 Interpretations of Mill on justice

Should a sympathetic interpretation of Mill retain all of these claims about our moral concepts? The contributors to this volume disagree about the correct answer to this question. Consider first [7a], Mill's claim about the connection between perfect moral obligations and moral rights. In his chapter, William Shaw points out several apparent counterexamples. We certainly appear to have moral obligations to act in specifiable ways at some particular times and places when it comes to such things as not perjuring ourselves when under oath, not paying less than our fair share for the national defense, and not avoiding jury duty if we are selected for it. If that is correct, then on Mill's account it should be the case that we fail to meet these moral obligations if and only if we violate someone's right. However, Shaw has his doubts about whether that is, in fact, correct.

> Arguably, however, this stretches the notion of a right too far. And, indeed, many philosophers take a rather restrictive view of rights,

> insisting that, from that fact that I ought to do something, even that I ought to do some specific action in a given situation, it does not necessarily follow that someone has a right that I act that way or that I act unjustly, as opposed to wrongly, if I fail to act in the required way.

In other words, there simply does not seem to be anyone whose right is violated if we perjure ourselves, if we pay too little in our taxes, or if we avoid jury duty. It is worth noting that, given Mill's claim about the close connection among our moral concepts, we cannot reject [7a] without also rejecting [7b] as well as at least one proposition in the conjunction which supports it – here either [2a] and [2b] or [6].

However, not all of the authors in this volume think that we should abandon [7a] and [7b]. Dale Miller's approach to this question is, in part, a response to the work of David Lyons (1994), who, like Shaw, rejects [7a] and [7b] but also contends that we should accept [6], rather than [2a] and [2b]. Lyons provides two reasons for this. First, he thinks that, if [2a] and [2b] were correct, then it would be possible for a moral obligation to be violated on a particular occasion even if it were not an obligation of justice. This, Lyons thinks, cannot be the case. Second, he also thinks that, if we understand Mill as accepting [2a] and [2b] rather than [6], then we would be forced to say that Mill holds that nearly all moral obligations are obligations of justice. And this too, Lyons affirms, cannot be so.

In response to Lyons – and, implicitly, to Shaw – Miller provides in his contribution a careful reading of chapter V of *Utilitarianism* – especially of paragraphs 14 and 15 – which is meant to support an alternative interpretation. According to what Miller calls *the equivalence approach*, [2a] and [2b] are correct, as are [6], [7a], and [7b]. In addition to marshalling a great deal of textual evidence for the equivalence approach, Miller also presents a subtle response to the worries that Lyons raises about [2a] and [2b]. In doing so, he also addresses some related issues raised recently by Walter Sinnott-Armstrong (2005). Of course, in order to embrace the equivalence approach wholeheartedly, one must have an even fuller discussion of these, something Miller himself provides not only here but in Miller (2010).

Fred Wilson is another contributor to this collection who accepts both [7a] and [7b]. While Wilson does not offer an extended defense of these claims against a critic such as Lyons, he does provide resources for an interesting line of response. Wilson adds to the content of claims such as [5] and [6] by pointing out that on Mill's view 'To violate a right

[is] to fail to do something to which another has a moral right to expect' (p. 129). If Wilson is right, then Mill's conception of the violation of moral rights is broader than might first be thought. I might violate your moral rights not only by unjustifiably assaulting you or taking your property but also simply by unjustifiably failing to act as I am expected to act. On this reading, we do in fact violate someone's rights when we perjure ourselves, when we pay too little in our taxes, and when we avoid jury duty. We violate the rights of members of the court in the first case, members of the nation in the second, and members of the community in the third. It is understandable why one might think that this response involves an overly broad notion of what a moral right is. But it is useful here to recall from (3) that Mill is thinking of a moral right as a claim that society ought to protect. And it is not hard to see Mill making a case that society ought to protect the claim of members of a court on witnesses not to lie, the claim of other taxpayers not to be burdened by free riders, and the claim by members of a community to get fair cooperation from one of its members.

If the relationship between moral rights and perfect moral obligations is at least controversial, what are we to think of the relationship between moral rights and justice? Though (4) commits Mill to the very strong claim that justice and rights are coextensive, not everyone agrees. However, Shaw is more sympathetic to Mill with regard to the relationship between rights and justice than he is about the relationship between rights and perfect moral obligations. Shaw stresses that 'Mill is not saying that murder is wrong because it is unjust, that this is what strikes us as abhorrent about it or that this is the reason morality condemns it. He is saying, rather, that because it violates the victim's rights, murder is unjust. And to me, at least, that seems perfectly true' (p. 67).

Of course, some critics of Mill think that this is precisely where he is weakest. As Wilson points out, these critics go back at least as far as William Whewell, who was Professor of Moral Philosophy and later also Master of Trinity College, Cambridge in Mill's own day. Mill explicitly takes the Principle of Utility to be the 'first principle' of morality (CW X, p. 234). As such, justice and rights must, ultimately, be subordinate to it. Once again, Mill is not coy about acknowledging this fact. He imagines being asked why someone has this or that right and tells us 'I can give no other reason than general utility' (CW X, p. 250). Moreover, Mill disputes 'the pretensions of any theory which sets up an imaginary standard of justice not grounded on utility' (CW X, p. 251). But, critics of Mill and of utilitarianism more generally urge, if a concern for utility

is prior to a concern for rights and justice, then these latter concepts will be run over roughshod whenever doing so maximizes aggregate happiness.

Mill scholars and utilitarians have responded to this line of criticism in a variety of ways, not all of which are mutually consistent. The contributors to this volume are no different in that respect. Some focus on the debunking aspects of Mill's treatment of justice. Wilson points to Mill's naturalism and presents Mill as blunting the force of his critics. As Wilson reports Mill thinking, 'given the naturalistic nature of justice, this concept has no intrinsic claim to be morally required: from naturalistic facts one cannot derive any claim that any principle is obligatory – "is" does not imply "ought" ' (p. 139). The point at issue here is not whether Mill thought justice was important. It should be obvious from the outline of Mill's moral concepts in section 2 of this chapter that he did. Rather, what is at issue is whether justice is an independent source of moral obligation. As Wilson shows, Mill thought that it was not.

Other contributors to this volume direct their attention to the limited scope that justice and other obligations have for conflict. Miller claims that, on his 'reading, the rules of justice could only rarely conflict with duties that the choice criterion classifies as imperfect. Since these duties only require us to do enough of something over time, if it were impossible to (say) be charitable on one occasion without acting unjustly, it would almost always be possible to do so on another and still fulfil the duty. A real conflict would occur only if it were impossible for some extended period of time to satisfy the imperfect duty without acting unjustly, and surely situations like this do not happen often' (p. 107).

Yet other authors seek to undermine the very notion that utility trumps justice in Mill's thinking. Mill does allow that 'particular cases may occur in which some other social duty is so important as to override any one of the general maxims of justice' (CW X, p. 238). But, as Shaw points out, there is a significant difference between holding that social utility overrides one of the general maxims of justice and holding that social utility overrides justice *simpliciter*. Shaw considers a case in which we must decide how best to remunerate especially talented workers, and he points out that

> there are two ways of conceptualizing this situation. One is to see ourselves as setting aside the ordinary maxims of justice and straightforwardly settling the question on utilitarian grounds. The other is to say that, guided by utility, we come down in support of one of the

> maxims, thus affirming that on balance justice requires paying (or not paying) the talented worker more. Understood this second way, we do not leave the realm of justice; rather, utility tells us which precept of justice carries greater normative weight. In hard cases justice may have different sides to it – different precepts may be at odds – but guided by utility we plump for one of them. The winning precept thus states what justice requires in this case, not just *pro tanto*, but all things considered. Justice itself remains indefeasible even if particular maxims do not. (p. 82)

However, as noted in section 2 of this chapter, Mill stops short of identifying justice and moral rightness. So how are we to understand Mill's thinking on this point? Miller offers some solace to those who think of Mill as a rule utilitarian. Miller's target is Lyons's hesitance to characterize Mill as a rule utilitarian. Lyons appears to characterize rule utilitarianism as being inconsistent both with [i] ranking actions in terms of their utilities and prefers actions with higher utilities – even if the preference in question is nonmoral – and with [ii] having at the foundations of one's moral theory the analysis of concepts such as *morally obligatory*. Miller maintains that Lyons's characterization of rule utilitarianism is overly narrow and that nothing Lyons shows to be the case is inconsistent with understanding Mill as a rule utilitarian in much the same way as Richard Brandt (1979) was and in a similar way to which Brad Hooker (2000) is a rule consequentialist: actions are to be understood in terms of their conformity with a set of rules that would, if widely internalized, bring about the greatest amount of utility or goodness, or at least as much utility or goodness as any alternative.

Despite the long-running battle over the question of whether Mill was an act utilitarian or a rule utilitarian, Shaw is wary of it for two reasons. First, the usual way of framing the debate involves an overly simple dichotomy. Shaw argues that Mill qualifies as neither an act utilitarian nor a rule utilitarian, on the usual way of understanding these positions. On the contrary, Mill sought to apply the standards of utilitarianism to a wide variety of phenomena, not to action alone. If Shaw is correct about this, then Mill is, in a certain sense, closer to the position known as 'global consequentialism' than might have been thought.[3] Second, if act utilitarianism were correct, then it would be morally obligatory to disobey social rules on occasions when doing so would bring about more utility than not doing so. However, this has the air of paradox to it, since this would make social rules otiose even though internalizing them can often lead to much better results than not doing so. It would be uncharitable, Shaw thinks, to attribute such a view to Mill.

Brink returns to the source of the debate between those who classify Mill as an act utilitarian and those who classify him as a rule utilitarian. Brink revisits the case made by Urmson (1953) that Mill was a rule utilitarian and concludes that all of the textual evidence provided by Urmson can be squared with an act utilitarian reading of him. However, Brink maintains that Lyons (1994) is correct in noting that there are other aspects of Mill's thinking on display in chapter V of *Utilitarianism* that cannot. Brink and Shaw appear to agree that there is more conceptual space available to Mill than is suggested by the usual dichotomy between act utilitarianism and rule utilitarianism, since Brink goes on to suggest that Mill's position in chapter V might be best understood as a form of what he calls 'sanction utilitarianism' (p. 44).[4] Brink explains that 'this account of duty defines the rightness and wrongness of an act, not in terms of its utility, as act utilitarianism does, but in terms of the utility of applying sanctions to the conduct, it is an indirect form of utilitarianism' (p. 47). Clearly, sanction utilitarianism has the advantage of synthesizing the Principle of Utility with a strengthened version of [1]. It might also be thought that it is closer to common-sense morality, in as much as it allows us to distinguish between acts that are wrong, acts that are permissible, acts that are obligatory, and acts that are supererogatory.

Nevertheless, sanction utilitarianism loses some of its charms on closer inspection. Brink suggests that act utilitarianism can shadow these distinctions in a way that makes it as least as plausible as sanction utilitarianism. Moreover, Brink argues that sanction utilitarianism has disadvantages that act utilitarianism lacks. In particular, it appears to get the order of explanation backwards. It is not that an act is wrong because we are warranted in punishing it; on the contrary, we are warranted in punishing the act because it is wrong. Furthermore, sanction utilitarianism is, according to Brink, problematic because of its status as a 'hybrid theory.' On the one hand, it determines when sanctions are warranted by directly applying the Principle of Utility. On the other hand, it determines an agent's duties only by indirectly applying the Principle. The worry is that an infinite regress looms, since sanctions themselves are actions concerning which agents can have duties. Brink concludes that Mill was simply ambivalent about the nature of morally right and morally wrong action. The elements of his thinking which suggest act utilitarianism (especially in chapter II of *Utilitarianism*) and the elements which suggest an alternative, such as rule utilitarianism or sanction utilitarianism (especially in chapter V of *Utilitarianism*), cannot be reconciled.

4 Mill and others on justice

John Stuart Mill and John Rawls are closely associated in the minds of many for a number of reasons. To begin with, few philosophers can compare with them in terms of their influence over their contemporaries and near-contemporaries. Mill's importance for – and influence over – nineteenth-century moral and political philosophy is difficult to overestimate, especially in the English-speaking world. Henry Balfour claimed that Mill's influence in Britain was on a par with that of Hegel in Germany and Aristotle in medieval European universities, as John Skorupski (1998, p. 1) rightly reminds us. If Rawls's influence has not been quite as large on the twentieth century, it has nevertheless been colossal. Thom Brooks and Fabian Freyenhagen (2005, p. vii) are hardly alone in claiming that 'John Rawls was perhaps the most important moral and political philosopher of the last century.' Moreover, Rawls's work on justice – especially his early work – explicitly aims to refute and replace work on justice done by Mill and others whom Rawls (1971, p. 22) calls 'the classical utilitarians.' As Rawls (1971, p. 26) famously argued, 'Utilitarianism does not take seriously the distinction between persons.' As a result, we need to look elsewhere for an account of justice. Unsurprisingly, Rawls maintains that we ought to accept his alternative account of justice. According to Rawls, basic institutions of a given society are just if, and only if, first, 'each person is to have an equal right to the most extensive scheme of equal basic liberties compatible with a similar scheme of liberties for others' and, second, social and economic inequalities are to be arranged so that:

> [a] they are to be of the greatest benefit to the least-advantaged members of society,
> [b] offices and positions must be open to everyone under conditions of fair equality of opportunity. (Rawls 1971, 60)

Of course, those who are sympathetic to Mill's view or to utilitarianism more generally are unlikely to take Rawls's criticism lying down. One line of response is to defend Mill's account of justice, either by showing that Rawls misinterpreted it or by showing that his arguments against it fail – or both. Another line of response is to attack Rawls's own theory of justice. To be sure, these two lines of response are not inconsistent with one another, and many who take up one also take up the other at some point.

But there is at least one more line of response for one sympathetic to Mill – namely, to show that the distance between Mill and Rawls on justice is far smaller than Rawls and others have thought. Though this line of response is underdeveloped in the otherwise massive literature on Rawls, Henry West's chapter in this collection does much to advance it. In order to make his case, West exploits the strong interest in liberty shared by both Mill and Rawls, as well as the importance that liberty has in a good human life. West stresses that both Mill's and Rawls's accounts of justice give priority to liberty but, once we take into consideration both ideal and nonideal theory, both also allow flexibility under unusual circumstances.

But Rawls is not the only contemporary author who can usefully be contrasted with Mill, as D.G. Brown shows in the chapter 'Justice and Political Liberalism.' Brown explores Martha Nussbaum's interpretation of – and proposed alternative to – Mill's Harm Principle. According to Mill,

> the sole end for which mankind are warranted, individually or collectively, in interfering with the liberty of action of any of their number, is self-protection. That the only purpose for which power can be rightfully exercised over any member of a civilized community, against will, is to prevent harm to others. His own good, either physical or moral, is not a sufficient warrant. He cannot rightfully be compelled to do or forbear because it will be better for him to do so, because it will make him happier, because, in the opinions of others, to do so would be wise, or even right. (CW XVIII, p. 217)

Brown notes that Nussbaum is roughly in agreement with Mill about the substance of the Harm Principle but is sharply in disagreement with Mill's justification for it, so much so that she offers her own alternative.

As Brown reads her, Nussbaum has two main complaints against Mill. The first of these is that the justification he offers gives the wrong kind of support for the broad liberties meant to be protected by the Harm Principle. In particular, Nussbaum appears to think that Mill is suggesting persons be treated as a mere means to bring about greater happiness, each generation providing more for the one that follows through its exercise of the Harm Principle and the resultant increases in human knowledge. But Brown thinks that Nussbaum's criticism misses its target. Mill, Brown maintains, presents the Harm Principle primarily by way of protecting individuals from the damage that can be done to them by imposition of the tyranny of the majority, not by way of maximizing utility. Indeed, Brown avers that Mill was 'simply not a maximizing consequentialist' (p. 231).[5]

Nussbaum's second complaint is that Mill fails to understand the nature of certain kinds of threats to liberty. This threat originates in an inegalitarian concern with, as it were, the liberty of the genius, that is to say, the value of freedom of thought and action for individuals with the greatest capabilities for using them for the creation of great works of art, scientific breakthroughs, and philosophical masterpieces. The worry, it would seem, is that, while liberty for the elite might be very valuable, liberty for those of us who are incapable of climbing anything near to these peaks of human achievement is thereby devalued. If the rest of us cannot produce the greatness of a Beethoven or a Newton or a Plato, then why do we warrant the same kind of liberty? However, Brown thinks that this worry rests on a mistake. Mill's concern is not simply with liberty, it is with *equal* liberty. In other words, the Harm Principle is meant to protect liberty for each individual consistent with the same amount of liberty for all.

Several authors in this volume continue the exploration of the relationship between justice and liberty. Of course, Mill wrote passionately about the limits to which others can infringe on one's liberty: 'That the only purpose for which power can be rightfully exercised over any member of a civilized community, against his will, is to prevent harm to others' (CW X, p. 223). But, as C.L. Ten notes in his chapter, Mill did not think that this claim applied to everyone. '[T]his doctrine,' Mill maintained, 'is meant to apply only to human beings in the maturity of their faculties,' not to 'young persons below the age which the law may fix as that of manhood or womanhood.' It is also not meant to apply to 'those backward states of society in which the race itself may be considered in its nonage' (CW X, p. 224). While few take issue with what Mill has to say about those who are immature in 'their faculties,' many do take issue with what Mill has to say about 'barbarians' – indeed, some find it downright offensive. The fact that Mill thinks it is sometimes justified for external powers to exercise despotism over barbarian societies is unlikely to make Mill's thinking any more palatable to those even slightly familiar with the history of colonial abuse in Mill's own time.

C.L. Ten, in his chapter, 'Justice for Barbarians,' wades into these troubled waters in order to clarify Mill's thought. Ten shows that Mill's position is far more subtle than it might first seem. Mill expresses doubts about the likely efficacy of imposing any form of government on a people, barbarous or otherwise, without a detailed and sympathetic understanding of the local traditions and conventions. Mill also condemns imposing a foreign set of ideas – including religious ideas – on an unwilling populace. As a result of these concerns, Mill argued against the permissibility of direct rule by a country such as Great Britain over another such as India. At best, what was warranted was indirect rule, in which the power structure of the ruled country is incorporated into the colonial administration of the ruling country. Importantly, Mill did not think that such indirect rule is justified by the fact that the ruling country is intrinsically superior to the ruled country. Indeed, as Ten explains, few public figures of Mill's day were as consistent and intense in their criticism of racist views. Moreover, Mill's opposition to racism was not limited to his writings. For example, while a Member of Parliament, he served as chairman of a committee that investigated atrocities against blacks committed under Governor Eyre. Though the committee was ultimately unsuccessful in its prosecution of Eyre, this was certainly not for lack of effort on Mill's part, as Ten shows.

The connections between the works of Mill and of David Hume are underexplored, and Jonathan Riley takes a large step toward changing this in his chapter. Riley explores the similarities between Hume's view of moral psychology and Mill's. In doing so, he shows a number of subtle and interesting connections between the two and, in the process, helps to flesh out Mill's somewhat dark reasoning about the so-called moral sentiment of justice, especially in chapter V of *Utilitarianism*. Riley also takes up the often-remarked-upon use of the term 'proof' in chapter IV of *Utilitarianism* and finds some deep connections between Hume and Mill here as well: 'Remarkably, Mill is following Hume in enlarging the meaning of the word proof to include ways besides logical demonstration of arriving at conclusions that reason is incapable of doubting' (p. 231).

The volume concludes with my own chapter, in which I take up Mill's attempt to manage nonutilitarian criticisms of the utilitarian account of justice. On Lyons's highly influential interpretation (1994), Mill's account of justice has both a conceptual side and a substantive side. While the former provides an analysis of such concepts as 'justice' and 'rights', the latter provides an explanation of when and where these concepts apply. If Lyons is correct, then Mill should be seen as arguing that utilitarians can allow for circumstances in which actions are wrong because they are unjust, while also claiming that the standards of right and wrong (as well as justice and injustice) are determined by the Principle of Utility, but I maintain that Lyons's interpretation is flawed. The distinction between the conceptual and the substantive levels of Mill's thinking does not hold up to scrutiny, and, even if it did, it would not support Lyons's reading of Mill. It would instead support a debunking interpretation of justice, an interpretation recently explored by Roger Crisp. Such a debunking interpretation suggests a very different response to the Weak Objection from Justice, one that many, but not all, utilitarians will find unwelcome.

Notes

1. Some notable exceptions include Lyons (1994), Bailey (1997), and Arneson (2000), as well as many of the contributors to this volume.
2. See also Brink (2005).
3. On global consequentialism, see Parfit (1984), Kagan (2000), and Pettit and Smith (2000).
4. See also Brink (2007, section 2.9).
5. See Jacobson (2008) for an argument that Mill was not a consequentialist at all.

References

Arneson, Richard (2000) 'Rawls versus Utilitarianism in Light of *Political Liberalism*,' in *The Idea of a Political Liberalism*, Victoria Davion (Lanham, MD: Rowman and Littlefield).

Bailey, James Wood (1997) *Utilitarianism, Institutions, and Justice* (Oxford: Oxford University Press).

Binmore, Ken (2005) *Natural Justice* (Oxford: Oxford University Press).

Brandt, Richard (1979) *A Theory of the Right and the Good* (Oxford: Clarendon).

Brink, David O. (2005) 'Consequentialism,' in *The Oxford Handbook of Ethical Theory*, David Copp (ed.) (Oxford: Oxford University Press).

Brink, David O. (2007) 'Mill's Moral and Political Philosophy,' in *Stanford Encyclopaedia of Philosophy*, http://plato.stanford.edu/entries/mill-moral-political, first published Tuesday October 9, 2007.

Brooks, Thom and Freyenhagen, Fabian (eds) (2005) *The Legacy of John Rawls* (London: Continuum).

Cohen, Gerald (1995) *Self-Ownership, Freedom, and Equality* (Cambridge, UK: Cambridge University Press).

Cohen, Gerald (2008) *Rescuing Justice and Equality* (Cambridge, MA: Harvard Belknap).

Crisp, Roger (1997) *Mill on Utilitarianism* (London: Routledge).

Daniels, Norman (2007) *Just Health* (Cambridge, UK: Cambridge University Press).

Gauthier, David (1986) *Morals by Agreement* (Oxford: Oxford University Press).

Grotius, Hugo ([1625] 1955) *Prolegomena to the Laws of War and Peace*, Francis Kelsey (trans.) (Indianapolis, Indiana: Bobbs-Merrill).

Hooker, Brad (2000) *Ideal Code, Real World* (Oxford: Oxford University Press).

Jacobson, Daniel (2008) 'Utilitarianism without Consequentialism: The Case of John Stuart Mill,' *Philosophical Review* 117(2), 159–91.

Kagan, Shelly (2000) 'Evaluative Focal Points,' in Hooker, Mason, and Miller (eds) *Morality, Rules, and Consequences* (Edinburgh University Press, Rowman and Littlefield), pp. 134–55.

Kant, Immanuel ([1797] 1996) *Metaphysics of Morals*, Mary Gregor (trans.) (Cambridge, UK: Cambridge University Press).

Kant, Immanuel ([1785] 1998) *Groundwork of the Metaphysics of Morals*, Mary Gregor (trans.) (Cambridge, UK: Cambridge University Press).

Lyons, David (1994) *Rights, Welfare and Mill's Moral Theory* (Oxford: Oxford University Press).

Miller, Dale E. (2010) *J. S. Mill: Moral, Social and Political Thought* (London: Polity).

Nagel, Thomas (1991) *Equality and Partiality* (Oxford: Oxford University Press).

Nozick, Robert (1974) *Anarchy, State, and Utopia* (New York: Basic Books).

Otsuka, Michael (2003) *Libertarianism without Inequality* (Oxford: Oxford University Press).

Parfit, Derek (1984) *Reasons and Persons* (Oxford: Oxford University Press).

Parfit, Derek (2011) *On What Matters* (Oxford: Oxford University Press).

Pettit, Philip and Smith, Michael (2000) 'Global Consequentialism,' in Hooker, Mason, and Miller (eds), *Morality, Rules, and Consequences* (Edinburgh University Press, Rowman and Littlefield), pp. 221–33.

Pufendorf, Samuel ([1673] 1991) *On the Duty of Man and Citizen according to Natural Law*, James Tully (ed.) and Michael Silverthorne (trans.) (Cambridge, UK: Cambridge University Press).

Rawls, John (1971) *A Theory of Justice* (Cambridge, MA: Harvard Belknap).

Rawls, John (1993) *Political Liberalism* (New York: Columbia University Press).

Robson, J.M. (ed.) (1969) *The Collected Works of John Stuart Mill: Essays on Ethics, Religion, and Society*, Vol. X (Toronto: University of Toronto Press).

Robson, J.M. (ed.) (1977) *The Collected Works of John Stuart Mill: Essays on Politics and Society Part 1*, Vol. XVIII (Toronto: University of Toronto Press).

Sandel, Michael (1982) *Liberalism and the Limits of Justice* (Cambridge, UK: Cambridge University Press).

Sandel, Michael (2009) *Justice: What's the Right Thing to Do?* (New York: Farrar, Straus and Giroux).

Scanlon, T.M. (1998) *What We Owe to Each Other* (Cambridge, MA: Harvard Belknap).

Sinnott-Armstrong, Walter (2005) 'You Ought to be Ashamed of Yourself (When You Violate an Imperfect Moral Obligation)', *Philosophical Issues* 15, 193–208

Skorupski, John (ed.) (1998) *The Cambridge Companion to Mill* (Cambridge, UK: Cambridge University Press).

Skyrms, Brian (1996) *Evolution of Social Contract* (Cambridge, UK: Cambridge University Press).

Urmson, J.O. (1953) 'The Interpretation of the Moral Philosophy of J. S. Mill,' *Philosophical Quarterly* 10, 33–9.

Part I

Mill's Moral Concepts

1 Mill's Ambivalence about Duty

David O. Brink

Consequentialists agree that deontic notions such as obligation, permission, and prohibition should be understood in terms of evaluative notions about the good. For instance, duty or obligation should be understood as serving or promoting the good in some way. In a familiar slogan, consequentialists believe that the good is prior to the right (Rawls, 1971). Utilitarians are consequentialists who conceive of the good in terms of happiness or well-being. Within the constraints set by consequentialist and utilitarian essentials, there are important family disputes. Consequentialists, in general, and utilitarians, in particular, disagree over the justification of consequentialist and utilitarian essentials, the proper conception of the good, in general, and happiness or well-being, in particular, and the exact relation between the good and the right.

On each of these issues, it is interesting and instructive to consider the views of John Stuart Mill, perhaps the most influential proponent of utilitarian and consequentialist ideas. Mill is especially interesting to consider on the relation between the good and the right, because his views, especially his claims in *Utilitarianism*, have been subject to such widely divergent interpretations. In what follows, I shall attempt to reconstruct Mill's theory of duty, abstracting, so far as possible, from his views about the justification of utilitarianism and about the proper conception of happiness or well-being.

There is a long tradition of reading Mill as an act utilitarian, who thinks that it is our duty to perform the action with the best consequences for human happiness. Act utilitarianism is a form of *direct* consequentialism because it makes the assessment of anything, including an action, depend upon its consequences. In his famous paper 'An Interpretation of the Philosophy of J.S. Mill,' J.O. Urmson (1953) argued against this act utilitarian reading of Mill and defended a rule utilitarian reading, according to which an act is obligatory, not because of its consequences, but if it conforms to a rule with optimal acceptance value. Rule utilitarianism is a form of *indirect* consequentialism, because it makes an action's deontic status depend, not on its consequences, but on its relation to something else – in this case, rules – that are evaluated by the value of their consequences. More recently, David Lyons (1994) has defended a different indirect reading of Mill's theory of duty, according to which right and wrong are determined by the utility of sanctioning conduct.

These three different utilitarian conceptions of duty are mutually inconsistent. Mill cannot consistently embrace more than one of these readings. After reviewing some of the evidence for the traditional act utilitarian reading, I consider Urmson's case for a rule utilitarian reading. Urmson draws attention to Mill's apparent concern with the felicific tendencies of classes of actions and his focus on secondary principles in moral reasoning. I argue that both of these considerations can be squared with act utilitarianism and so do not require us to depart from the traditional act utilitarian reading. However, I agree with Lyons that in Chapter V of *Utilitarianism* Mill introduces a different form of indirect utilitarianism that is inconsistent with act utilitarianism. Because I think that Mill's other claims in *Utilitarianism* are best interpreted in act utilitarian terms, I believe that Chapter V makes Mill's overall position ambivalent about the relation between the good and the right. I conclude by exploring some apparent differences between the two forms of utilitarianism to which Mill is attracted. In particular, I suggest that some apparent advantages of Mill's indirect utilitarianism look spurious upon closer examination.

1 Direct and indirect utilitarianism

In order to understand what is at stake among some different interpretations of Mill's theory of duty, we need to make some now generally familiar distinctions. In particular, we need to distinguish between direct and indirect utilitarianism.

Direct utilitarianism: Any object of moral assessment (e.g. action, motive, policy, or institution) should be assessed by and in proportion to the value of its consequences for the general happiness.

Indirect utilitarianism: Any object of moral assessment should be assessed, not by the value of its consequences for the general happiness, but by its conformity to something else (e.g. norms or motives) that has (have) good or optimal acceptance value.

So formulated, direct and indirect utilitarianism are general theories that apply, at least in principle, to any object of moral assessment. But our focus here is on right action or duty. Act utilitarianism is the most familiar form of direct utilitarianism applied to action, whereas the most common indirect utilitarian theory of duty is rule utilitarianism.

Act utilitarianism: An act is right insofar as its consequences for the general happiness are at least as good as any alternative available to the agent.

Rule utilitarianism: An act is right insofar as it conforms to a rule whose acceptance value for the general happiness is at least as great as any alternative rule available to the agent.

This conception of act utilitarianism is both *maximizing*, because it identifies the right action with the best available action, and *scalar*, because it recognizes that rightness can come in degrees, depending on the action's proximity to the best.[1] The right act is the optimal act, but some suboptimal acts can be more right and less wrong than others. Similarly, this conception of rule utilitarianism assesses rules in both maximizing and scalar fashion.

Act utilitarianism appears to say that we should adhere to familiar moral precepts about honesty, fidelity, and nonmaleficence only when doing so has the best consequences. It is a counterintuitive doctrine to the extent that we regard some of these precepts as categorical moral rules or principles. Rule utilitarianism may seem less counterintuitive, because it can explain why one ought to adhere to certain rules or precepts, even when doing so does not have the best consequences, provided doing so is generally optimal. Act utilitarianism must condemn following rules when doing so is suboptimal; rule utilitarianism need not. But not everyone agrees that this makes rule utilitarianism superior to act utilitarianism. Some think that we are wrong to embrace categorical moral rules and principles. Though these rules and principles might be good rules of thumb, they are not exceptionless generalizations. Moreover, rule utilitarianism may seem ad hoc. If utility is the appropriate test for rules, then why shouldn't we assess actions by the same criterion? Isn't rule utilitarianism a form of irrational rule worship? I raise these issues here, not to take a stand on them, but to indicate what might be at stake in the debate between direct and indirect utilitarianism.

2 Utilitarianism as a standard of conduct

Chapter II of *Utilitarianism* purports to explain what utilitarianism is. In an early and famous passage, Mill describes that doctrine in this way:

> The creed which accepts as the foundations of morals 'utility' or the 'greatest happiness principle' holds that actions are right in proportion as they tend to promote happiness; wrong as they tend to produce the reverse of happiness. By happiness is intended pleasure and the absence of pain; by unhappiness, pain and the privation of pleasure. (CW X, p. 210)

For obvious reasons, this famous passage is sometimes called the Proportionality Doctrine.

As we will see, the Proportionality Doctrine has been interpreted in both act utilitarian and rule utilitarian ways. But, before we get to these issues, we should attend to a different question about the sort of principle that utilitarianism is. We might expect a utilitarian (act or rule) to apply the utilitarian principle in her deliberations. Consider act utilitarianism for a moment. We might expect such a utilitarian to be motivated by pure disinterested benevolence and to deliberate by calculating expected utility on each and every occasion for action. But it is a practical question how to reason or be motivated, and direct utilitarianism implies that this practical question, like all practical questions, is correctly answered by what would maximize utility. Utilitarian calculation is time-consuming and often unreliable or subject to bias and distortion. For such reasons, we may better approximate the utilitarian standard if we don't always try to approximate it. Mill says that to suppose that one must always consciously employ the utilitarian principle in making decisions

> is to mistake the very meaning of a standard of morals and confound the rule of action with the motive of it. It is the business of ethics to tell us what are our duties, or by what test we may know them; but no system of ethics requires that the sole motive of all we do shall be a feeling of duty; on the contrary, ninety-nine hundredths of all our actions are done from other motives, and rightly so done if the rule of duty does not condemn them. (CW X, pp. 219–20)

In his *Introduction to the Principles of Morals and Legislation*, Jeremy Bentham ([1789] 1970) made a similar point, denying that utilitarian calculations should be made on every occasion. Later utilitarians, such as Henry Sidgwick (1907), have emphasized this point, insisting that utilitarianism provides a *standard* of right action, not necessarily a *decision procedure*.

> Finally, the doctrine that Universal Happiness is the ultimate *standard* must not be understood to imply that Universal Benevolence is the only right or always the best *motive* of action. For, as we have observed, it is not necessary that the end which gives the criterion of rightness should always be the end at which we consciously aim: and if experience shows that the general happiness will be more satisfactorily obtained if men frequently act from other motives than pure universal philanthropy, it is obvious that these other motives are reasonably to be preferred on Utilitarian principles. (1907, p. 413)

If utilitarianism is itself the standard of right conduct, not a decision procedure, then what sort of decision procedure should the utilitarian endorse, and what role should the principle of utility play in moral reasoning? As we will see (Section 4), Mill thinks that much moral reasoning should be governed by secondary precepts or principles about such things as fidelity, fair play, and honesty that make no direct reference to utility but whose general observance does promote utility. These secondary principles should be set aside in favor of direct appeals to the utilitarian first principle in cases in which adherence to the secondary precept would have obviously inferior consequences or in which such secondary principles conflict (CW X, pp. 220–1 and pp. 225–6).

We can now specify more precisely that the question that concerns us here is what kind of utilitarian standard Mill endorses.

3 Act utilitarianism

Several of Mill's characterizations of utilitarianism imply or at least suggest a form of direct utilitarianism, specifically act utilitarianism. Chapter II, we saw, is where Mill purports to say what the doctrine of utilitarianism does and does not say. In the opening paragraph, he tells us that utilitarians are 'those who stand up for utility as the test of right and wrong' (CW X, p. 209). According to the Proportionality Doctrine, introduced in the next paragraph, utilitarianism holds 'that actions are right in proportion as they tend to promote happiness; wrong as they tend to produce the reverse of happiness' (CW X, p. 210). Later in that chapter, he says that it requires that 'utility or happiness [be] considered as the directive rule of human conduct' (CW X, pp. 213–14). Still later in Chapter II, he describes utilitarianism as a 'standard of what is right in conduct' (CW X, p. 218). Even Chapter V, which will eventually introduce some indirect elements, begins with Mill asserting that utilitarianism is 'the doctrine that utility or happiness is the criterion of right and wrong' (CW X, p. 240). These passages all seem to endorse a form of direct utilitarianism, specifically act utilitarianism.

4 Rule utilitarianism?

But not everyone agrees. J.O. Urmson famously defended a rule utilitarian reading of Mill. One of Urmson's reasons for this rule utilitarian reading appeals to Mill's reliance on various rules and secondary principles in moral reasoning. We will examine that rationale shortly. But, perhaps surprisingly, Urmson also appeals to the Proportionality Doctrine as requiring a rule utilitarian interpretation of Mill.

Felicific tendencies

Recall that the Proportionality Doctrine says, in part, that utilitarianism holds that actions are right in proportion as they tend to promote happiness; wrong as they tend to produce the reverse of happiness (CW X, p. 210). Urmson claims that we can make sense of an action's tendency to produce good or bad consequences only as a claim about what is true of a *class* or *type* of actions. Token actions produce specifiable consequences; only types of actions have tendencies. On Urmson's interpretation, Mill is really saying that an action is right if it is a token of a type of act that tends to have good or optimal consequences. But then the Proportionality Doctrine would espouse a form of rule utilitarianism. This is natural interpretive claim. But several considerations count against Urmson's interpretation of the Proportionality Doctrine.

First, it was common among the Philosophical Radicals to formulate utilitarianism, as the Proportionality Doctrine does, in terms of the felicific tendencies of individual actions. For instance, Bentham does this early in his *Principles*.

> By the principle of utility is meant that principle which approves or disapproves of every action whatsoever, according to the tendency which it appears to have to augment or diminish the happiness of the party whose interest is in question: or, what is the same thing in other words, to promote or oppose that happiness. I say of every action whatsoever; and therefore not only every action of a private

> individual, but of every measure of government. ([1789] 1970) Chapter I, Paragraph 2; cf. Chapter I, Paragraphs 3 and 6)

Here Bentham clearly ascribes the felicific tendency to action tokens, and he equates an action's felicific tendency with the extent to which it promotes utility. Later, Bentham repeats this understanding of tendencies.

> The general tendency of an act is more or less pernicious, according to the sum total of its consequences: that is, according to the differences between the sum of such as are good, and the sum of such as are evil. ([1789] 1970) Chapter VII, Paragraph 2; cf. Chapter IV, Paragraph 5)

John Austin, who was clearly a rule, rather than an act, utilitarian, nonetheless shared Bentham's understanding of the felicific tendencies of particular acts, as he makes clear in *The Province of Jurisprudence Determined.*

> Now the *tendency* of a human action (as its tendency is thus understood) is the whole of its tendency: the sum of its probable consequences, insofar as they are important or material: the sum of its remote and collateral, as well as of its direct consequences, in so far as any of its consequences may influence the general happiness. ([1832] 1954, Lecture II, Paragraph 38)

In the first passage from Bentham and in this passage from Austin, there is a concern with expected, rather than actual, utility, presumably because they are concerned in these passages with the calculation of expected utility required when one is trying to apply the utilitarian standard. But presumably neither wants to formulate the utilitarian standard itself in terms of expected, rather than actual, utility.[2] If we abstract from this apparent concern with expected utility, Austin and Bentham are claiming that action tokens have felicific tendencies and that an action's felicific tendency consists in the value of its actual consequences. We might call this the *extensional* reading of the felicific tendencies of action tokens.[3] But, if we interpret Mill's Proportionality Doctrine against the background of these extensional claims held by his utilitarian forbears, then we have strong evidence against Urmson's reading and in favor of an act utilitarian reading of the Proportionality Doctrine.[4]

Second, we might note another, related extensional reading of felicific tendencies within the Proportionality Doctrine. Particular actions have many consequences that are distributed both across persons and across times. The felicific or hedonic valence of these various consequences can be mixed. A given act may have consequences that are good for A and B but bad for C, or bad for A and B in the short run but better for them in the long run. We could speak of an action's tendency to promote happiness either as a way of picking out its beneficial consequences or perhaps as a way of signaling that its beneficial consequences outweigh or predominate over its harmful consequences. Sometimes, Bentham does just this.

> Sum up all the values of all the *pleasures* on the one side, and those of all the *pains* on the other. The balance, if it be on the side of pleasure, will give the *good* tendency of the act upon the whole, with respect to the interests of that *individual* person; if on the side of pain, the *bad* tendency of it upon the whole. ([1789] 1970) Chapter IV, Paragraph 5)

But then the Proportionality Doctrine would be asserting that an action is right insofar as it has beneficial consequences or insofar as its beneficial consequences predominate. But these are direct act utilitarian claims.

Third, Mill sometimes understands tendencies as *powers* or *dispositions* of things to produce a certain sort of effect that will produce that effect unless some countervailing force interferes. For instance, in his understanding of the laws of mechanics in *A System of Logic*, Mill denies that an object subjected to a force always moves in the direction of the force.

> To accommodate the expression of the law to the real phenomena, we must say, not that the object moves, but that it *tends* to move, in the direction and with the velocity specified. We might, indeed, guard our expression in a different mode, by saying that the body moves in that manner unless prevented, or except insofar as prevented, by some counteracting cause. (CW VII, p. 444)

But tendencies in this sense are possessed not only by types of things but also by tokens. Moreover, tokens have the tendency even when they don't manifest it (produce the associated effect) due to interference. If Mill understands talk of tendencies in the Proportionality Doctrine in this way, then there's no need to read him, as Urmson does, as talking about types of actions, rather than action tokens. He would be ascribing to token actions powers to produce pleasure or pain – powers which, though present, may be masked by interfering factors.

But if we read Mill's tendency talk in the Proportionality Doctrine in this dispositional way, then he is endorsing something other than act utilitarianism, as traditionally conceived. Act utilitarianism is a form of direct utilitarianism, and it identifies the rightness of an act with the value of its consequences. These are actual consequences. But the dispositional version of the Proportionality Doctrine denies this. For, on this view, rightness tracks not actual value but dispositional value – not actual consequences but the consequences an action would produce were it not interfered with. This view might be equivalent to rule utilitarianism if an action's dispositional value were always the same as the normal or average value of the consequences of that type of action. If so, then there would be merit to Urmson's rule utilitarian reading of the Proportionality Doctrine, even though he would be wrong to defend it by appeal to the claim that only action types have tendencies. However, it is not reasonable to assume that dispositional value is the same as usual or average value, for a genuine disposition may be regularly or systematically masked if interference is regular. Water may boil at 100°C at sea level, but few samples of water may boil at that exact temperature due to interfering conditions, such as impurities in the water or atmospheric pressure that is lower or higher than at sea level.

So a dispositional reading of proportionality wouldn't result in rule utilitarianism. But it would result in an odd form of utilitarianism – one that implied that an action might be right even though it doesn't have good consequences, even though it does not belong to a class of actions that generally have good consequences, and even though that same action might not have good consequences in nearby possible worlds. This leads me to think that, even though Mill clearly understands tendencies as dispositions or powers that might not be manifest in some contexts, this is not how he understands talk of tendencies in the Proportionality Doctrine. There it seems more plausible to read him as assuming a purely extensional reading of tendencies of the sort employed by Bentham and Austin in their own canonical statements of utilitarianism.

Secondary principles

But Urmson does not appeal only to the Proportionality Doctrine to support his rule utilitarian interpretation. He also defends this interpretation as a reading of Mill's claims about the importance of secondary principles and rules in our moral reasoning. He recognizes that an act utilitarian might appeal to rules or principles as rules of thumb in doing utilitarian calculations, but he insists that Mill's secondary principles are not mere rules of thumb.

We can see the need for rules and principles that do not refer to utility by remembering Mill's distinction between a moral standard and a decision procedure (CW X, pp. 219–20). In his *Autobiography* Mill notes the case for pursuing our own happiness indirectly.

> I never, indeed, wavered in the conviction that happiness is the test of all rules of conduct, and the end of life. But I now thought that this end was only to be attained by not making it the direct end. Those only are happy (I thought) who have their minds fixed on some object other than their own happiness; on the happiness of others, on the improvement of mankind, even on some art or pursuit, followed not as a means, but as itself an ideal end. Aiming thus, at something else, they find happiness by the way. (CW I, p. 145)

The need for indirection in the pursuit of one's own happiness is sometimes called the paradox of egoism or prudence. It requires that one pursue things other than one's own happiness for their own sakes in order to be happy. Mill treats these plural ends as secondary principles. He holds similar views about the need for secondary principles in the promotion of universal happiness. For instance, in *Utilitarianism* he defends the utilitarian's appeal to various moral precepts as secondary principles (CW X, pp. 225–6). But it's not entirely clear how these secondary principles are related to the utilitarian first principle. Mill's discussion of the indirect pursuit of one's own happiness suggests one possible relationship.

> Secondary principles are false targets for the successful pursuit of one's primary objective, as when one shouldn't think too hard about how to make a free throw if one wants to increase one's chances of making the shot or when one aims to the left of the green so as to compensate for a slice in one's golf swing.

However, the immediate context of discussion in Chapter II of *Utilitarianism* suggests that Mill is there focusing on a different relationship.

> Secondary principles are generally but imperfectly reliable guides to doing what will maximize happiness.

Secondary principles, so understood, might sound like mere rules of thumb. But Mill does not regard them as mere heuristics in a utility calculation. They don't themselves make reference to utility, and he thinks they should be adhered to uncritically in ordinary circumstances. He goes so far as to describe the rule against lying as 'sacred' (CW X, p. 223). He seems to believe that secondary principles, such as the principle against lying, often satisfy two conditions.

[1] Following the principle generally but imperfectly leads to optimal results.
[2] One cannot in general reliably discriminate whether or, if so, when adherence to the principle would produce suboptimal results.

When these two conditions are met, Mill believes, agents should follow these principles automatically and uncritically most of the time. In these cases, agents consult only secondary principles; they do not use them as heuristics in a utility calculation. They have genuine deliberative autonomy. But to say this is not to say that agents should never consult the utilitarian first principle or assess the acceptance value of secondary principles. They should periodically step back and review, as best they can, whether the principle continues to satisfy conditions (1) and (2). Also, they should set aside these secondary principles and make direct appeal to the principle of utility in unusual cases in which it is especially clear that the effects of adhering to the principle would be significantly suboptimal and in cases in which secondary principles, each of which has a utilitarian justification, conflict (CW X, pp. 220–1 and pp. 225–6). But, otherwise, they should regulate their conduct according to these secondary principles without recourse to the utilitarian first principle. Regulating one's behavior in this way by secondary principles is what will best promote happiness. Mill summarizes this picture in *A System of Logic*.

> I do not mean to assert that the promotion of happiness should be itself the end of all actions, or even all rules of action. It is the justification, and ought to be the controller, of all ends, but it is not itself the sole end. There are many virtuous actions, and even virtuous modes of action (though the cases are, I think, less frequent than is often supposed) by which happiness in the particular instance is sacrificed, more pain being produced than pleasure. But conduct of which this can be truly asserted, admits of justification only because it can be shown that on the whole more happiness will exist in the

> world, if feelings are cultivated which will make people, in certain cases, regardless of happiness. (CW VIII, p. 952)

Mill makes similar claims in his essay 'On Bentham:'

> We think utility, or happiness, much too complex and indefinite an end to be sought except through the medium of various secondary ends, concerning which there may be, and often is, agreement in persons who differ in their ultimate standard; and about which there does exist a much greater unanimity among thinking persons, than might be supposed from their diametrical divergence on the great questions of moral metaphysics.... Those who adopt utility as a standard can seldom apply it truly except through the secondary principles; those who reject it, generally do no more than erect those secondary principles into first principles. It is when two or more of the secondary principles conflict, that a direct appeal to some first principle becomes necessary; and then commences the practical importance of the utilitarian controversy... (CW X, pp. 110–11)

Mill's claims about the nature and importance of secondary principles and precepts that are and ought to be regulated by utilitarian first principles form an important part of his views about moral reasoning.

His utilitarian justification of discrete secondary principles is intended as a contrast with the intuitionism of William Whewell and others. As he makes clear in his essay 'Whewell on Moral Philosophy,' Mill thinks that the intuitionist wrongly treats familiar moral precepts as ultimate moral factors whose justification is supposed to be self-evident to reason. By contrast, Mill's account of secondary principles recognizes their importance in moral reasoning but insists that they are neither innate nor infallible; they are precepts that have been adopted and internalized because of their acceptance value, and their continued use should be suitably regulated by their ongoing comparative acceptance value. Far from undermining utilitarian first principles, Mill thinks, appeal to the importance of such moral principles actually provides support for utilitarianism.

It seems clear that Mill is assigning to secondary principles or rules a role that goes beyond rules of thumb in a utilitarian calculation. In the passage from *A System of Logic* above he claims that utility justifies which principles or rules we follow. Does this commit Mill to rule utilitarianism? Urmson thinks it does. John Rawls may too.

Rawls (1999) motivates a rule utilitarian justification of punishment by appeal to a difference between legislative and judicial attitudes toward rules. Rawls asks us to distinguish the legislative issues of whether to punish conduct, which conduct to punish, and how to punish such conduct from the judicial issue about the conditions under which particular individuals ought to be punished. This is, Rawls thinks, a special case of the more general distinction between reasons for having a practice and the reasons that regulate its proper operation. Forward-looking utilitarian reasons are relevant to these legislative issues, but only backward-looking retributive reasons are relevant to addressing the judicial issue.

> The decision whether or not to use the law rather than some other mechanism of social control, and the decision as to what laws to have and what penalties to assign, may be settled by utilitarian arguments; but if one decides to have laws then one has decided on something whose working in particular cases is retributive in form. (1999, p. 23)

This is a rule utilitarian approach to punishment. Interestingly (as Rawls himself notes), Mill begins his own account of the relationship between first principles and secondary principles in *A System of Logic* by making the same distinction between legislative and judicial perspectives on punishment (CW VIII, pp. 943–4). So perhaps he too is drawing rule utilitarian conclusions.

But Mill's claims about secondary principles are not inconsistent with act utilitarianism. For one thing, though Mill does not treat secondary principles as mere rules of thumb in utilitarian calculation, he does not think that they should be followed uncritically or independently of their consequences. He thinks that they should be set aside in favor of direct appeal to the principle of utility when following them would be clearly suboptimal or when there is a conflict among secondary principles.

Moreover, act utilitarianism permits one to act on discrete moral precepts or principles that make no direct reference to utility if this results in one performing the optimal action. Indeed, the act utilitarian can allow the agent to follow principles or rules even when this sometimes results in suboptimal acts being performed. Recall that act utilitarianism is a species of direct utilitarianism, which assesses things by their (actual) consequences. But the direct utilitarian assesses things other than actions, including motives, principles, and rules. Now it might be true that for a particular agent the rules with the optimal acceptance value direct him to perform actions, some of which are suboptimal. If he cannot reliably identify in advance those cases in which adherence to the rule would be suboptimal, or if he is not sufficiently fine-grained psychologically to deviate from the rule here where doing so is optimal without deviating from the rule in other cases where it is not, then he will do more good by following the rules uncritically even though he knows that by doing so he will perform some suboptimal actions. In such a situation, a direct utilitarian should want the agent to follow the optimal rules, rather than perform the optimal action. This would be rule utilitarianism (not direct utilitarianism) only if we made the further claim that the right action is to follow the optimal rules. But the direct utilitarian will refuse this further move. She will say that the right action is the optimal action, but that for some agents it can in principle be best to act from optimal motives, rather than perform the right action. The suboptimal actions the agent thus performs will be wrong, but they can be cases of *blameless wrongdoing*, perhaps even *praiseworthy wrongdoing*.[5]

For the most part, Mill gives no indication that he does not accept this direct utilitarian justification of acting from optimal rules or motives, even when this might result in suboptimal acts. However, there is one passage that suggests the indirect utilitarian account. In the middle of Chapter II of *Utilitarianism* Mill argues that utilitarianism permits most people most of the time to concentrate on promoting the well-being of a comparatively small circle of people and that only a few are required to concern themselves with promoting the human good impartially on a regular basis. He goes on to say:

> In the case of abstinences indeed – of things which people forbear to do, from moral considerations, though the consequences in the particular case might be beneficial – it would be unworthy of an intelligent agent not to be consciously aware that the action is of a class which, if practiced generally, would be generally injurious, and that this is the ground of the obligation to refrain from it. (CW X, pp. 219–20)

Here, Mill commits himself to an indirect utilitarian conception of duty if he says that an act is right or required by duty, though suboptimal, because it is an instance of a rule with optimal acceptance value. That is certainly a natural reading of this passage. But it introduces inconsistency with the direct utilitarian claims Mill makes elsewhere.

Of course, one could claim that his talk of 'obligation' here is loose and not to be taken literally. An act utilitarian who believes that there are cases of blameless or even praiseworthy wrongdoing could claim that Mill is saying only that the agent has a good reason or justification to follow the optimal rule even in particular cases in which doing so is suboptimal and, hence, by act utilitarian lights, wrong. So, when Mill says that the ground of the obligation is the acceptance value of the practice, he really only means that this is the agent's reason for following the optimal practice, not a ground of obligation or duty to forbear in the particular case. This reading has the advantage of making this passage consistent with Mill's other commitments to act utilitarianism, but it has the disadvantage of requiring a nonliteral reading of the passage.

Instead of endorsing a loose reading of the passage, the act utilitarian might advocate greater attention to Mill's actual language. There are two different things Mill says in this passage that make the rule utilitarian reading of the passage problematic or at least nonmandatory.

First, notice that Mill discusses cases in which it is good to follow a practice of forbearance even though this means foregoing beneficial consequences in particular cases. He says we have reason to regard it as our duty to abstain from certain actions even when these would have beneficial consequences. He says that the prohibited actions would be beneficial, not that they would be optimal. But then he does not actually assert that we have a duty to perform suboptimal acts.

But there is a second, independent way to resist the rule utilitarian reading. Suppose, for the sake of argument, Mill is thinking about cases in which abstinence is suboptimal. He does not say that it is our duty to abstain even when doing so is suboptimal. Instead, he says 'it would be unworthy of an intelligent agent not to be consciously aware that the action is of a class which, if practiced generally, would be generally injurious, and that this is the ground of the obligation to refrain from it.' But, then, he is saying that a good agent will regard duty as consisting in conformity to rules with optimal acceptance value – not that duty will so consist. The direct utilitarian agrees that agents with limited powers of discrimination might do best by following optimal rules even though this may produce some individual actions that are suboptimal and, hence, by her lights, wrong. So the direct utilitarian might think that it was best for an agent to regard her duty as consisting in conformity with the best rules, even if her duty actually consisted in what was optimal. Once we see that 'the ground of the obligation' falls within the scope of what it would be 'worthy of an intelligent agent' to consider, we can see how the passage admits of a direct, act utilitarian reading after all.

To say that we can reconcile the abstinence passage with direct utilitarianism is not to say that this is the most natural reading of the passage or that there is nothing to be said for a rule utilitarian reading. But, if we continue to abstract, for the moment, from complexities to be introduced in Chapter V of *Utilitarianism* (discussed below), then, given Mill's commitments to direct utilitarianism elsewhere, a direct utilitarian reading of the abstinence passage appears to be the only way for him to maintain a consistent position. The fact that we can read the abstinence passage in a way that is consistent with direct utilitarianism is, therefore, reason to do so. This allows us to read Mill's claims about secondary principles in a way that is consistent with his commitment to direct utilitarianism, though not without some interpretive strain. Whatever Mill may have said, it should be clear that his principal claims about the importance of secondary principles do not, as such, force a choice between direct, act utilitarianism and indirect, rule utilitarianism. *A fortiori*, it does not provide reason to reject the act utilitarian strand in Mill's formulation of the utilitarian doctrine.[6]

5 Sanction utilitarianism

So far, the picture we get is that Mill pretty consistently endorses act utilitarianism as a standard of right conduct or duty, even if he does not require it to be a decision procedure or to supply a set of motives. Though he believes in the importance of secondary rules that can and should regulate much moral reasoning, this does not require any departure from direct utilitarianism. However, Chapter V of *Utilitarianism* introduces claims about duty, justice, and rights that are hard to square with direct or act utilitarianism.

> For the truth is, that the idea of penal sanction, which is the essence of law, enters not only into the conception of injustice, but into that of any kind of wrong. We do not call anything wrong unless we mean to imply that a person ought to be punished in some way or other for doing it – if not by law, by the opinion of his fellow creatures; if not by opinion, by the reproaches of his own conscience. This seems the real turning point of the distinction between morality and simple expediency. (CW X, p. 246)

Here Mill defines wrongness and, by implication, duty, not directly in terms of the nature of the action or its consequences but indirectly in terms of appropriate responses to it. He appears to believe that one is under an obligation or duty to do something just in case failure to do it is wrong and that an action is wrong just in case some kind of external or internal sanction – punishment, social censure, or self-reproach – ought to be applied to its performance. This test distinguishes duty from expediency (CW X, pp. 246–7). Not all suboptimal or inexpedient acts are wrong, only those to which one ought to apply some sort of sanction (at least, self-reproach).

Justice is a proper part of duty. Justice involves duties that are perfect duties – that is, duties that are correlated with rights.

> Justice implies something which it is not only right to do, and wrong not to do, but which some individual person can claim from us as a matter of right. (CW X, pp. 246–7)

An act is unjust just in case it is wrong and violates someone's rights (CW X, pp. 249–50). Someone has a right just in case she has a claim that society ought to protect by force of law or public opinion.

> When we call anything a person's right, we mean that he has a valid claim on society to protect him in the possession of it, either by the force of law, or by that of education and opinion. If he has what we consider a sufficient claim, on whatever account, to have something guaranteed to him by society, we say that he has a right to it. If we desire to prove that anything does not belong to him by right, we think this is done as soon as it is admitted that society ought not to take measures for securing it to him, but should leave it to chance, or to his own exertions. (CW X, p. 250)

Mill makes or implies several claims here. Let's try to distinguish some of them and see how he relates them.

[1] An act is wrong iff some sort of sanction ought to be applied to its performance.
[2] An act is obligatory or one's duty iff failure to do it is wrong.
[3] Hence, an act is obligatory or one's duty iff some sort of sanction ought to be applied to the failure to do it.
[4] An act is permissible iff it is not wrong to perform it.
[5] Hence, an act is permissible iff it is not the case that some sort of sanction ought to be applied to its performance.
[6] Not all inexpedient or suboptimal acts are wrong.

[7] Hence, it is not always one's obligation or duty to perform the optimal act.
[8] Hence, some suboptimal acts are permissible.
[9] Hence, there can be supererogatory acts.
[10] Justice is a species of duty in which the failure to act justly is not only wrong but also violates rights.
[11] Someone has a right to x iff society ought to protect her claim to x by force of law or public opinion.
[12] Hence, unjust acts are wrongs that society ought to prohibit by force of law or opinion.
[13] Hence, just acts are duties that society ought to require by force of law or opinion.

Notice that these relationships among duty, justice, and rights and other deontic notions do not yet introduce any utilitarian elements. But Mill does think that whether sanctions ought to be applied to an action – and hence whether it is wrong – and whether society ought to enforce an individual's claim – and hence whether she has a right – both depend upon the utility or expediency of doing so (CW X, p. 250). However, he does not say precisely what standard of expediency he has in mind. In particular, he does not say whether something counts as wrong just in case it is optimal to sanction that conduct or just in case it would be beneficial to sanction it, and so forth. The class of wrong acts is narrower if we require that sanctions be optimal than if we require that they be merely beneficial. Unless otherwise noted, I will ignore this interesting question about the proper utilitarian standard for applying sanctions.

Because this account of duty defines the rightness and wrongness of an act, not in terms of its utility, as act utilitarianism does, but in terms of the utility of applying sanctions to the conduct, it is an indirect form of utilitarianism. Because justice is a species of duty, it inherits the indirect character of sanction utilitarianism. In 'Mill's Theory of Morality' and other essays, David Lyons (1994, Chapters 2 and 3) has drawn attention to this indirect aspect of Mill's utilitarianism. Lyons does not have a name for this form of indirect utilitarianism. Because it makes the rightness and wrongness of conduct depend upon the utility of sanctioning that conduct in some way, we might call it *sanction utilitarianism*. Because sanction utilitarianism is a species of indirect utilitarianism, it is inconsistent with act utilitarianism.

While I am indebted to Lyons's analysis of Mill's theory of duty in Chapter V of *Utilitarianism*, I disagree with his interpretation on one point and dispute the significance he attaches to sanction utilitarianism.

It is worth noticing that Lyons's interpretation of Mill's theory of duty is *doubly* indirect. It is indirect, as we have seen, because it makes an action's rightness or wrongness a function not of its utility but rather of the utility of others responding to it in certain ways. But on Lyons's reading Mill's theory is indirect in another way as well.

> To call an act wrong is to imply that guilt feelings, and perhaps other sanctions, would be warranted against it. But sanctions assume coercive rules. *To show an act wrong, therefore, is to show that a coercive rule against it would be justified.* (1994, p. 55)

Lyons believes that for Mill an action's deontic status turns, not on its utility, but on the utility of sanctioning responses, not to it, but to actions of that type or class. This second layer of indirection is the appeal to rules, shared with rule utilitarianism. However, I see no justification for this second layer of indirection. In particular, I see no evidence that Mill wants to introduce rules or principles into his formulation of the utilitarian standard. Of course, as we have seen, he is a firm believer in the need for secondary principles in ordinary moral deliberations. But this is a claim about how we are likely to best satisfy the utilitarian standard, not a claim about the formulation of the standard itself. When Mill defines wrong action in terms of sanctions, he says that an act is wrong if *it* ought to be sanctioned in some way, not if it's enjoined by a principle, violations of which ought to be sanctioned. If so, sanction utilitarianism is only singly indirect, which means that it is even further removed from the sort of indirection embodied in rule utilitarianism. Sanction utilitarianism is really a distinct form of indirect utilitarianism.

Lyons concludes from the fact that Mill's indirect account of duty is not act utilitarian that Mill is not an act utilitarian. But, whereas I agree with the premise, the conclusion does not follow. The fact that Mill sometimes makes claims that do not fit with act utilitarianism does not mean that he does not elsewhere make commitments to act utilitarianism. Lyons (1994, p. 50 and pp. 59–60) reminds us that Mill sometimes identifies utilitarianism as a theory of ends.

> Questions about ends are, in other words, questions about what things are desirable. The utilitarian doctrine is, that happiness is desirable, and the only thing desirable as an end; all other things being desirable only as a means to that end. (CW X, p. 234)

It is true that utilitarianism is in part a theory of ends or the good; it insists that the good is happiness or well-being. But it is also a theory of the right, as both direct and indirect forms of utilitarianism recognize. The problem is simply that Mill is attracted to different utilitarian conceptions of right action. While the account of duty in chapter V represents an indirect form of utilitarianism, Mill elsewhere – and on several occasions – assigns utility a direct role in the determination of right and wrong action. We examined these in Section 3 above. The natural conclusion is that Mill does not have a consistent theory of duty. The introduction of indirect utilitarian ideas in Chapter V of *Utilitarianism* into an account of utilitarianism that is otherwise act utilitarian reveals a fundamental tension in Mill's thought about duty.

6 Sanction vs. act utilitarianism

Given Mill's ambivalence between direct and indirect utilitarianism, it is natural to inquire whether one view is more plausible than the other. Some of Mill's claims in Chapter V suggest a possible advantage that sanction utilitarianism might have. In articulating sanction utilitarianism, Mill claims that it allows him to distinguish duty and expediency and claim that not all inexpedient acts are wrong; inexpedient acts are only wrong when it is good or optimal to sanction them. This suggests that sanction utilitarianism may be preferable to act utilitarianism, because it has a more plausible account of the relation among different deontic categories.

Consider some of the implications of act utilitarianism. Act utilitarianism implies that I do wrong every time I fail to do the very best action, even when the suboptimal act that I perform is very good indeed. That may seem harsh and overly demanding. To see why, consider a familiar fourfold deontic distinction:

[a] wrong or forbidden,
[b] permissible,
[c] obligatory, and
[d] supererogatory

According to common-sense thinking, the obligatory is just a proper part of the permissible, and there are many permissible acts that are neither obligatory nor wrong. Common sense also recognizes a class of supererogatory acts that are above and beyond the call of duty.

By contrast, act utilitarianism seems unable to account for this fourfold distinction. Because it makes the optimal obligatory and the suboptimal wrong, it appears to expand the domain of the forbidden. Act utilitarianism also collapses the distinction between the permissible and the obligatory, treating all nonobligatory acts as impermissible. Moreover, act utilitarianism recognizes no supererogatory acts. If the optimal is already one's duty, there appears to be no room for the supererogatory.

By contrast, sanction utilitarianism does not appear to have these problems. It offers a distinct account of each category.[7]

[a] Wrong or forbidden acts are those whose performance it is optimal to blame.
[b] Permissible acts are those whose performance it is not optimal to blame.
[c] Obligatory acts are those whose omission it is optimal to blame.
[d] Supererogatory acts are permissible acts that are especially expedient.

In this way, sanction utilitarianism appears to respect this common fourfold distinction and, in particular, to make room for the supererogatory.[8]

Is this a genuine advantage of sanction utilitarianism? The direct utilitarian can and should distinguish between the moral assessment of an act and the moral assessment of the act of praising or blaming that act. Each should be assessed, the direct utilitarian claims, by the utility of doing so. But then it is possible for there to be wrongdoing (a suboptimal act) that is blameless or even praiseworthy. But then the direct utilitarian can appeal to the same distinctions among praiseworthiness and blameworthiness that the sanction utilitarian appeals to, while allowing that these distinctions line up differently than her own deontic distinctions.

[a] Acts whose performance it is optimal to blame. This class will include only those suboptimal (wrong) acts that rise to the level of meriting blame.
[b] Acts whose performance it is not optimal to blame. This class will include optimal (obligatory) acts and some, but not all, suboptimal (wrong) acts that do not merit any kind of blame.
[c] Acts whose omission it is optimal to blame. This class would include only those acts whose nonperformance was so suboptimal (wrong) as to merit blame.
[d] Acts whose performance it is not optimal to blame and whose performance it is optimal to praise. This class will include especially expedient acts, including the optimal (obligatory) act and several slightly suboptimal (wrong) acts.

Because this fourfold distinction is made, not directly in terms of deontic status, but in terms of patterns of praise and blame, it represents a kind of *pragmatic* reconstruction of the common-sense classification.

While there is no *a priori* guarantee that the direct utilitarian fourfold classification in terms of praise and blame will track perfectly the commonsense classification of deontic status, there is some reason to think that it will sort options in roughly the same ways and to wonder whether the direct utilitarian's classification might not provide reflectively acceptable guidance and correction where the commonsense classification provides uncertain or questionable guidance. In any case, it is hard to see how sanction utilitarianism could be preferable to act utilitarianism here, because they offer the same classification in terms of praise and blame. The only difference is that, whereas sanction utilitarianism ties rightness and wrongness to praise and blame, act utilitarianism does not. But this looks more like a difference in moral book-keeping systems than a substantive moral difference.

However, sanction utilitarianism appears to have disadvantages that act utilitarianism does not. One such cost is that sanction utilitarianism appears to provide the *wrong sort of reason* for thinking an action wrong. It makes the wrongness of an act depend upon the appropriateness of punishing or, more generally, sanctioning it. But this inverts what many would regard as the usual dependency between duty and punishment. Many think that punishment is appropriate for wrong acts because they are wrong. This requires grounding their wrongness in some independent account; it is not the suitability for punishment that makes an act wrong. Retributivism is the view that punishment should be consequential on, and proportional to, the wrongness of the conduct in question. But then the retributivist owes us some independent account of what makes actions wrong. Usually, this debt is paid in deontological currency. By contrast, direct consequentialism must deny that an act's wrongness is either a necessary or a sufficient condition for punishment, because whether an act should be punished depends on the consequences, not of the original action, but of the act of punishing it. Though they disagree about whether punishment is always and only consequential on wrongness, the direct consequentialist and the retributivist agree on the need for an account of an action's wrongness that is prior to and independent of its suitability for punishment. It is only sanction consequentialism that must deny the explanatory priority of wrongness to punishment.

Another disadvantage of sanction utilitarianism is its *hybrid* structure. Sanction utilitarianism is impurely indirect. For, while it provides an indirect utilitarian theory of duty, the account it provides of when sanctions should be applied to conduct is direct – it depends upon the consequences of applying sanctions. This isn't just the worry that sanction utilitarianism is a *mixed* theory – combining direct and indirect elements in an unmotivated or ad hoc way – though that would be cause for concern too. There is a deeper worry afoot. Sanction utilitarianism provides an indirect utilitarian account of the conditions under which an action – any action – is right or wrong. This general indirect criterion is that any action is wrong to which one ought to attach sanctions. But sanction utilitarianism goes on to explain when one ought to attach sanctions in direct utilitarianism terms of whether doing so would be optimal (or, perhaps, beneficial). But imposing sanctions is a kind of action, and we can ask whether the imposition of a particular sanction would be right or wrong. The general criterion implies that we should answer this question about the rightness of applying sanctions in sanction utilitarian terms, namely, by asking whether it would be right to sanction the failure to apply sanctions. This introduces a second-order sanction, whose rightness we can now ask about. We seem to be off on an infinite regress of sanctions. This is already cause for concern, inasmuch as this infinite regress looks vicious, because there appears to be no determinate fact to ground an answer to the original question about whether it is right to apply the first-order sanction. But matters are worse for sanction utilitarianism, inasmuch as it implies a direct utilitarian answer to the question of whether it is right to apply sanctions that is inconsistent with the general criterion. The trouble is that sanction utilitarianism says two mutually inconsistent things.

[1] Any act is right iff it is optimal to apply sanctions to its omission (the indirect claim).
[2] Applying sanctions is right iff doing so is optimal (the direct claim).

As far as I can see, the combination of [1] and [2] renders sanction utilitarianism internally inconsistent.

In the face of these worries about sanction utilitarianism, it may be tempting to try to square sanction utilitarianism with act utilitarianism by noticing that in the crucial passage introducing sanction utilitarianism Mill says that 'we do not *call anything wrong* unless we mean to imply that a person ought to be punished in some way or other for doing it – if not by law, by the opinion of his fellow creatures; if not by opinion, by the reproaches of his own conscience' (CW X, p. 246, emphasis added).

One might argue that Mill is giving an account of when we *call* something wrong, not when it *is* wrong. Whereas being wrong is, as the act utilitarian claims, a matter of being suboptimal, we only bother to call something wrong if it rises to the level that it would be good or optimal to sanction. We might call this a kind of *pragmatic* reading of sanction utilitarianism. It would be like the pragmatic strategy considered earlier in this section for the fourfold distinction among the wrong, the permissible, the obligatory, and the supererogatory. Considered in itself, this act utilitarian reading of the significance of sanction utilitarianism is reasonably plausible. The problem is that the surrounding text makes it difficult to sustain this reading without strain. For in the previous sentence Mill says that 'the idea of penal sanction...enters...into any kind of wrong,' and in the sentence immediately following the statement of sanction utilitarianism he says 'that this seems to be the real turning point of the distinction between morality and simple expediency.' Here, he seems to be speaking in his own voice and insisting on distinguishing one's duty from what is or would be optimal.

7 Conclusion

The different strands in Mill's utilitarian conception of duty require disentangling. In his central exposition of the utilitarian standard in Chapter II Mill commits himself to direct utilitarianism and its act utilitarian conception of duty in multiple passages. In that same chapter, Mill focuses on the felicific tendencies of actions and assigns a significant role to rules within moral reasoning, both of which have been taken to commit him to a an indirect utilitarian conception of duty, such as rule utilitarianism. However, these claims are fully reconcilable with direct utilitarianism. The abstinence passage may suggest rule utilitarian claims, but even this passage admits of a direct utilitarian reading. Overall, there is very strong support for a traditional act utilitarian reading of Mill's explanation of utilitarian essentials in *Utilitarianism* and little or no compelling support for a rule utilitarian reading. But in Chapter V Mill does introduce indirect utilitarian ideas in the doctrine of sanction utilitarianism. I don't see how to reconcile these direct and indirect elements in Mill's conception of duty.

Our survey of the comparative costs and benefits of sanction and act utilitarianism is no doubt incomplete. But it suggests that, despite its initial appeal, it is unclear that sanction utilitarianism enjoys real advantages over act utilitarianism, and that sanction utilitarianism is, in fact, more problematic than act utilitarianism. If so, then we may wish that

Mill had more clearly endorsed no more than the pragmatic reading of sanction utilitarianism. Or, if we count the number of passages expressing one or the other of these two conceptions of duty, we may want to insist that act utilitarianism is Mill's *considered* view. Sympathetic as I am to these interpretive suggestions, I don't think that we can avoid the conclusion that Mill was in fact ambivalent between these direct and indirect utilitarian conceptions of duty.[9]

Notes

1. This conception of act utilitarianism might be contrasted with *satisficing* act utilitarianism, which says that an act is right just in case its consequences for the general happiness are *good enough*. Though satisficing act utilitarianism is also a form of direct utilitarianism, Mill shows no signs of being attracted to it, and I will not discuss it further here.
2. In Bentham's case, this is reasonably clear from his doubts about the actual utility of trying to calculate expected utility in some circumstances ([1789] 1970, Chapter IV, Paragraph 6). However, the matter is complicated by the fact that Bentham treats both certainty and propinquity (temporal proximity) as intrinsic dimensions of pleasures that affect their intrinsic value ([1789] 1970, Chapter IV, Paragraphs 2–3). But here, I think, Bentham is confusing the standard and its application. Certainty and propinquity are not features of pleasures themselves, but of their relation to planners, and they affect not actual utility, but expected utility.
3. I call it an extensional reading of the felicific tendency of an act, even though it can apply to possible or hypothetical acts, because the felicific tendency of a hypothetical act consists in what would be the actual, not the probable, consequences of such an act, were it performed.
4. My claims here are indebted to Berger (1984, pp. 73–8).
5. It might be thought that the optimal action and the action based on optimal motives could not come apart in this way, because the negative effects of departing from optimal rules must count against the optimality of departing from optimal rules. This is a complicated issue. Our actions do affect our motives and dispositions. But one act does not a motive or disposition make, from which it follows, I believe, that we cannot assume that the best action is always the same as the action required by the best motives.
6. Some writers understand indirect utilitarianism as including any utilitarian theory that permits psychological indirection, in the form of false targets or secondary principles, as a way of satisfying the utilitarian standard. But, as I have argued, these forms of indirection do not require that the standard itself be formulated in indirect terms. Our focus has been on whether Mill's standard itself is direct or indirect.
7. Recall that Mill's sanction utilitarianism is agnostic about whether the utilitarian standard for applying sanctions should be optimality or something less, such as net benefit. For ease of comparison with act utilitarianism, I focus on the optimality criterion. But similar claims would apply, *mutatis mutandis*, for the comparison with the net benefit criterion.

8. In 'Auguste Comte and Positivism' Mill discusses the need to recognize categories of the permissible but not obligatory and the supererogatory (CW X, pp. 337–8), but he does not say or imply that this is a problem for act utilitarianism or an argument for sanction utilitarianism.
9. Earlier versions of some of this material were presented at the triennial meetings of the International Society for Utilitarian Studies at Dartmouth in August 2005, a UCSD History of Philosophy Roundtable in March 2007, the University of Pennsylvania in March 2007, a philosophy and law seminar at Georgetown University in February 2008, the University of California, Santa Barbara in May 2008, and the University of Texas in October 2008, and benefited from feedback on those occasions. In writing and revising this essay, I am conscious of intellectual debts of various kinds to Richard Arneson, Garrett Cullity, Dale Dorsey, Sam Freeman, Alan Fuchs, Paul Guyer, Michael Hardimon, Monte Johnson, Charlie Kurth, David Lyons, Christopher McMahon, James Messina, John Mikhail, Mark Murphy, Alastair Norcross, Henry Richardson, Sam Rickless, Don Rutherford, Susan Sauvé Meyer, Eric Watkins, Aaron Zimmerman, and Matt Zwolinski.

References

Austin, John ([1832] 1954) *The Province of Jurisprudence Determined*, H.L.A. Hart (ed.) (New York: Noonday Press).

Bentham, Jeremy ([1789] 1970) *An Introduction to the Principles of Morals and Legislation*, J. Burns and H.L.A. Hart (eds) (London: Athlone Press).

Berger, Fred (1884) *Happiness, Justice, and Freedom: The Moral and Political Philosophy of John Stuart Mill* (Los Angeles: University of California Press).

Lyons, David (1994) *Rights, Welfare, and Mill's Moral Theory* (New York: Oxford University Press).

Rawls, John (1971) *A Theory of Justice* (Cambridge: Harvard University Press).

Rawls, John (1999) 'Two Concepts of Rules,' reprinted in his *Collected Papers*, S. Freeman (ed.) (Cambridge: Harvard University Press).

Robson, J.M. (ed.) (1969) *The Collected Works of John Stuart Mill: Essays on Ethics, Religion, and Society*, Vol. X (Toronto: University of Toronto Press).

Robson, J.M. (ed.) (1974a) *The Collected Works of John Stuart Mill: A System of Logic Ratiocinative and Inductive Part 1, Vol. VII* (Toronto: University of Toronto Press).

Robson, J.M. (ed.) (1974b) *The Collected Works of John Stuart Mill: A System of Logic Ratiocinative and Inductive Part 2, Vol. VIII* (Toronto: University of Toronto Press).

Robson, J.M. and Stillinger, J. (eds) (1981) *The Collected Works of John Stuart Mill: Autobiography and Literary Essays*, Vol. I (Toronto: University of Toronto Press).

Sidgwick, Henry (1907) *The Methods of Ethics*, 7th ed. (New York: Macmillan).

Urmson, J.O. (1953) 'The Interpretation of the Moral Philosophy of J. S. Mill', *Philosophical Quarterly* 10, 33–9.

2
Justice, Rights, and Rules in Mill's Utilitarianism

William H. Shaw

1 Introduction

Among the most important of Mill's many contributions to the utilitarian tradition is the space he finds within utilitarianism for justice, rights, and rules. In doing so, he lays the building blocks of an attractive and viable form of utilitarianism – a subtle, indirect type of utilitarianism that is resistant to a wide range of familiar criticisms. A number of philosophers these days, myself included, find themselves drawn to a utilitarianism of the sort Mill adumbrated.[1] However, experts on Mill disagree over the precise interpretation of his normative theory. And no one denies that some passages in Mill's various writings on ethics are open to rival readings and that others are difficult to reconcile with one another. He neglects to fill some gaps in his arguments and leaves some interesting questions unanswered. Moreover, Mill wrote in a different time. Some issues that were important to him are less important to us, and vice versa.

This chapter does not examine all aspects of Mill's normative theory. Rather, it focuses on his account of justice and the importance he assigns to rights and rules. I begin by pointing out some distinctive features of Mill's way of framing the justice–utility issue. I then go on in Section 3 to examine his basic theory of justice, paying special attention to the parallel he draws between it and the familiar distinction between perfect and imperfect duties. Section 4 discusses his view of rights, explaining what Mill adds to Bentham, while Section 5 outlines Mill's rejoinder to the charge that utility is too unreliable a standard on which to base justice and probes some of the obscurities in his discussion of conflicts between different principles of justice and between justice and other normative considerations. I conclude with some reflections on the difficulties of classifying Mill as either an act or a rule utilitarian.

2 Mill's concerns and ours

The natural place to begin, of course, is with Chapter V of *Utilitarianism*, Mill's extended analysis of the connection between justice and utility. There he observes that an important source of resistance to utilitarianism comes from the fact that people have a strong and distinct sense (or 'sentiment' or 'feeling') of justice, a sense of justice that seems to them to have nothing to do with utility, but rather to reflect 'an inherent quality in things' (CW X, p. 240). A major goal of Mill in this chapter is to show how 'the subjective mental feeling of justice' can be explained in a way that is consistent with a utilitarian account of ethics, according to which 'justice [is] only a particular kind or branch of general utility' (CW X, pp. 240–1).

Before going further, we should note two ways in which the issues that engage Mill diverge from those that tend to be at the center of today's debates over utilitarianism and justice. The first is the psychological focus of Mill's discussion – his concern in this chapter to explain the origin and strength of our sentiment of justice. This stands in marked contrast to the nonpsychological orientation that typifies most contemporary normative philosophy. True, moral psychology continues to occupy some philosophers, just as it always has, and in the last few years in particular a number of them have begun wrestling with the question of what empirical psychology might possibly teach us about ethics. But these discussions have had little or no impact on the ongoing debate over utilitarianism and, in particular, over the relation between utility and justice. Utilitarians today wish to establish, and their critics to deny, that in some way or other the principles of justice reduce to, or are subordinate to, the principle of utility. But neither side is much interested in the psychological side of the question. Contemporary utilitarians seem not to care much about how people come to have the nonutilitarian moral principles that so many of them clearly seem to have. For their part, critics of utilitarianism typically stake a lot on the fact that we have moral intuitions or considered moral beliefs that conflict, or seem to conflict, with utilitarianism. However, they display little interest in the psychological origin of these judgments. Rather, they take these moral intuitions or considered beliefs as fixed points, with which any successful normative theory must, by and large, tally –that is to say, with a little give and take here, and some adjustments and revisions there. Although some utilitarians acquiesce, to various degrees, in this popular 'reflective equilibrium' methodology, others dismiss the whole approach, arguing that people's moral intuitions reflect only their upbringing and the social attitudes around them and, hence, lack the probative force that the critics think they have when they try to enlist them against utilitarianism. But beyond this brusque and summary dismissal of 'intuition' utilitarians of this stripe do not go.

That Mill takes up the psychological side of the justice–utility question is a little surprising in light of Chapter III of *Utilitarianism*. There he contends that the precepts of customary morality, that is, of the positive or conventional morality of the society in which we have been raised, are the only ones that are likely to feel obligatory in themselves. Any other system of morality will seem to us to lack this binding force. 'When a person is asked to believe,' Mill writes, 'that this [customary] morality derives its obligation from some general principle around which custom has not thrown the same halo, the assertion is to him a paradox' (CW X, p. 227). He goes on to argue that, given the right social circumstances, all the internal and external sanctions that now support conventional morality and make it seem so necessary might attach with equal or greater strength to the principle of utility. It thus seems open to Mill, based on his stance in Chapter III, to brush aside as philosophically unimportant the putative fact that people experience the feeling of justice as pointing to some quality of things separate from their utility.

Why doesn't he do so? One can only surmise that he thought the apparently nonutilitarian character of our sentiment of justice was more of an obstacle to accepting utilitarianism than is the nonutilitarian character of other moral sentiments and that therefore, for his essay to be effective, it needed to do more than simply dismiss as irrelevant people's sense that justice is independent of utility. Further, as Chapter V makes clear, Mill does not want to debunk justice or to reduce its distinct and distinctively forceful claim on us. Rather, he wants to resuscitate justice on utilitarian terrain while at the same time retaining our sense of its demands as more serious and more compelling than are morality's other requirements.

In addition to the psychological orientation of Mill's discussion, there is a second difference between the way he frames the justice–utility issue and the way we tend to think about it today. As he sees it, although nonutilitarians believe that in principle justice is distinct from utility, they acknowledge that justice is 'never…disjointed from it in fact,' at least not 'in the long run' (CW X, p. 240).[2] This subtle view contrasts with that of most contemporary critics of utilitarianism. They typically contend that justice and utility do indeed conflict, and they relish pointing to situations in which utilitarianism requires, or is alleged to require, a course of action that runs contrary to the requirements of justice as these are normally understood (or that violates what we take to be people's rights or fails to respect some basic principle of common-sense morality). By contrast, the nonutilitarianism that Mill saw himself as wrestling with grants that justice and long-run utility are coextensive, but maintains that utility (or lack of it) is not the reason something is just (or unjust).

As utilitarians frequently point out, most of the alleged counterexamples to utilitarianism – intended to show that doing the utilitarian thing will sometimes require one to act unjustly, to ride roughshod over rights, or to ignore some elementary principle of morality – are not only improbable but deeply implausible, given what we know about human beings. They argue that for many reasons it will not, and indeed cannot, be the case that – to take a few well-worn examples – hanging an innocent man, supporting chattel slavery, killing a depressed and friendless derelict, or torturing a young girl to make her terrorist father talk will maximize net happiness. Mill did not have to engage on this argumentative front. His opponent does not argue that utilitarianism will sometimes enjoin unjust actions, only that it fails to capture what it is that makes something just (or unjust).

Things might be more complicated than this, however. On what basis might a critic who concedes that, the world being what it is, justice and utility do not diverge, and never will, nevertheless affirm that justice is not based on utility – that utility is not the reason something is just or unjust? One possibility is that the critic believes that, even if justice and utility invariably coincide in our world, there are possible worlds in which the two diverge.[3] And, to make this theoretical point, the critic would have no option but to introduce far-fetched counterexamples. For my own part, I believe that it is an open question how seriously any normative theory must take hypothetical scenarios involving possible worlds in which human beings or the circumstances of their lives are quite different from what we know them to be in our world. In any case, it is certainly unlikely that Mill would have worried about such examples, had he been presented with them. Moreover, by grounding the principles of justice in the real world, Chapter 5 makes objections based on distant counterfactuals beside the point.

3 What is justice?

Some people view justice as coextensive with right. The right thing to do is the just thing to do, and vice versa. Some ancient moralists may have believed something like this, equating justice and righteousness or seeing justice as the sum of our virtuous relations with others. Some utilitarians have identified the two, as well. For them, something is just if and only if it maximizes happiness.

Most philosophers, however, interpret justice in a narrower sense, maintaining that it is not the whole of morality. As they see it, the complaint that something is 'unjust' is more specific than the complaint that it is 'wrong' or 'immoral.' Not all wrongs, and certainly not all failures to maximize utility, are unjust. What, then, makes an act, policy, or institution unjust? Unfortunately, the terms *just* and *unjust* are somewhat vague and open-ended, and different people use them in different ways. Still, as Mill helpfully points out, talk of justice or injustice typically revolves around a few related ideas. Specifically, Mill contends that injustice consists in [1] violating someone's moral or legal rights (insofar as the latter do not rest on laws that infringe anyone's moral rights), [2] a person's failing to get what he or she deserves, [3] breaking faith with someone, violating one's engagements, or disappointing expectations that one has knowingly and voluntarily created, [4] not acting impartially in matters where favor and preference do not properly apply, or [5] treating people unequally in situations where equality is called for. Mill may have overlooked the fact that justice is also often used to mean *fairness*. Maybe he saw point [3] as covering fairness. But [3] doesn't seem to capture the fact that justice seems also to concern [i] the fair treatment of (members of) groups of people and [ii] the fair compensation of prior injuries. Perhaps, though, Mill thought that points [5] and [2] adequately covered these aspects of fairness.

Rights, equality, fairness, desert, impartiality – these do seem to be the focal points of talk of justice and injustice. Many people would leave the matter here, treating the concept of justice as a family resemblance notion, not something that can be defined or analyzed in terms of necessary and sufficient conditions. Mill, however, goes on to develop an account of the concept of justice that ties together these diverse strands. 'In our survey of various popular acceptations of justice,' Mill writes, 'the term appeared generally to involve the idea of a personal right.' He continues:

> Whether the injustice consists in depriving a person of a possession, or in breaking faith with him, or in treating him worse than he deserves, or worse than other people who have no greater claims – in each case the supposition implies two things: a wrong done, and some assignable person who is wronged...It seems to me that this

> feature in the case – a right in some person, correlative to the moral obligation – constitutes the specific difference between justice and generosity or beneficence. Justice implies something which it is not only right to do, and wrong not to do, but which some individual can claim from us as his moral right. (CW X, pp. 246–7)

Justice thus represents only a subset of morality, namely, those obligations which some person or persons can claim from us as a matter of right. We act wrongly in Mill's view whenever we fail to fulfill our moral obligations. We act unjustly when we not only act wrongly but also violate someone's rights.

Perfect and imperfect duties

Mill links his account of the concept of justice to the traditional distinction between duties of perfect and duties of imperfect obligation. Duties of the first kind require us to act (or refrain from acting) in some specific or specifiable way at a prescribed time and place. Thus, if I have an obligation to bail you out of jail or to assess your teaching performance fairly and objectively or to refrain from double-crossing you, robbing you, or sticking a knife in your chest, this is a perfect obligation: what I am to do (or not do) is fully and completely specified. Morality inflexibly requires me to do or not do certain precise things. By contrast, my moral obligation to be charitable is imperfect because I am not obliged to be charitable in any particular way or to any particular person or at any exact time. Rather, there are various ways in which I can discharge that duty, and I am free to choose among them. Mill maintains that this distinction between perfect and imperfect duties 'exactly coincides with that which exists between justice and the other obligations of morality.' These two sets of distinctions coincide because 'duties of perfect obligation are those duties in virtue of which a correlative *right* resides in some person or persons' whereas 'duties of imperfect obligation are those moral obligations which do not give birth to any right' (CW X, p. 246).[4]

This thesis might be questioned, however. In *On Liberty*, Mill affirms that society may rightfully compel us to give evidence in court, to bear our fair share of the common defense and other necessary joint work of society, to save a fellow creature's life, or to protect the defenseless against ill usage (CW XVIII, pp. 224–5; cf. p. 277). These certainly seem to be duties of perfect obligation, not imperfect obligation, as these terms are usually understood – they are, after all, not merely a matter of generosity or beneficence – but would failing to fulfill any of these obligations violate the rights of 'some assignable person'? Perhaps it would. One might, after all, maintain that each of my 300 million fellow Americans has a right that I pay my fair share of taxes, that the citizens of my town have a right that I not duck jury duty, or that the injured stranger whom I happened upon has a right that I stop and lend assistance. Arguably, however, this stretches the notion of a right too far. And, indeed, many philosophers take a rather restrictive view of rights, insisting that, from that fact that I ought to do something, even that I ought to do some specific action in a given situation, it does not necessarily follow that someone has a right that I act that way or that I act unjustly, as opposed to wrongly, if I fail to act in the required way.

By contrast, as I have intimated, some people take an expansive view of rights, maintaining not only that every dereliction of a specifiable duty violates someone's rights but, even more capaciously, that every wrongful action does so.[5] This second contention seems especially strained and implausible. It preserves the connection between justice and rights, but only by merging all of morality into justice and erasing any difference between perfect and imperfect obligations.

Justice and the violation of rights

There may be reason, then, to abandon Mill's linking of rights and perfect duties. But what about the linking of justice with rights, which is the thesis that really matters here? That it is unjust to violate someone's rights might seem uncontroversial – at least as a general principle – but there are some philosophers who deny it. They believe that some wicked things, such as assaulting, killing, or stealing from someone, do not do an injustice to the victim even though they violate his or her rights.[6] This strikes me as counterintuitive, although these thinkers may be correct that what impresses one as wrongful about such actions is not, or at least not immediately, that there has been an injustice. However, Mill is not saying that murder is wrong because it is unjust, that this is what strikes us as abhorrent about it, or that this is the reason morality condemns it. He is saying, rather, that, because it violates the victim's rights, murder is unjust. And to me, at least, that seems perfectly true.

The philosophers who doubt this truth do not affirm that violating someone's rights by assaulting, killing, or stealing from him is a just course of action, merely that it is not unjust. Are there, then, situations in which contravening someone's rights would be positively just (as opposed to merely not unjust)? Perhaps, but convincing examples are difficult to come by, because, if we believe that an envisioned course of action is just despite an apparent rights violation, then we are inclined to think, not that a genuine right has been violated, but rather that it has been appropriately curtailed, delimited, or overridden. Or we may believe that the envisioned course of action is the most just course open to us, that is, that it is the just thing to do overall, even though it involves infringing a right and is, thus, unjust in that particular respect.

Suppose we grant, as I believe, that, whenever someone's rights have been violated, the person has been treated unjustly. Does the converse hold – that is, is it ever possible to act unjustly without violating someone's rights? To begin with, it is worth noting that we sometimes describe policies, institutions, and socioeconomic structures as unjust, where this does not appear to entail that anyone is acting unjustly, or even acting at all, or that anyone's rights are being violated. If, for example, you are a Rawlsian and you live in the United States, then you will almost certainly believe that you live in an unjust society, one that fails to instantiate the difference principle. But to say that because of this your rights (or anyone else's rights) are being violated seems dubious. If so, then perhaps we cannot say that injustice always involves the violation of rights, even if Mill is right in maintaining that one's acting unjustly always does involve this.

But is it correct that, whenever one acts unjustly, one violates someone's rights? Consider some examples: [1] It has been suggested that, although it would be unjust for Brenda to omit Irene from her will despite Irene's long years of sacrifice and service to her, Irene has no right to an inheritance.[7] As a matter of law, presumably, this is true, but Irene may have a moral entitlement based on expectations that Brenda created. [2] Suppose that I choose to be a free rider with respect to some important collective endeavor. One might agree that I act unfairly and hence unjustly, but have I violated anyone's rights? Well, if the free riding in question is serious enough for us to consider my conduct unjust, then perhaps it is not far-fetched to affirm that those who cooperate have a right that I not defect. [3] One might believe, as Mill does, that justice requires giving people what they deserve – returning good for good and evil for evil[8] – and therefore that it is unjust to prevent, or perhaps simply to fail to ensure, a criminal's receiving the punishment he deserves. Does this injustice necessarily violate someone's rights? One might side with Kant and Hegel here and affirm that a criminal has a right to be punished, which right I violate by unjustly allowing him to avoid punishment. Or perhaps my unjust act violates the rights of the victim – although this contention is more plausible for some crimes than for others (for example, counterfeiting or insider trading).

Because these examples are inconclusive, we are not forced to abandon the thesis that injustice always involves a violation of rights. If so, and if the converse thesis that all rights violations are unjust seems plausible, should we, then, endorse Mill's linking of justice and rights? The pertinent moral terminology, I think, lacks sufficient stability and consistency in ordinary usage for any theory like Mill's to capture everyone's moral and linguistic intuitions. One might thus content oneself with affirming that Mill's theory holds in general and for the most part, even if not in every case. Alternatively, if one finds Mill's theory illuminating and insightful, then one may be willing to revise a few stray linguistic intuitions in order to bring one's judgments in line with Mill, thus using his theory to anchor a kind of terminological reflective equilibrium.

4 Rights and utilitarianism

As we have seen, Mill equates the realm of justice with the realm of rights. That something is a matter of justice entails not only that it is the right thing to do (and that failing to do it would be wrong), but also that it is something that someone can claim from us a matter of right. What is it to have a right? Rights are 'legitimate and authorized expectations' (CW X, p. 250). More particularly, for one to have a moral right to something is to have 'a valid claim on society to protect him in the possession of it' (CW X, p. 250). Mill goes on to assert that utility determines when one has such a claim. This is a normative thesis, but there is nothing distinctively utilitarian about either Mill's account of justice as a matter of rights or his characterization of moral rights as entitlements or expectations that society should uphold. The latter are conceptual or metaethical theses which could be endorsed from various normative perspectives.

Before proceeding further, it is worth pausing to address a possible objection to Mill's account of rights. To have a right is 'to have something which society ought to defend me in the possession of' (CW X, p. 250). But, if 'ought implies can', then, if society cannot make good on my claim to x or defend my possession of it, it seems to follow that I have no right to x. This is counterintuitive. However, we can get around this objection if we take Mill to mean that society ought to endeavor to protect me in the possession of x ('by force of law or... education and opinion'), not that it must always succeed in doing so. What about cases in which society is utterly powerless, even in principle, to secure my possession of x? Although society can preserve my property against many threats, it cannot ward off acts of God. It can defend my life against various attacks, but not against the inevitability of death. In response, one could either concede that there can be no such rights or else maintain that it is sufficient that society does what it can (as little as that may be) to resist the irresistible. Either way, I don't see a serious problem for Mill.

That a moral right is broadly speaking a claim that society ought to (try to) uphold seems undeniable. Whatever account one gives of moral rights – what rights we have, why we have them, where they come from, what is important about them – one must surely think that society ought to recognize and defend them. How could it be otherwise? But, even if the class of rights is coextensive with (or at least a subset of) the class of claims that society should uphold, different normative theories will understand or expand on this point in different ways. For Mill, a right is nothing other than a valid claim, and one has that claim because of the utility of society's protecting claims of that sort. Utilitarianism thus determines what claims society should affirm and protect; these claims, then, constitute our rights. By contrast, nonutilitarian rights theorists reverse this explanatory order. Although affirming that, if one has a right, society should protect it, they identify the rights that people have independently of considerations of social utility. For them, my right to x is the reason that society should protect me in the possession of it, whereas for the utilitarian that society should protect my claim to x is the reason I have a right to x.

Mill believes that justice is the 'most sacred and binding part' of morality because it consists in upholding 'certain classes of moral rules, which concern the essentials of human well-being more nearly, and are therefore of more absolute obligation, than any other rules for the guidance of life' (CW X, p. 255). And these rules, as we have seen, are the ones that identify people's moral rights. This is the core of what is probably Mill's greatest contribution to utilitarianism, namely, the idea that the long-run maximization of well-being requires the identification and endorsement of certain moral rules and rights, which in normal circumstances take categorical, sometimes nearly absolute, precedence over immediate determinations of utility.

Beyond Bentham

To be sure, Bentham had earlier recognized and affirmed the importance of legal and other institutional rights. Although he notoriously ridiculed talk of natural rights, Bentham understood well the necessity, if we are to maximize well-being, of institutionalizing certain rights that protect an individual's freedom of action from infringement by others, including the state. Indeed, it is difficult to see how a welfare-maximizing legal system could fail to entrench certain entitlements, such as the right to personal property or the right to be free from assault and other bodily invasions. The task for utilitarians, of course, is to determine the exact set of rights, the institutionalization of which will produce the most desirable results.

When a right is established, then one is free to act in a certain way (or must be treated in a certain way) without regard to considerations of direct or immediate utility – at least in normal circumstances. Following Bentham, this is not a point that utilitarians reluctantly acknowledge; they insist upon it. When institutionalized, rights provide people with certain protections or a realm of choice that is not subject to direct calculation of utility. If you have a right to control access to your home, then you may admit and exclude whomever you wish; you do not have to allow homeless people to sleep in your living room even if doing so would be likely to increase net happiness. Having specified or delineated a right in the first place so that people's having and exercising that right will promote well-being as much as possible, it would then be counterproductive for utilitarians to disregard, override, or permit its abrogation in individual cases. If we support a certain right on grounds of utility, then we must tolerate cases in which its exercise fails to maximize well-being.[9] Practically speaking, it is impossible to institutionalize a right (and reap the benefits that this brings) and at the same time condemn its exercise or routinely license its violation in an effort to harvest greater utility.

Naturally, utilitarians will circumscribe the rights they endorse in various ways or build certain readily identifiable exceptions into them so as to maximize utility. The right to free speech does not permit one to defame others, and, although homeowners have rights over their property, the law may legitimately prohibit them from storing toxic chemicals or restrict what they may build on their land. But, once we have institutionalized a right that has already been specified and delimited so as to maximize well-being, there will be no feasible way to authorize violations of it simply on the ground that doing so would increase utility in that particular case.

Mill goes further than Bentham, however, and upholds on utilitarian grounds moral rights that are not institutionally based. Today most utilitarians follow Mill in recognizing the importance of not just legal, but also moral, rights. That is, they believe that there are certain claims or entitlements that it promotes social utility to recognize and protect, even if these rights are not legally formalized. They want people to acknowledge that others have rights and to be firmly minded to respect those rights, refrain from violating them, and to push, where relevant and feasible, for their institutionalization. Moreover, there is a strong utilitarian case for upholding certain rights as basic human rights and insisting as adamantly as possible that individuals are always and everywhere entitled to be treated in certain ways whether or not that is required by the legal system under which they live. These human rights include personal liberty and freedom of movement, freedom of religion, expression, and inquiry, freedom from arbitrary imprisonment or execution and from arbitrary deprivation of property or livelihood. Widely recognized rights such as these correspond to certain vital human interests, interests that are central to our lives going well. Respecting these rights promotes human flourishing; violating them almost invariably diminishes human well-being. By identifying as human rights certain fundamental sources of well-being or preconditions for people's faring well, utilitarians attempt to safeguard the most basic interests of individuals and prevent governments and powerful groups from trampling on them. This is why justice is 'the claim we have on our fellow-creatures to join in making safe for us the very groundwork of our existence,' a claim 'that assumes [the] character of absoluteness,' that 'becomes a moral necessity' (CW X, p. 250), and that is marked 'by the sterner character of its sanctions' (CW X, p. 259).

5 Utility and the conflicting claims of justice

Critics of utilitarianism, Mill writes, urge 'that utility is an uncertain standard, which every different person interprets differently' and that therefore 'there is no safety but in the immutable, ineffaceable, and unmistakable dictates of justice' (CW X, p. 251). Knowing what will promote happiness is difficult, they argue, and people are bound to differ when estimating consequences. This makes the standard of utility an inexact and unreliable basis for guiding our conduct and, more specifically, for determining what is just and what is not. When the same sort of criticism is advanced these days, it is more often framed in terms of rights, with the opponent of utilitarianism arguing that it cannot provide a secure basis for rights, especially human rights. As one representative critic writes, 'if the ultimate basis for institutionalizing one set of rights-defining practices rather than another is utilitarian, then those core human rights have a most uncertain basis'.[10] Not only are people likely to disagree about which principles and practices will best promote utility in the long run, he argues, but also, even if they did agree, utilitarianism's empirical and consequentialist orientation entails that the rights or principles of justice that it does identify will be at best tentative and provisional, subject to change as circumstances change. Thus, 'it is an open, quasi-empirical question whether other practices, abhorrent to rights advocates, might not produce greater utility.' For reasons like this, critics of utilitarianism, both now and in Mill's time, urge that that justice and rights are 'totally independent of utility' (CW X, p. 251).

Mill finds little merit in this line of criticism. He insists, to the contrary, that 'there is as much difference of opinion, and as much discussion, about what is just as about what is useful to society' (CW X, p. 251). If the dictates of justice were as unambiguous as the critics of utilitarianism contend, he argues, then 'it is hard to understand ... why so many things appear either just or unjust, according to the light in which they are regarded' (CW X, p. 251). Indeed, 'in the mind of one and the same individual, justice is not one rule, principle, or maxim, but many which do not always coincide in their dictates' (CW X, p. 251). Turning the critic's argument on its head, Mill contends that, without utilitarianism to provide a determinate standard of justice, one is left with a plethora of competing principles, all of which seem to have some plausibility but which are mutually incompatible. Mill develops this point by considering the conflicting views that people have of the justice of [1] punishment in general, [2] particular sentencing practices, [3] rival standards of taxation, and [4] paying talented workers more than less skilled workers.

Just remuneration

Let us focus on [4]: is it just or not to pay talented workers more than less talented workers? There are, Mill writes, two possible answers to this question. On the one hand, one can argue that 'whoever does the best he can deserves equally well,' that he ought not to be disadvantaged through no fault of his own, that those with 'superior abilities have already advantages more than enough ... without adding to these a superior share of the world's goods,' and that, if anything, 'society is bound in justice rather to make compensation to the less favored for this unmerited inequality of advantages than to aggravate it.' On the other hand, one can argue with equal plausibility that because 'society receives more from the efficient laborer ... society owes him a larger return' and that because 'a greater share of the joint result is actually his work ... not to allow his claim to it is a kind of robbery.'

We thus have two competing principles of justice, both of which seem plausible: 'Justice has in this case two sides to it, which it is impossible to bring into harmony, and the two disputants have chosen opposite sides; the one looks to what it is just that the individual should receive, the other to what it is just that the community should give' (CW X, p. 253). From his or her own point of view, each disputant is unanswerable. 'Any choice between them, on grounds of justice,' Mill continues, 'must be perfectly arbitrary.' The only sensible way to resolve such controversies is by appealing to the utilitarian standard: 'Social utility alone can decide the preference.' The same point holds for examples [1], [2], and [3]. 'From these confusions [of conflicting principles of justice] there is no mode of extrication other than the utilitarian' (CW X, p. 254).

Mill's line of argument does not prove the superiority of a utilitarian approach, but his examples illustrate well 'the loose and irregular manner in which supposed principles of justice grow up' (CW X, p. 252) and provide a powerful rejoinder to the contention that utility provides a less certain standard than do the various conventional principles of justice. Mill is making a general point and therefore does not explain specifically how he thinks a utilitarian approach would resolve the examples he discusses. However, in the *Principles of Political Economy*, he takes up an issue very much like [4] when he contrasts a 'communistic' system of distribution in which workers divide the produce equally without regard to the quantity of work done with a less extreme system of socialism in which remuneration is proportioned to labor. The communistic principle, he writes, 'appeals to a higher standard of justice, and is adapted to a much higher moral condition of human nature' whereas 'the proportioning of remuneration to work done... when it depends on natural difference of strength or capacity... is in itself an injustice: it is giving to those who have; assigning most to those who are already most favored by nature.' This does not settle the matter, however, because remuneration in proportion to work, 'although a compromise with the selfish type of character formed by the present standard of morality, and fostered by the existing social institutions... is highly expedient; and... is far more likely to prove immediately successful than an attempt at a higher ideal' (CW, II, p. 210).

Mill's stance connects with his belief that a central tenet of justice is the duty to treat each as he or she deserves. In the present context, though, that ideal represents too high a standard for us to attempt to achieve, at least 'until education shall have been entirely regenerated.' It would be wrong, however, to conclude that for Mill adopting remuneration in proportion to work done is simply a matter of expediency trumping justice. First, such remuneration is 'just... insofar as the more or less of the work is a matter of choice;' it is not always and everywhere unjust. Second, as was clear in Mill's discussion of [4], there are principles of justice that support it even if we come to believe that other principles of justice are ultimately more compelling.

Maxims and principles

After discussing [4] and his other examples, Mill goes on to expound his utilitarian view that justice concerns those moral rules, the maintenance of which is vital to human well-being. Their observance preserves peace among human beings. Moreover, we each have 'the strongest and most direct inducements for impressing [them] upon one another... the strongest interest in publishing and enforcing [them] by word and deed' (CW X, p. 255). Among these moral rules are those against 'wrongful aggression or wrongful exercise of power over someone' (CW X, p. 255)[11] as well as 'the principle of giving to each what they deserve' (CW X, p. 256), which requires us to assist benefactors, maintain friendships, keep promises, and, more generally, not disappoint expectations we have at least tacitly encouraged.

'Most of the maxims of justice current in the world,' Mill writes, are 'simply instrumental to carrying into effect [these] principles of justice' (CW X, p. 257). The maxims he has in mind – for example, that one is responsible only for one's voluntary actions, that it is unjust to condemn a person without a hearing, or that punishment ought to be proportional to the crime – loom large in the law, as do the maxims of equality and impartiality, which in the eyes of everyone enjoy an 'exalted rank... among the precepts of justice.' These various maxims are not, it seems, secondary or subordinate principles that provide a more specific, practical, or user-friendly guide to what justice requires. Rather, they are instrumental in the sense that they are 'a necessary condition of the fulfillment of other obligations of justice.' In particular, adherence to them facilitates 'inflicting punishment when due' and 'awarding to each person his right.' In addition to serving this function, equality and impartiality may be considered 'as corollaries from the principles already laid down,' in particular, the duty to treat each according to his deserts; indeed, Mill suggests, they are implicated in the very meaning of the greatest happiness principle itself (CW X, p. 257).

There is some obscurity here, at least with regard to terminology, and it is unclear whether Mill sees 'maxims,' 'precepts,' and 'principles' as operating at different levels or, indeed, whether he draws any consistent distinctions among these terms. As previously discussed, most people subscribe to various principles of justice that do not always coincide in their instructions; as a result, there is a range of opinion about what justice requires in hard cases and hence, for Mill, a need to subordinate these commonsensical principles to the standard of utility. It is the 'common umpire' (CW X, p. 225). But, if this is so, can the various, often conflicting principles of justice really be the 'the most sacred and binding part' of morality (CW X, p. 255), 'more absolute and imperative' than 'any other rules for the guidance of life' (CW X, p. 239)?

From a utilitarian perspective, it is easy to see that certain rules and rights 'stand higher in the scale of social utility' (CW X, p. 238). Consider, to take an instance close to Mill's heart, the liberty principle. Based on 'utility in the largest sense' and 'grounded on the permanent interests of man as a progressive being' (CW XVIII, p. 224), Mill's principle holds that only self-protection can justify interfering with someone's liberty. For Mill, this principle is nearly absolute, and his adherence to it models what it is for a utilitarian to embrace something as a fundamental right. Consider, likewise, the human right not to be tortured, the right to practice the religion of one's choice or no religion at all, or the right to be secure against arbitrary imprisonment or deprivation of property. For a utilitarian of Mill's persuasion, these rights would be close to absolute, ranking among the most stringent of moral requirements, because of the enormous long-term utility that comes from society's respecting them. They are, moreover, unlikely to conflict with any rival rights or principles of justice.

Precisely defining and delimiting these fundamental rights and basic moral rules in a way that ensures that propagating and defending them will maximize long-run utility may not always be easy. There will inevitably be borderline cases. But, with regard to what are widely regarded today as basic human rights, we should not overlook the multitude of cases about which there is a firm consensus – the moral equivalent of what lawyers would call 'black letter' law cases, that is, in which no one doubts that the rights in question hold and where one is hard pressed to imagine any countervailing moral consideration. This is what utilitarians are trying to achieve when they identify and uphold certain rights and rules as a fundamental matter of justice. They want our commitment to these rights and rules to be inflexible, not subject to direct utilitarian calculation in anything other than the most extraordinary of circumstances.

Mill deserves credit for this insight, but he sometimes diverts the reader from it by emphasizing how the ordinary principles of justice can conflict in specific cases, thus implying that they represent, at best, only *prima facie* or *pro tanto* obligations. We should endorse those principles, take them seriously, and follow them when they do not conflict with other principles, but many of them are manifestly of secondary moral importance, unlike, say, the right to be free from arbitrary arrest, which, although also grounded in utilitarian considerations, is virtually never to be set aside. Mill never quite captures this contrast or explicitly recognizes that normative principles (maxims, precepts, rules, standards) come in various degrees of specificity and have different weights. He does not distinguish clearly enough between justice claims that are merely *prima facie* and easily overridden, those that are nearly absolute and rarely, if ever, superseded, and those that are really all-things-considered judgments about what is just or unjust in some particular situation. He also leaves vague the extent to which utilitarianism will require revision of our various conventional principles of justice.

Can justice be overridden?

The principles of justice protect 'certain social utilities' that are more absolute and imperative 'than any others are as a class (though not more so than others may be in particular cases)' (CW X, p. 239).[12] Despite the great utility that comes from upholding justice and respecting rights, 'particular cases may occur in which some other social duty is so important as to override any one of the general maxims of justice' (CW X, p. 238). Here Mill is envisioning, not cases in which different principles of justice collide, but rather ones in which net benefit prevails over the requirements of justice. For example, 'to save a life, it may not only be allowable, but a duty, to steal or take by force the necessary food or medicine, or to kidnap and compel to officiate the only qualified medical practitioner.' Mill's example assumes that the person whose life is in jeopardy does not have a right that we save it or does not have a right that we save it in that particular way (for example, by stealing a car to take the person to the hospital rather than waiting for an ambulance); otherwise, doing so would be a matter of justice or, at least, involve a conflict of rights. The example also assumes that the circumstances are truly out of the ordinary, for, as we have seen, utilitarians who, like Mill, take rules seriously will not put them aside in every situation in which following them might be expected to produce less than optimal results.

In the extraordinary cases Mill has in mind, however, 'we usually say, not that justice must give way to some other moral principle, but that what is just in ordinary cases is, by reason of that other principle, not just in the particular case' (CW X, p. 238). This 'useful accommodation of language' preserves the 'indefeasibility attributed to justice' and rules out our having to concede that there 'can be laudable injustice.' About this matter, unfortunately, Mill says nothing more. Reference to what 'we usually say' and to a 'useful accommodation of language' might suggest that he is merely pointing to an intriguing feature of ordinary moral discourse, one with little or no intrinsic or independent significance. But one suspects that Mill intends something deeper, namely, that it is good on utilitarian grounds to preserve the idea of justice as indefeasible, even if this involves some linguistic elasticity.

Unhappy with this elasticity, one might insist instead that, when we say that what is ordinarily just is not just in the case at hand, we are implicitly revising, refining, or delimiting the principle in question. Instead of a simple rule, like 'Keep your promises,' what we really have is a more complicated rule: 'Keep your promises unless a life is at stake.' And it is true that, when we endorse some basic right or rule, we often hold, not there are exceptions to it or cases in which it does not hold, but rather that the rule or right, when properly formulated, incorporates certain qualifications. Thus, the right to free speech does not, to take Holmes's famous example, include the right to shout fire in a crowded theater. Instead of seeing ourselves as overriding this right or making a necessary, utility-driven exception to it, we can say that free expression does not, and never did, include *that*.[13] But there is a problem with proceeding too far along these lines. Both rule utilitarians and sophisticated act utilitarians want people to internalize a commitment to certain basic rules and rights, but the utility of their doing so is contingent on those rules and rights being psychologically salient and simple enough to be readily understood, remembered, and applied. Build too many utility-motivated qualifications into a rule and you make it too cumbersome to be easily learned, too unwieldy to be a useful guide in practice.

Mill is here considering situations in which utility overrides a dictate of justice (whether we describe it this way or not), a dictate that is unchallenged by any other consideration of justice, but what about those cases – such as the remuneration of talented workers – in which the maxims of justice conflict? In those cases, his discussion seemed to imply that there is no question of trying to preserve the indefeasibility of justice. In deciding how to remunerate talented laborers, we are torn between two or more maxims of justice; therefore, utility properly decides the question. Still, there are two ways of conceptualizing this situation. One is to see ourselves as setting aside the ordinary maxims of justice and straightforwardly settling the question on utilitarian grounds. The other is to say that, guided by utility, we come down in support of one of the maxims, thus affirming that on balance justice requires paying (or not paying) the talented worker more. Understood this second way, we do not leave the realm of justice; rather, utility tells us which precept of justice carries greater normative weight. In hard cases justice may have different sides to it – different precepts may be at odds – but, guided by utility, we plump for one of them. The winning precept thus states what justice requires in this case, not just *pro tanto*, but all things considered. Justice itself remains indefeasible even if particular maxims do not.

6 Concluding reflections

We should not let the obscurities and vagaries in Mill's account of justice and utility eclipse his overall achievement. This chapter has touched on only some aspects of his utilitarianism, but, in developing his theory of justice and rights, Mill provides, I have argued, the crucial elements for constructing a subtle and plausible utilitarian normative theory, one that is largely indirect in its orientation. Mill may not have fully accomplished that task himself, but utilitarians have much to learn from him and are wise to build on his account of justice and on his insistence that utilitarians should acknowledge, respect, and adhere to certain moral rights and rules.

This insistence is salutary, but it has led some contemporary commentators to conclude, prematurely, that Mill was a rule utilitarian (and, implicitly, that all sensible utilitarians should be, too). This is too large an issue to treat adequately here, but a few comments seem appropriate in this final section. As typically formulated, rule utilitarianism affirms that an action is wrong if and only if it conflicts with rules, the general adoption of which by society would maximize well-being. Otherwise, the action is permissible. Utility determines the rules, but, once the rules are identified, they are not to be overridden by direct appeals to utility. As John Austin ([1832] 1995, p. 49) put it, 'Utility [should] be the test of our conduct, ultimately, but not immediately... Our rules [should] be fashioned on utility; our conduct on our rules.' By contrast, act utilitarians are usually thought to maintain, as J.J.C. Smart did, that, although the ordinary rules of morality may be useful aids to decision-making in ordinary situations, they are simply 'rules of thumb,' which one should not hesitate to put aside if doing so is likely to increase overall benefit (Smart and Williams, 1973, p. 42). Rule utilitarians, by contrast, acknowledge no direct imperative to maximize utility.

Some scholars affirm, and others deny, that Mill permits direct appeals to utility to override moral rules. At the end of Chapter 2 of *Utilitarianism*, Mill writes that 'secondary' principles inevitably have exceptions to them and 'that hardly any kind of action can safely be laid down as either always obligatory or always condemnable' (CW X, p. 250), which suggests a casual, Smart-like view of rules. On the other hand, as we have seen, Chapter 5 frequently emphasizes the profound importance, and near exceptionless character, of the rules of justice, and it is nearly impossible to interpret these passages as holding that they are only rules of thumb. Although Mill does not explicitly say so, adherence to these rules and respect for the rights that correspond to them should be a matter of conscience for a well brought-up person, which implies that there is 'a mass of feeling which must be broken through in order to do what violates' these rules and which, if we do violate them, 'will probably have to be encountered afterwards in the form of remorse' (CW X, p. 228). A strict act utilitarian interpretation of Mill is also difficult to square with the importance he places on cultivating a commitment to veracity (CW X, p. 223) or with his lauding the importance of a love of virtue for its own sake (CW X, p. 236).

Two interpretative errors have helped make the long-running debate over whether Mill was an act or rule utilitarian seem so intractable. One of them is assuming that there is a simple dichotomy between act and rule utilitarianism. Like Bentham, Mill wanted to apply the utilitarian standard to a wide range of objects – to the assessment of institutions, social policies, character traits, dispositions, and motivations as well as moral rules and, yes, individual actions. And he may plausibly have believed that no one realm of utilitarian assessment automatically takes precedence over the others.

A second error is to assume that, if one accepts the act utilitarian criterion that an action is right if and only if it maximizes utility, then one must ignore rules whenever one believes that doing so is likely to make for a better outcome. To the contrary, however, having people firmly inclined to act in certain rule-designated ways – and to feel guilty about failing to do so – can have enormous social benefit. This is because it produces good results to have people strongly disposed to act in certain predictable ways, ways that generally (but perhaps not always) maximize happiness. 'Any other plan,' Mill wrote, 'would not only leave everybody uncertain what to expect, but would involve perpetual quarreling: and hence general rules have to be laid down for people's conduct to one another, or in other words, rights and obligations must…be recognized' (CW XV, p. 762). But the benefits of rights and rules – benefits that will be treasured equally strongly by those who adhere to an act utilitarian criterion of right and wrong – cannot be secured if people are permitted, let alone encouraged, to break the rules whenever they believe that doing so would be for the best.

If these two errors are avoided, one sees that Mill does not necessarily have to be classified as a rule utilitarian, despite the importance he places on rights and rules. Two further considerations also complicate one's interpreting Mill as a straightforward rule utilitarian. One is that he clearly allows (as we have seen) utility to decide cases in which two or more rules conflict and even to override the requirements of justice. Sophisticated act utilitarians, like R.M. Hare, typically adopt this stance. They take rules seriously but fall back on direct utilitarian calculation when those rules conflict. This point, however, is not decisive, because rule utilitarianism could include among its rules the directive that conflicts among them are to be resolved by direct appeal to utility.

The second is a passage from the *Logic*, in which Mill distinguishes situations in which there is

> a necessity that some rule, of a nature simple enough to be easily understood and remembered, should not only be laid down for guidance, but universally observed, in order that the various persons concerned may know what they have to expect: the inconvenience of uncertainty on their part being a greater evil than that which may possibly arise, in a minority of cases, from the imperfect adaptation of the rule to those cases

from situations

> in which there does not exist a necessity for a common rule, to be acknowledged and relied on as the basis of society life; where we are at liberty to inquire what is the most moral course under the particular circumstances of the case.

He thus concludes:

> In some things our conduct ought to conform itself to a prescribed rule; in others, it is to be guided by the best judgment which can be formed of the merits of the particular case (CW VIII, pp. 1,154–5).

In this contested area of interpretation, no single passage from Mill can be considered conclusive, and the evidentiary value of this particular one is compromised by the fact that, for whatever reason, Mill dropped it from the third edition of *Logic* when he revised the section of the book that contained it. Still, the passage counts against the claim that Mill embraced (or consistently embraced) rule utilitarianism in its standard form. Although he insists here on the importance of observing moral rules, he evidently believes that it would be infeasible and perhaps counterproductive to attempt to identify (utility-maximizing) rules covering all conduct and all situations. This, in turn, suggests that Mill may have inclined, at least at certain points in his thinking, toward a sophisticated, largely indirect form of utilitarianism that transcends the simple act–rule dichotomy.

Notes

1. For my own approach to utilitarianism, see Shaw (1999).
2. Later, Mill writes: 'It has always been evident that all cases of justice are also cases of expediency' (CW X, p. 259).
3. G.E. Moore's critique of hedonistic utilitarianism takes an analogous form. See Moore ([1912] 2005, pp. 23–8, and 'Editor's Introduction,' pp. xiv–xvi).
4. Mill describes the perfect/imperfect terminology as 'ill-chosen.' He presumably thought that his way of capturing the distinction was more precise and theoretically superior.
5. For example, Mill imagines a moralist who believes 'that mankind…have a right to all the good that we can do them' (CW X, p. 246).
6. Lyons (1994, p. 85). Anthony Quentin (1973, p. 74) writes, more cautiously, that these actions 'are not exactly unjust, at any rate in the current sense of that word.'
7. The argument (without the names) comes from Crisp (1997, pp. 162–3), who draws on Miller (1976, p. 57).
8. See CW X, p. 242, p. 256; pp. 257–8.
9. Contrary to what David Lyons argues (1980 and 1994, Chapter 6).
10. Fishkin (1984, pp. 103–4).
11. The word *wrongful* might seem redundant because the identification of an action as contrary to the utility-justified rules already marks it as wrong. Presumably, Mill wishes to indicate that the principles of justice do not forbid all forms of aggression and every sort of exercise of power over others.
12. This appears to contradict Mill's statement in the same paragraph 'that all cases of justice are also cases of expediency.' Because Mill knew well that even the best rule will sometimes produce inexpedient or suboptimal results, he could only have meant that justice coincides with expediency in general or in the long run.
13. In 'Whewell on Moral Philosophy,' Mill writes that 'the existence of exceptions to moral rules is no stumbling-block…. The essential is, that the exception should be itself a general rule' and thus 'of definite extent' and not leave 'the expediencies to the partial judgment of the agent in the individual case' (CW X, p. 183).

References

Austin, John ([1832] 1995) *The Province of Jurisprudence Determined*, W.E. Rumble (ed.) (Cambridge: Cambridge University Press).

Crisp, Roger (1997) *Mill on Utilitarianism* (London: Routledge).

Fishkin, James (1984) 'Utilitarianism and Human Rights,' in *Human Rights*, Ellen Frankel Paul, Fred D. Miller Jr., and Jeffrey Paul (eds) (Oxford: Basil Blackwell), pp. 103–7.

Lyons, David (1980) 'Utility as a Possible Ground of Rights,' *Noûs*, vol. 14, no. 1 (March).

Lyons, David (1994) *Rights, Welfare, and Mill's Moral Theory* (New York: Oxford University Press).

Miller, David (1976) *Social Justice* (Oxford: Oxford University Press).

Mineka, F.E. and Lindley, D.N. (eds) (1972): *The Collected Works of John Stuart Mill: The Later Letters of John Stuart Mill 1849–1973 Part II*, Vol. XV (Toronto: University of Toronto Press).

Moore, G.E. ([1912] 2005) *Ethics*, W.H. Shaw (ed.) (Oxford: Oxford University Press).

Quentin, Anthony (1973) *Utilitarian Ethics* (LaSalle, Ill.: Open Court).

Robson, J.M. (ed.) (1965) *The Collected Works of John Stuart Mill: Principles of Political Economy Part 1*, Vol. II (Toronto: University of Toronto Press).

Robson, J.M. (ed.) (1969) *The Collected Works of John Stuart Mill: Essays on Ethics, Religion, and Society*, Vol. X (Toronto: University of Toronto Press).

Robson, J.M. (ed.) (1974) *The Collected Works of John Stuart Mill: A System of Logic Ratiocinative and Inductive Part 2*, Vol. VIII (Toronto: University of Toronto Press).

Robson, J.M. (ed.) (1977) *The Collected Works of John Stuart Mill: Essays on Politics and Society Part 1*, Vol. XVIII (Toronto: University of Toronto Press).

Shaw, William H. (1999) *Contemporary Ethics: Taking Account of Utilitarianism* (Oxford: Blackwell).

Smart, J.J.C. and Williams, Bernard (1973) *Utilitarianism: For and Against* (Cambridge: Cambridge University Press).

3
Mill's Division of Morality

Dale E. Miller

1 Introduction

My object in this chapter is to arrive at a clearer understanding of Mill's 'division of morality,' by which I mean the division that he draws between justice and the rest of morality. While much that he has to say on this subject is not clear, two points are. One concerns his terminology. Mill uses *perfect obligation* to denote moral obligations that are obligations of justice and *imperfect obligation* to denote those that are not. The other clear point is that he takes all and only those moral obligations that are correlated with rights to be perfect obligations. Both of these points are made explicitly in the fifteenth paragraph of the fifth chapter of *Utilitarianism*, to which I will hereafter refer as *5:15*. This lengthy paragraph seems to be the only passage in which Mill explicitly speaks to the division of morality, and it reads in part:

> This, therefore, being the characteristic difference which marks off, not justice, but morality in general, from the remaining provinces of Expediency and Worthiness; the character is still to be sought which distinguishes justice from other branches of morality. Now it is known that ethical writers divide moral duties into two classes, denoted by the ill-chosen expressions, duties of perfect and of imperfect obligation; the latter being those in which, though the act is obligatory, the particular occasions of performing it are left to our choice, as in the case of charity or beneficence, which we are indeed bound to practise, but not towards any definite person, nor at any prescribed time. In the more precise language of philosophic jurists, duties of perfect obligation are those duties in virtue of which a correlative right resides in some person or persons; duties of imperfect

> obligation are those moral obligations which do not give birth to any right. I think it will be found that this distinction exactly coincides with that which exists between justice and the other obligations of morality. (CW X, pp. 246–7)

David Lyons is going to figure importantly in my discussion for two reasons. First, I will largely take for granted a basic approach to understanding Mill's moral theory reading that I have defended in other recent work. This approach, which I describe in the next section, is mostly drawn from Lyons. Second, though, Lyons has already written about Mill's division of morality from the standpoint of this approach, and on this particular subject our conclusions are very different. I will frame my discussion as a rebuttal to his.

2 A rule utilitarian reading of Mill[1]

In a series of papers that were published in the 1970s and 1980s, Lyons develops an interpretation of Mill that depicts him as holding quite a sophisticated version of utilitarianism. In common with several other 'revisionary' readings of Mill that appeared in roughly the same period or thereafter, Lyons's interpretation attaches considerable significance to the fifteenth paragraph of Chapter V of *Utilitarianism*, which reads in part:

> We do not call anything wrong, unless we mean to imply that a person ought to be punished in some way or other for doing it; if not by law, by the opinion of his fellow-creatures; if not by opinion, by the reproaches of his own conscience. This seems the real turning point of the distinction between morality and simple expediency. (CW X, p. 246)

Several interpreters, Lyons included, suggest that Mill is offering what amounts to an analysis of the concept of morally wrong action in this passage, one that entails that an action cannot be wrong unless it would be appropriate, which is to say justified, for the agent to be punished for it.[2] While 5:15 does not obviously single out guilt as having a closer conceptual connection with the notion of morally wrong action than any other punishment, Lyons regards it as uncharitable to Mill to read him as saying that an action that is appropriately punished only by external sanctions is morally wrong. According to Lyons (1994, p. 53), there are certain parts of the law that the state is justified in enforcing, at least by fines, even though it would be 'implausible' to suggest that those who violate these laws have done anything morally wrong: 'Laws that establish useful routines or guidelines for business practices, for example, do not give moral obligations.' Thus Lyons concludes that:

> Mill seems to be saying that wrong acts are those for which guilt feelings are appropriate. ... When the stakes are high and additional grounds can accordingly be given, social measures may be justified, such as public condemnation and legal punishments. But these are added on, as the case demands. (1994, p. 53)

Lyons takes Mill's answer to the question of what actions are justifiably punished by guilt to invoke the notion of moral rules. As Lyons understands Mill, a person's conscience 'enforces' (my term) rules that she has 'internalized' (Lyons's term), that is, come to feel guilty about violating them as a result of her experiences. By and large, contemporaneous members of the same society will internalize the same rules. Lyons therefore attributes to Mill the view that an action is wrong if the agent and the rest of her society (or at least her contemporaries within her society) ought to internalize a rule that forbids actions of that type.

So far, no mention has been made of Mill's utilitarianism. According to Lyons, though, happiness maximization is Mill's criterion for determining what rules the members of a given society ought to internalize. As evidence for this part of his reading, Lyons (1994, p. 52) adduces Mill's support for Bentham's 'rigorously utilitarian' (Lyons's phrase) theory of punishment, a theory that Mill says that Bentham left 'nearly complete.' In applying this criterion, of course, it would be necessary to take into account the costs associated with the moral education necessary to get people to internalize different sets of rules.

While Lyons (1994, pp. 53–5) does not think that the external sanctions – in the form of either legal penalties or informal social sanctions like ostracism – figure in Mill's analysis of the concept of morally wrong action, he does still believe that there is a contingent connection between an action's being wrong and the external sanctions. When people have internalized a rule against an action-type, they will tend to want to respond to other people who perform actions of that type with some form of punishment; however, they can choose to refrain from inflicting punishment on someone else if they recognize that there is sufficient reason for them to do so. And, since every punishment causes unhappiness, there are bound to be rules that it would be expedient for people to internalize but not for society to enforce through legal or informal social punishments. In some cases, in other words, the marginal costs of using external sanctions in addition to the internal sanction will exceed the marginal gains.

The moral theory that Lyons attributes to Mill says that an action is wrong if it is forbidden by the rules whose general acceptance by the members of the agent's society would be maximally expedient – where accepting a rule is understood to mean internalizing it. This certainly looks like a rule utilitarian view, although Lyons (1994, p. 58 and p. 113) stops short of applying this label to it, saying only that it 'resembles' or 'shares the spirit and intention' of rule utilitarianism. Lyons (1994, p. 119) gives two reasons for this reticence, but both are somewhat puzzling. One is that Mill applies the criterion of happiness maximization to individual actions in addition to sets of rules. Lyons (1994, p. 50) says that Mill is committed to 'ranking acts according to their utilities' and 'preferring' those that rank higher, even though he does not have an act utilitarian moral theory and this preference has no bearing on his evaluation of acts' moral standing. The other is that his argument for his moral theory – the argument that Lyons (1994, p. 78) takes to lie implicit in Mill's writings – starts with an analysis of moral concepts. Lyons only makes these points in passing, though, and he says little to explain why either of these considerations should disqualify Mill from being a rule utilitarian. Gerald Gaus (1998), therefore, seems to be correct when he says that 'these two points only imply that Mill is not a rule utilitarian if one adopts a fairly narrow view of rule utilitarianism' and that 'it does seem that Lyons' (1994, p. 291) interpretation of Mill is a rule utilitarian one in the usual, broader sense of the term. More specifically, the view that Lyons attributes to Mill is a version of 'ideal code' rule utilitarianism, according to which actions are wrong if they are forbidden by the moral code (that is, the set of moral rules) whose general acceptance would be happiness-maximizing.

3 Lyons on Mill's division of morality

A scenario:

> You have recently donated a large amount of money, relative to your income, to provide relief to the citizens of a much poorer country that borders your own. Driving through an inhospitable and unpopulated border region between the two countries, you encounter someone who is clearly entering your country illegally, with several young

children in tow. This family is obviously on the brink of dying of thirst, and you have an ample supply of water with you.

We can safely take for granted that Mill would believe you have an obligation to save the lives of this family, the fact that you have already been quite charitable toward the people of this poorer nation notwithstanding. (This is not to say that he would not think that you have other obligations as well, such as an obligation to contact the appropriate authorities.) But does he believe that your duty to provide assistance in this case is a perfect or an imperfect one? In other words, does he believe that the people whom you have stumbled upon have a right to your assistance? Or, to offer one more formulation of the question, would Mill consider a failure to help on your part to constitute an injustice? This question is a specific instance of the general question to which Lyons and I give conflicting answers.

The best way to introduce Lyons's answer may be to start with *On Liberty*. Lyons takes the liberty principle to permit interference with an individual's conduct whenever this would conduce to preventing harm to someone else. On this reading, the liberty principle places fewer restrictions on society's use of coercion than it would if it only allowed society to interfere with conduct that would itself harm someone else: coercion can be used against A to prevent B from being harmed, even if the danger to B does not come from A (1994, pp. 92–6). Lyons also takes Mill to embrace a 'principle of enforcing morality' in *On Liberty*, according to which actions that the liberty principle would preclude society from interfering with are never morally wrong (1994, p. 131). In consequence, all of the moral obligations that Mill takes us to have can be distinguished into those that forbid us to perform actions that would result in our doing harm to unwilling others ourselves and those that require us to take steps to protect other people from harm, steps that might include either acting as 'Good Samaritans' by acting as individuals to rescue other people from potential harm or participating in protective institutions like the court system (through serving as witnesses or jurors, for example). We are neither forbidden to do every action that might harm someone else without her consent nor obligated to do all that we can to protect others from harm, as Lyons reads Mill. What specific kinds of things we are forbidden or required to do will ultimately depend on what moral rules it would best promote happiness for people to internalize. But any moral obligations that we have will fall into one of these two categories.

As Lyons (1994, pp. 118–23) reads him, Mill takes this distinction between obligations not to harm others ourselves and obligations to protect from harm to map perfectly onto the distinction between obligations that do and do not have correlative rights. When we have an obligation not to cause other people harm ourselves, they have a right that we not harm them, but when we have an obligation to protect others from harm, they do not generally have a right to protection. Still, if on a given occasion we have an obligation to do something that conduces to protecting another person against harm, but we do something else instead, then our act breaches our obligation even if she had no right to our protection. So, on this account, the family at the border has no right to your help and the obligation to keep them from dying of thirst is not an obligation of justice. Yet you have still acted wrongly if you do not help them.

Lyons's interpretation is at odds with a part of the passage from 5:15 that I quoted in the introduction. At this point, it will be useful to introduce some terminology (that is mine, not Lyons's). In the portion of 5:15 previously quoted, Mill provides two different criteria for distinguishing perfect from imperfect obligations. First he tells us that with imperfect duties 'though the act is obligatory, the particular occasions of performing it are left to our choice', then he adds that in 'duties of perfect obligation are those duties in virtue of which a correlative right resides in some person or persons; duties of imperfect obligation are those moral obligations which do not give birth to any right.' Since the first of these criteria foregrounds the notion of choice, we can call it the 'choice criterion.' The second can then be called the 'rights criterion.' Mill offers 'the case of charity or beneficence' as an example of a duty that is classified as imperfect by the choice criterion. At least I will assume that these are two names for the same duty; Mill never makes clear how charity and beneficence are related. Our discretion to decide on which occasions we will fulfill this obligations apparently extends not just to choosing the moments at which we will be charitable but also whom we will benefit. The implication is that one simply has to be 'charitable enough' over a period of time, for example, and any combination of charitable acts that together constitute doing enough suffice to fulfill the obligation. Presumably, any moral obligation that leaves agents free to choose on what occasions they will fulfill it will similarly require them only to do enough of something over time. In contrast, perfect duties leave agents no comparable discretion. That is not to say that they do not leave *any* discretion: if I have an obligation to pay you £20, and you have a right to get £20 from me, then I might have the discretion to choose between giving you a £20 note or two £10 notes or (perhaps) a check. Or, if my obligation is to pay you by tomorrow, then I might have a choice between waiting until then or going ahead and paying you today. When he presents the choice criterion, though, Mill is obviously thinking in terms of much broader discretion than this.

Lyons (1994, p. 117) recognizes that his interpretation clashes with Mill's discussion of the choice criterion. However, he maintains that we should 'ignore' this part of 5:15 and take only what Mill says about the rights criterion as his 'official' account of the division of morality. As I read Lyons, this is meant to be an act of interpretative charity. Not only is Mill's 'analysis of justice ... incomplete,' in Lyons's (1994, p. 124) judgement, but the view that we have to ascribe to Mill if we take what he says about the choice criterion seriously is deeply flawed. Hence interpreting this aspect of Mill's thought requires 'reconstruction,' as opposed to straightforward exegesis, 'because Mill does not address the matter directly but also because his views need some sympathetic refinement in the process of interpretation' (1994, p. 109). I admit to finding Lyons's talk of 'reconstruction' slippery and a little ambiguous. Does reconstructing Mill's view mean trying to work out his position on the basis of inadequate clues or does it mean improving on Mill's view while trying to remain within the spirit of his thought? I am exclusively interested in doing the first of these, and if Lyons actually intends to do the second then our views do not in fact clash. I will assume, though, that Lyons also intends to capture Mill's own account of the division of morality.[3]

While he does not explicitly disentangle them, Lyons seems to have two related but distinct reasons for thinking that the choice criterion gives an entirely unacceptable account of the division of morality. The first is that he takes it to have a peculiar implication, namely that it can never be the case that a moral obligation that is not an obligation of justice can be violated by an agent's action on a particular occasion. Lyons illustrates this point with the obligation of charity:

> If charity is obligatory only 'imperfectly', in the way Mill suggests, then the connection between such an obligation and the morality of conduct is *too* loose for his purposes. For in that case no particular acts of charity are ever required of any person. Moreover, from one's failing to perform a charitable act on a given occasion, when he has the opportunity to do so and no overriding obligation pertains, we *cannot ever* infer that he has breached his moral obligation to be charitable and has acted wrongly. (1994, p. 116)

Lyons does not seem to think that there is any problem with Mill's characterization of charity *per se*, but he denies that all of our non-justice obligations are like charity in this respect: '[I]t does seem possible for someone to act wrongly by breaching a moral obligation without at the same time acting unjustly' (1994, p. 116).

Lyons's second reason for thinking that the choice criterion yields an unacceptable account of the division of morality is that it leads to nearly all of morality's being subsumed under justice. There are not many moral obligations that can plausibly be understood to require us only to do enough of something over a period of time, after all, and if these are the only moral duties that are not part of justice then by far the greater part of morality will lie within the realm of justice. Lyons sees this implication as objectionable for two different reasons.

The first is that there are certain obligations that require specific things from us at specific times – they are not obligations that merely require us to do enough of something over time, in other words – and yet that we have independent grounds for thinking should not be classified as obligations of justice. As examples, Lyons offers certain duties to ourselves, such as those not to commit suicide or engage in self-mutilation. (Mill, of course, does not believe that we have obligations to ourselves, but this, as Lyons (1994, p. 116) notes, is irrelevant in this context, since 'the idea of a duty to oneself does not seem unintelligible and should be allowed for by an analysis of moral obligations or an *analytic* division of morality, such as Mill's'). These duties to self do not give us any choice about when to fulfill them; insofar as we are obligated not to commit suicide, after all, we are obligated at every moment to refrain entirely from killing ourselves, not to avoid killing ourselves too much over a given span of time. Yet to call this an obligation of justice would be 'implausible,' according to Lyons (1994, p. 116). By inappropriately classifying this and other obligations as obligations of justice, this way of distinguishing between justice and the rest of morality 'tends to overpopulate' justice (1994, p. 137).

The second reason that Lyons considers it objectionable to ascribe to Mill an account of the division between justice and the rest of morality according to which most of morality is subsumed under justice is that this would enmesh Mill in an inconsistency. At one point in 5:15, a few lines after the portion quoted previously, Mill makes it clear that he thinks that other moralists have made a mistake by 'merg[ing] all morality in justice,' that is, failing to recognize that there are non-justice obligations (CW X, pp. 246–7). According to Lyons (1994, p. 139), though, attributing the view in question to Mill 'would render Mill's expressed concern about 'merging all morality in justice' misleading, at best, justified only by his recognition of imperfect obligations such as charity.' And this, Lyons says, would be 'unsatisfying.'

Lyons sees the account of the division of morality that we get if we ignore the choice criterion and take account only of the rights criterion to be a significant improvement. On this account, at least as Lyons develops it, the non-justice part of morality includes all of our obligations to protect others from harm. Some of these may, like charity, require us to do only enough of something over time, but others will require us to perform specific acts at specific times, like giving water to the family at the border. The realm of justice will shrink accordingly, comprising only those obligations that amount to prohibitions on our causing different varieties of harm to others; these, according to Lyons, are the only obligations that Mill takes to have correlative rights. This is a vast improvement, Lyons thinks, over an account of the division of morality based on the choice criterion, although he still does not regard it as adequate. He maintains that even it overpopulates justice to an extent, because not every obligation that has a correlative right is in fact an obligation of justice. According to Lyons (1994, p. 144), while 'Rape, torture, cruelty, and unwarranted assault...violate the victims' rights,' these acts 'would not normally be characterized as injustices.'

While I believe that Lyons misunderstands Mill's way of dividing morality, I do want to acknowledge that there is a fair amount of text in Chapter V of *Utilitarianism* that seems *prima facie* to support his reading. For example, Mill (CW X, p. 255) writes that 'The moral rules *which forbid mankind to hurt one another*...are more vital to human well-being than any maxims, however important, which only point out the best mode of managing some department of human affairs.' Since this passage comes in the midst of a discussion of the rules or principles of justice, it is not much of a stretch to assume that he means to identify the rules of justice with those moral rules that forbid us to hurt each other. Indeed, Mill's entire discussion of the 'sentiment of justice' may appear to lend support to Lyons's reading. Mill's stated purpose in Chapter 5 is to answer the objection that the strong moral emotions associated with cases of perceived injustice are incompatible with a utilitarian account of justice. Mill rebuts this objection by giving an associationist psychological explanation of how these strong emotions could become attached to moral rules that forbid us to hurt one another.

It is also worth noting that, on Lyons's interpretation of Mill, it will still often turn out to be the case that, when we have an obligation to protect other people from harm, they do have a right to our protection. Mill is insistent in *Utilitarianism* that justice requires us to follow through when we have encouraged people to expect a certain benefit from us and to base their plans on receiving it. Under these conditions, to deny them this benefit is to harm them. He also insists that, by accepting benefits from others, we encourage them to expect that we will reciprocate in their own time of need:

> Good for good is also one of the dictates of justice... He who accepts benefits, and denies a return of them when needed, inflicts a real hurt, by disappointing one of the most natural and reasonable of expectations, and one which he must at least tacitly have encouraged, otherwise the benefits would seldom have been conferred. (CW X, p. 256)

As Lyons rightly points out, Mill understands this obligation of reciprocity very broadly. Mill believes that, simply by accepting the protections we enjoy as a result of our society's protective institutions and the customary Good Samaritan requirements built into its positive morality, we encourage our compatriots – all of them – to expect us to contribute toward providing them with the same protections. Mill explains this in *On Liberty*:

> [E]very one who receives the protection of society owes a return for the benefit, and the fact of living in society renders it indispensable that each should be bound to observe a certain line of conduct towards the rest. This conduct consists, first, in not injuring the interests of one another... and secondly, in each person's bearing his share (to be fixed on some equitable principle) of the labours and sacrifices incurred for defending the society or its members from injury and molestation. (CW XVIII, p. 276)

So Mill takes us to have what Lyons (1994, pp. 139–42) calls a 'second-order obligation of reciprocity' to take certain steps to protect other members of our own society from harm. Having encouraged them to expect our help, we become a cause of harm to them ourselves if we fail to follow through. This obligation is an obligation of justice, and it does give rise to a correlative right. This second-order obligation accounts for some of the specific features in the scenario with which I introduced this section. The case is designed to be one in which the circumstances that give rise to the obligation of reciprocity do not obtain, since the people needing protection are neither members of our society nor 'invited guests.' On Lyons's interpretation, Mill could not say that they have a right to help, even though he could still say that we have an obligation to help and no choice about whether to do so.

4 The choice criterion reconsidered

The alternative to Lyons's reading – if not the only possible alternative, the only one that seems to be a live option – is an interpretation of 5:15 that says that the choice and rights criteria are coextensive, inasmuch as any obligation that does not require agents only to do enough of something over time, with the occasions on which they do it left to their choice, has a correlative right. This interpretation would say, in other words, that, whenever a person is obligated to fulfill an obligation on a particular occasion, there is someone who has a right to their doing so. Since it says that the two criteria are equivalent, we can call this the 'equivalence' reading of Mill. There is no substantive disagreement between this interpretation and Lyons's about what Mill takes us to be morally obligated to do. The two interpretations entirely agree about what moral obligations Mill takes us to have. They disagree about which of these obligations give rise to correlative rights, however, and hence also about where the boundaries of justice are to be drawn within the wider sphere of morality.

The equivalence reading also finds support in *Utilitarianism*. First, obviously enough, there is the portion of 5:15 in which Mill introduces the choice criterion. While I am certainly in favor of charitable readings of Mill, I worry that Lyons sets aside this stretch of text too easily. It is one thing to favor one reading of an ambiguous passage over another based on charity, another thing to ignore a passage altogether. Even this may be justified sometimes, of course, especially when there is ample text that favors a different reading and when the passage in question seems to be endorsing a seriously defective view (although Mill's language here is itself not very precise and might mean no more than that the language of rights is more technical). But some high thresholds must be met in these areas for this move to be justified, and much of the argumentation in the rest of this section will be aimed at showing that they are not met here. In addition, it is easier to justify the decision to ignore a passage if one has a story to tell about why it was written, that is, how the figure in question became confused or what it is she was trying to say but ended up saying badly.

Lyons offers no explanation for why Mill introduces the choice criterion. He can always claim, of course, that the fact that Mill characterizes the language of the rights criterion as 'more precise' than that of the choice criterion could be taken as a sign that he means to distance himself a little from the choice criterion. But, if he believes that there are imperfect obligations that do not merely require us to do enough of something over time, then why mention the choice criterion in the first place? On Lyons's interpretation, those obligations, like charity, that only require us to do enough of something over time are examples of imperfect obligations, but they are only examples and not especially representative ones. If Mill does not in fact think that the choice criterion is at least a good first approximation of the division of morality, then it is utterly mysterious why he should call attention to it; it would have been obvious to him that he was inviting confusion by doing so.

Second, the following lines from 5:15, which appear later than those that I have quoted so far, are very suggestive:

> It seems to me that this feature in the case – a right in some person, correlative to the moral obligation – constitutes the specific difference between justice, and generosity and beneficence... No one has a moral right to our generosity or beneficence, because we are not bound to practice these virtues toward any given individual... Wherever there is a right, the case is one of justice, and not the virtue of beneficence... (CW X, pp. 246–7)

Clearly Mill is saying here that charity and beneficence are examples of moral obligations without correlative rights, which makes them imperfect obligations according to the rights criterion. This much is quite explicit. What is not said so explicitly, but is nonetheless implied, is that these are the *only* duties that he takes us to have that are imperfect according to the rights criterion. The last sentence in particular strongly suggests this. Obviously it would not be fair for me to put this construction on the text if anything that Mill said before or between the statements that I just quoted suggested that charity and beneficence are only examples of obligations without correlative duties. However, he says nothing of the sort (although 5:15 is too long for me to establish this by quoting it in its entirety). And, in the absence of any statement to this effect, the claim that he means to say that morality can be divided without remainder into perfect obligations of justice with correlative rights and the imperfect obligations of charity or generosity and beneficence is the natural reading of the text.[4] This claim is clearly inconsistent with Lyons's interpretation.

Third, there is Mill's formal account of rights. Mill says that:

> When we call anything a person's right, we mean that he has a valid claim on society to protect him in the possession of it, either by the force of law, or by that of education and opinion ... If we desire to prove that anything does not belong to him by right, we think this done as soon as it is admitted that society ought not to take measures for securing it to him, but should leave him to chance, or to his own exertions. (CW X, p. 250)

This is a fairly bare-bones analysis of what it means to say that someone has a right. It requires no more for it to be the case that an individual I has a right to Φ than that a moral rule be justified requiring some agent A to give I Φ on demand. At first glance, it may look here as if Mill thinks that additional moral rules must be justified in order for I to have a right to Φ from A, namely rules requiring other individuals or society at large to come to I's aid if A refuses to fulfill her obligation (at least if I demands this). Note, though, that Mill says that society can protect a rights-holder through 'education.' This suggests that he thinks it suffices for an individual to have a right to Φ that it be expedient for society to instill in its members a rule requiring them to give her Φ. (That he believes that when a rule has been widely internalized people will tend to impose informal external sanctions on people who violate it, in the absence of a particular reason not to, accounts for his speaking of education and opinion together.) Mill may well believe that there are justified moral rules that require us to intervene when certain rights of other people are being violated, but he does not seem to make the existence of rights contingent upon justifiability of such rules.

To appreciate the significance of Mill's analyzing what it is for someone to have a right in this way, think back to the scenario with which I introduced the last section. In that scenario, Lyons would agree that my society ought to 'take measures' for securing my assistance for the family that is in danger. It should have already used its power over my education to bring it about that I would internalize a rule requiring me to provide this assistance, and, if I do not, then in the absence of some particular reason not to it should use at least the power of opinion to make me pay for the omission. Thus, not only do I have an obligation to be a Good Samaritan, but the family has a right to my doing so.

Finally, fourth, there is this seldom-remarked-on passage, which I take to be nearly decisive:

> Thus the moralities which protect every individual from being harmed by others, either directly or by being hindered in his freedom of pursuing his own good, are at once those which he himself has most at heart, and those which he has the strongest interest in publishing and enforcing by word and deed... Now it is these moralities primarily which compose the obligations of justice. The most marked cases of injustice, and those which give the tone to the feeling of repugnance which characterises the sentiment, are acts of wrongful aggression, or wrongful exercise of power over some one; the next are those which consist in wrongfully withholding from him something which is his due; in both cases, inflicting on him a positive hurt, either in the form of direct suffering, or of the privation of some good which he had reasonable ground, either of a physical or of a social kind, for counting upon. (CW X, p. 256)

This passage is important in two different ways. First, it represents compelling evidence that Mill believes that the rules of justice include more than rules that forbid various acts that would harm other people. If the moral rules that 'protect every individual from being harmed by others...*primarily* compose the obligations of justice,' the implication is that they do not *exclusively* compose them. Likewise, if the cases of injustice that involve violations of these rules, through either wrongful aggression or wrongful disappointment of someone's legitimate expectations, constitute '*the most marked* cases of injustice,' the implication is that they do not constitute the *only* such cases.

Second, this passage undermines much of the *prima facie* textual evidence for Lyons's reading. It points to the fact that Mill considers a certain subset of the rules of justice – a proper subset, albeit one that comprises a large majority of these rules – to be of far more significance than the rest. They are more significant not only because of their number but also because violations of them do no more damage to human well-being than violations of the other rules that meet the formal or abstract definition for being rules of justice. We might call these rules the 'core' of justice, and of course they are precisely the rules that Lyons contends that Mill takes to be the whole of justice. The fact that Mill believes that the core rules of justice are so much more important than the rest explains why he would focus on them exclusively in much of Chapter V, as when he writes that 'The moral rules *which forbid mankind to hurt one another*... are more vital to human well-being than any maxims...' or when he discusses the sentiment of justice (CW X, p. 256). These are the rules to which the sentiment attaches, after all, and these are the rules that the critics whom Mill is answering allege cannot be justified only by their utility. Even if there happen to be some other rules that are formally rules of justice, if they do not have the same 'powerful sentiment' attached to them then they are not important in that context (CW X, p. 240).

Admittedly, one passage near the end of Chapter V does not fit entirely easily with this reading:

> It appears from what has been said, that justice is a name for certain moral requirements, which, regarded collectively, stand higher in the scale of social utility, and are therefore of more paramount obligation, than any others; though particular cases may occur in which some other social duty is so important, as to overrule any one of the general maxims of justice. Thus, to save a life, it may not only be allowable, but a duty, to steal, or take by force, the necessary food or medicine, or to kidnap, and compel to officiate, the only qualified medical practitioner. In such cases, as we do not call anything justice which is not a virtue, we usually say, not that justice must give way to some other moral principle, but that what is just in ordinary cases is, by reason of that other principle, not just in the particular case. (CW X, p. 259)

Here Mill does seem to speak of what I have called the core rules of justice as if they were the only rules of justice. Ostensibly, he is describing cases in which perfect obligations, those entailed by the rules of justice, are being trumped by imperfect ones. But, on my reading, the rules of justice could only rarely conflict with duties that the choice criterion classifies as imperfect. Since these duties only require us to do enough of something over time, if it were impossible to (say) be charitable on one occasion without acting unjustly, it would almost always be possible to do so on another and still fulfill the duty. A real conflict would occur only if it were impossible for some extended period of time to satisfy the imperfect duty without acting unjustly, and surely situations like this do not happen often. What Mill describes as instances of the rules of justice being trumped by non-justice rules are really cases of the core rules of justice being trumped by rules of justice that lie outside the core, that is, rules that forbid us from harming others being trumped by rules that require us to protect others from harm. But, if my reading forces us to see Mill as guilty of slack drafting here, in virtue of referring to the core of justice as if it were the whole, then at least this lapse is easier to understand than the one of which he is guilty on Lyons's reading, when he initially formulates the distinction between perfect and imperfect duties in terms of the choice criterion. At least the core rules of justice, the part that he mistakes for a whole in this case, are the most numerous and the most representative examples of the larger class to which they belong.

I take myself to have shown so far that the textual support for what I have called the equivalence reading of Mill on the division of morality is on the whole stronger than that for Lyons's interpretation. Lyons also argues, however, that there are serious problems with the view that the equivalence reading attributes to Mill, and if these problems are real and are serious enough then someone might still be inclined to favor Lyons's interpretation on the basis of charity despite its poorer fit with the text. So I want to mount a qualified defense of the proposition that the only non-justice moral obligations are those that only require us to do enough of something over time. I will not try to show that this is the true account of what separates justice from the rest of morality or even that it is a better account than the one that Lyons attributes to Mill, but I will argue that it is not as absurd as Lyons makes it out to be.

One reason that Lyons criticizes the claim that all imperfect duties are of the sort that only require us to do enough of something over time is that it is never the case that any particular action violates such a duty. Walter Sinnott-Armstrong, as it happens, holds a similar view:

> An important implication of this distinction is that a single action can violate a perfect moral obligation but not an imperfect moral obligation. Any single act of lying violates the obligation not to lie. Any single act of killing violates the obligation not to kill. However, no single act of passing by a beggar violates the imperfect moral obligation to help the needy. If it did, then that moral obligation would become a perfect moral obligation. Instead of a single act, what does violate an imperfect obligation is not doing enough acts of the kind that you have an imperfect obligation to do or doing too many acts of a kind that you have an imperfect obligation not to do. (2005, p. 199)

It seems to me that Lyons and Sinnott-Armstrong are mistaken about this. There are obvious questions, ones that I cannot address here, about how we could specify what it means to be (say) 'charitable enough' over a given period of time. Certainly it would be necessary to take into account not just how many times an agent acted charitably, but also (at least) how much she gave, her means and the different degrees of urgency with which the different people toward whom she had the opportunity to act charitably needed help. That specifying this is difficult may be a problem for Mill, but if so then it is a problem for him on more or less every reading, Lyons's included, and it is a problem for our ordinary morality as well. Yet however we specify what counts as doing enough, there will be occasions at which an agent is facing her 'last chance,' that is, occasions at which she will not have done enough unless she acts charitably at that time. *Contra* Lyons, if an agent does not act charitably at one of these junctures then we can infer that she has breached her obligation. Granted, we could not draw that inference only by observing her behavior on that one occasion; we would need to know her prior track record. But after that one occasion she will have breached an obligation that she had not breached previously. And, *contra* Sinnott-Armstrong, the fact that the agent has reached her last chance does not convert her imperfect obligation into a perfect one. Imperfect obligations give us broad discretion about the occasions on which we will fulfill them. The fact that the agent has reached the point where she must act charitably or breach her obligation in virtue of how she has exercised her discretion on previous occasions does not morph the obligation into one that does not allow this discretion.

Lyons also criticizes the view that the equivalence reading attributes to Mill for the fact that this means that nearly all of morality is subsumed under justice. He contends both that this results in certain duties being classified as duties of justice when they clearly are not, such as certain duties to ourselves, and that it would be inconsistent for Mill to hold such a view given his recognition that it is a mistake to merge all of morality into justice. This second point cuts little ice. Even if charity is the only duty that requires us only to do enough of something over time, and hence is the only duty that is not part of justice on the view that the equivalence reading ascribes to Mill, it is not so negligible that Mill would effectively be guilty of merging all of morality into justice himself.

Lyons's contention that the view of the division of morality that Mill holds on the equivalence reading classifies certain duties as obligations of justice when they clearly are not does require more attention. The easy answer is that Lyons may be guilty of taking a particular account of the division of morality for granted when this matter in fact remains fairly controversial. The point at which it is most readily apparent that

Lyons is taking a controversial view for granted comes when he claims that even the view that he attributes to Mill overpopulates justice, since offenses like rape and murder violate rights yet are not injustices. While it may not be obvious that these offenses are injustices, surely there is no consensus that they are not. Perhaps there is more likely to be a consensus to the effect that some of the additional moral failures that are classified as injustices on the view that I take Mill to hold really are not. Even this is not certain, though: would there really be widespread agreement that it would not be an injustice to refuse the border crossers water? And, even if the view that the equivalence reading attributes to Mill is somewhat at odds with commonly accepted views about the contours of justice, this only means that Mill's conception of justice is to some extent revisionary. It is not so much at variance with our normal understanding of justice as to render the concept unrecognizable.

But Lyons's example of duties to self to illustrate his point is well chosen. On the view that I take Mill to hold, duties not to kill or mutilate ourselves would have correlative rights. These would be rights against ourselves, and *prima facie* there is something vaguely weird about that notion. To be clear, my reading of Mill does not entail that he takes us to have such rights. But it entails that he believes that if we did have such duties to ourselves – which seems like an intelligible possibility, as Lyons notes, even though Mill denies that we do – then we would have rights against ourselves also. If the possibility of rights against ourselves is unintelligible, then this would be a problem for Mill. Given Mill's analysis of what it is to have a right, though, the idea of a right against ourselves is not a conceptual impossibility. To say that someone has such a right only means that society should try to use its influence over her education to get her to internalize a rule that prevents her from doing something harmful to herself. The apparent weirdness of the notion comes from the fact that we normally operate with a more robust conception of what it is to have a right. Here, too, Mill offers a conception that is revisionary but that does not render the concept of which it is a specification unrecognizable.

5 Conclusion

Admittedly, the foregoing discussion makes fairly heavy weather of a relatively minor point of disagreement. Yet the point remains that Lyons gives us insufficient reason to disregard what Mill says about the choice criterion. Perhaps the view that the only non-justice obligations are those that leave agents considerable discretion about when to fulfill them and require them only to do enough of something over time does not offer the best account of the division between justice and the rest of morality. Nevertheless, the considerations that I have raised here argue forcefully that this is Mill's considered opinion.[5]

Notes

1. I discuss and defend this reading further in Miller (2006; 2010a, Chapter 6; 2010b) and (2011).
2. Commentators besides Lyons (and myself) who do so include Dryer (1969), Copp (1979), Gray (1996), Crisp (1997), Fuchs (2006), and Brown (2010).
3. Lyons would actually have us disregard not only the choice criterion but also the terms 'perfect obligation' and 'imperfect obligation,' for he takes Mill to use these terms only in connection with the choice criterion. Lyons asserts that 'Mill provides no general name for the moral obligations that fall outside the realm of justice,' and so Lyons uses the label 'nonjustice obligations' for this purpose (1994, p. 109). On this point, however, Lyons simply misreads Mill, for 'imperfect obligation' *is* Mill's general name for obligations that fall outside the realm of justice. *Pace* Lyons, Mill never 'expresses dissatisfaction with the terminology of 'perfect' and 'imperfect' obligation' (1994, p. 116). In the portion of 5:15 quoted at the outset of this paper, Mill presents the distinction between obligations that do and do not have correlative rights not as an alternative to the language of perfect and imperfect obligations but as a more precise way of explicating this language. He writes, for example, that 'duties of imperfect obligation are those moral obligations which do not give birth to any right.' For Mill, therefore, 'imperfect obligation' and 'non-justice obligation' are synonymous, however he might distinguish between justice and non-justice obligations.
4. While it is unclear how Mill means us to understand the relation between beneficence and charity or generosity in *Utilitarianism*, as I have already noted, it does appear that he uses 'beneficence' differently in *Utilitarianism* and *On Liberty*. In *Utilitarianism*, the obligation of beneficence only requires us to do enough of something over time. In *On Liberty*, Mill refers to our 'Good Samaritan' obligations as duties of 'individual beneficence,' but he does not seem to think of them as being limited in this way. That is, he does not seem to think of 'saving a fellow creature's life, or interposing to protect the defenceless against ill-usage' as things that we only need to do enough of over time. Nor is this the only case of a technical term that is used differently in these two texts; in Miller (2010a, Chapter 7), I show that his use of 'interest' in the two essays is also inconsistent.
5. I am grateful to Beth McHose and Leonard Kahn for their comments on earlier versions of this chapter.

References

Brown, D.G. (2010) 'Mill's Moral Theory: Ongoing Revisionism,' *Politics, Philosophy and Economics* 9(1), 5–45.

Copp, David (1979) 'The Iterated-Utilitarianism of J. S. Mill,' *New Essays on John Stuart Mill and Utilitarianism, Canadian Journal of Philosophy*, Supplementary Volume V, 75–98.

Crisp, Roger (1997) *Mill on Utilitarianism* (London: Routledge).

Dryer, D.P. (1969) 'Mill's Utilitarianism,' *The Collected Works of John Stuart Mill: Essays on Ethics, Religion, and Society*, Vol. X (Toronto: University of Toronto Press).

Fuchs, Alan (2006) 'Mill's Theory of Morally Correct Action,' *The Blackwell Guide to Mill's Utilitarianism*, Henry West (ed.) (Malden, MA: Blackwell).

Gaus, Gerald F. (1998) 'Mill's Theory of Moral Rules,' *John Stuart Mill's Social and Political Thought: Critical Assessments*, G.W. Smith (ed.) (London: Routledge).

Gray, John (1996) *Mill on Liberty: A Defence*, 2nd ed. (London: Routledge).

Lyons, David (1994) *Rights, Welfare and Mill's Moral Theory* (Oxford: Oxford University Press).

Miller, Dale E. (2006) 'Mill's Theory of Sanctions,' *The Blackwell Guide to Mill's Utilitarianism*, Henry West (ed.) (Malden, MA: Blackwell).

Miller, Dale E. (2010a) *J. S. Mill: Moral, Social and Political Thought* (London: Polity).

Miller, Dale E. (2010b) 'Brown on Mill's Moral Theory: A Critical Response,' *Politics, Philosophy and Economics* 9(1), 47–66.

Miller, Dale E. (2011) 'Mill, Rule Utilitarianism, and the Incoherence Objection,' *John Stuart Mill and the Art of Life*, Ben Eggleston, Dale E. Miller and David Weinstein (eds) (Oxford: Oxford University Press).

Robson, J.M. (ed.) (1977) *The Collected Works of John Stuart Mill: Essays on Politics and Society Part 1*, Vol. XVIII (Toronto: University of Toronto Press).

Robson, J.M. (ed.) (1969) *The Collected Works of John Stuart Mill: Essays on Ethics, Religion, and Society*, Vol. X (Toronto: University of Toronto Press).

Sinnott-Armstrong, Walter (2005) 'You Ought to be Ashamed of Yourself (When You Violate an Imperfect Moral Obligation),' *Philosophical Issues* 15, 193–208.

4
John Stuart Mill on Justice

Fred Wilson

1 To begin: Mill, justice, and utility

John Stuart Mill defended utilitarianism; indeed, he was its leading defender in the Victorian era. Mill was also the advocate of a radical reform in British politics and society, and his proposals were all rooted in the Principle of Utility as he understood it. For the utilitarian, all other moral rules were subsidiary to the Principle of Utility. This includes the principles of justice. But this giving priority to utility was challenged by those who defended the primacy of justice, and there are those who continue so to challenge Mill's account of morality and of justice. This chapter aims to give an exposition of Mill's views on these issues, and to offer, partially at least, a defense of those views, or at least to show that they are not so wildly short of the truth as they are presented as being.

2 Introduction[1]

This chapter defends utilitarianism not primarily by positive argument (though Mill does propose what he deems to be a proof of sorts of the Principle of Utility) but instead largely through replies to the critics of utilitarianism. The Principle of Utility is itself developed only so far as needed for these replies, but in spite of this inexactitude the replies are for the most part cogent. It is in this context of replying to critics that Mill locates his important discussion of *justice*. He states and clarifies the Principle of Utility and replies to a variety of objections in Chapters I through III. In Chapter IV he provides an argument that he takes to justify the Principle of Utility. This chapter, 'Of What Sort of Proof Is the Principle of Utility Susceptible?,' proposes an argument that is neither deductive nor inductive, but one which Mill at least takes to be convincing. It is an argument which is not as simplistic as many have suggested, but is nonetheless an argument that few have found convincing. Be that as it may, our own main concern here is his views on justice. This is the topic to which Mill turns in Chapter V, 'On the Connection between Justice and Utility,' in which the idea of many is taken up, that Justice is a final and conclusive argument against his Principle. This argument against Mill's thesis, that the Principle of Utility is the basic moral principle, is based on the claim that this Principle is inconsistent with the claims of Justice as a more fundamental moral principle. For example, one might achieve maximal happiness if one allows that the distribution include the knave, one who is unworthy of such a reward. Or one might achieve maximal happiness by letting a few be very happy while letting the remainder lead miserable lives. Or, again, you cannot break a solemn promise simply because so acting would be somewhat to your advantage; a minor advantage is trumped by the moral right of the promisee that the promise be kept – promise-breaking is *just wrong*; nothing could be stronger or more evident than that. Examples like these make it certain, it is held, that utility, an appeal to mere pleasure, cannot justify, ever, such a firm moral judgment as the Principle that promises ought to be kept, or cannot justify a distribution of goods that is simply unfair. In any such case (one can think of others) Mill's Principle appears to be satisfied but in a way that is obviously unjust, and, since we can all recognize that the Principle of Justice, and not the Principle of Utility, is the one that clearly *ought* to prevail, it follows that Mill's Principle cannot have the status he claims for it of being our basic moral rule. It is this argument that Mill addresses in Chapter V, where he attempts to defend his position that the Principle of Utility ought to be our basic moral rule: if, he argues, the claims of Justice ought, as indeed they ought, to be recognized, then that is only because those claims are justified by the Principle of Utility – which, therefore, remains the fundamental principle, undisturbed by the claims of justice: those claims are far from conflicting with Mill's Principle; conformity to the rule or rules of justice can be justified only by appeal to that Principle of Utility.

3 Mill's Principle of Utility[2]

Mill's thought had its origins in Bentham, who tells us that 'By the principle of utility is meant that principle which approves or disapproves of every action whatsoever, according to the tendency which it appears to have to augment or diminish the happiness of the party whose interest is in question: or, what is the same thing in other words, to promote or to oppose that happiness.' And Bentham ([1789] 1970, Chapter 1) emphasizes that this applies to 'every action whatsoever.' One cannot appeal to some Principle of Justice to claim that an act which violates the Principle of Utility is nonetheless the right thing to do because Justice demands it.

Mill, in his essay on *Utilitarianism*, takes up apparent counterexamples to the claimed fundamental nature of the Principle of Utility, such as those that we have mentioned. In this essay he explains his Principle of Utility in this way:

> The creed which accepts as the foundation of morals Utility, or the greatest Happiness Principle, holds that actions are right in proportion as they tend to promote happiness, wrong as they tend to produce the reverse of happiness. (CW X, p. 210)

He elaborates by adding that 'By happiness is intended pleasure and the absence of pain; by unhappiness, pain and the privation of pleasure.' And he further adds that '... the theory of life on which this theory or morality is grounded... [is that] pleasure, and freedom from pain, are the only things desirable as ends; and that all desirable things (which are as numerous in the utilitarian as in any other scheme) are desirable either for the pleasure inherent in themselves, or as a means to the promotion of pleasure and the prevention of pain' (CW X, p. 210).[3]

And then, in this essay on *Utilitarianism*, after defending the Greatest Happiness Principle against a variety of objections, Mill comes to consider what he takes to be the strongest of all: 'In all ages of speculation, one of the strongest obstacles to the reception of the doctrine that Utility or Happiness is the criterion of right and wrong have been drawn from the idea of Justice.' He explains:

> The powerful sentiment, and apparently clear perception, which the word recalls with a rapidity and certainty resembling an instinct, have seemed to the majority of thinkers to point to an inherent quality in things; to show that the Just must have an existence in Nature as something absolute – generically different from every variety of the Expedient [that is, what is conducive to happiness or pleasure], and, in idea, opposed to it, (as is commonly acknowledged) never in the long run, disjoined from it in fact. (CW X, p. 240)

Duty may in the end be absolute, but God at least will reward the virtuous with happiness. Mill attempts to meet this objection in Chapter V of *Utilitarianism*.

The objection from Justice finds its support, Mill is here making clear, in a metaphysics in which Justice has an objective ground in the ontological structure of the universe. Now, Mill does not here, in *Utilitarianism* itself, elaborate or call into question this metaphysics: he more or less takes for granted that it is without serious support. But it will, I think, be appropriate right here for us, at the beginning of our discussion of Mill on Justice and its relation to Utility, to lay out this metaphysics. For we can, I suggest, best understand Mill's position on justice and the argument of Chapter V only if we do place it in some of the broader context of Mill's thought and the thought of those who defend Justice.

4 Mill's opposition: the defenders of justice

We can start by recalling that Mill was a great admirer of Plato, or, rather, Socrates. Thus, Mill in his account of eliminative induction placed the falsification of hypotheses as central to the experimental method, and he tended to see a precursor in Socrates, when he refuted, showed to be false, an opponent's views on, for example, the definition of justice or virtue, by finding some sort of counterexample to the proffered definition. Further, he saw Plato's distinction between a form, such as justice itself, and its instances, in this case instances of justice, instances such as ensuring each receives a fair share of some good or keeping a promise to return a book.

This Platonic vision was taken up and defended by the Victorian philosopher of science, William Whewell,[4] who, as Professor or Moral Philosophy and later also Master of Trinity College, Cambridge, felt it was incumbent on him to look after the morals of his undergraduates. To this end he lectured on both moral philosophy and its history, and in these lectures laid out his Platonic account of morality and defended it, mainly by criticizing its critics.

Forms of actions were morally right or just, he argued, provided that they were instances of the transcendent form or idea defining what is Right. Humans are naturally inclined to do what is Right – this is their moral nature – but they have other inclinations, in particular bodily urges aiming at gratifications of a sensory kind. These are natural too, but in our human nature their proper place is that of being subordinate to our moral nature. However, these urges can lead to corruption in the sense that they can, unless controlled, lead us to act contrarily to our nature and to do what is wrong, that is, not right (Whewell, 1862, pp. 43ff). But we do have the means to control these urges that tend to our own corruption. Humans have the capacity to know, have a rational intuition of, their own natural form, and have the rational capacity to discover the best means to achieve their ends (Whewell, 1862, pp. 84ff). So, knowing their metaphysical nature, that is, their natural ends, they can recognize that the best means towards those ends – towards doing what is Right or just, in other words – is to control and to keep their bodily urges to their proper place as subordinate to their moral nature. Within the category of being Right, there are various principles, those dealing with security, those dealing with relations in the family, those dealing with civil society, and so on; the basic principles in each area falling under the form of rightness are known *a priori*, like the axioms of geometry, though they may in the course of history, again like the axioms of geometry, be at first grasped but imperfectly and only rise to full conscious clarity as we experience the operations of these transcendent forms in the events in and actions into the world of ordinary sensible experience. 'The Conceptions of the fundamental Rights of Man are universal, and flow necessarily from the Moral Nature of Man: the Definitions of these Rights are diverse, and are determined by the Laws of each State' (Whewell, 1845, vol. I, p. 77).[5]

5 Objective justice criticized and defended once more

The first in the British tradition to critically attack Platonism was Thomas Hobbes. Hobbes argued that there is nothing beyond the world as we encounter it in our everyday sensory experience of things. There are therefore no forms, no transcendent ontological structures that provide an objective grounding for morality.

Bentham was to take up Hobbes's position with regard to any *a priori* morality – to suppose otherwise, that there is somehow an objective, ontologically true, morality, is an illusion; to suppose that there is such an ontologically grounded morality simply enables one to take one's own prejudices as truths grounded in the objective reality of things – prejudices which allow it to seem an objective truth that some can with rightness exploit others – humans do seek their own pleasure, and these prejudices enable the few to attain a great deal of pleasure in this world while the many work for meager reward to ensure the few their way of life. Rather than these norms which justify the well-being of the few and the servitude of the many, the norm, Bentham argued, ought to be the greatest happiness for the greatest number.

As for moral feelings, Bentham also argued, again following Hobbes, these arise through processes of mental association. Associationism was taken to be a solidly founded scientific theory, differing from physics not in its form as a confirmed scientific theory but only in its subject matter – physics dealt with planets and stones, associationism with things mental. It was a theory of learning: if events of kind A were repeatedly experienced as accompanied by, or followed by, events of kind B, then in consciousness ideas of kind A were regularly accompanied by ideas of B. The basic laws go back to Aristotle on memory, but for the anti-Platonist empiricists of the eighteenth and nineteenth centuries it became a general theory of mind.

6 Our idea of justice that is to be analyzed

Now, our sense of justice is in fact a strong motive – try making an inequitable distribution of candy among kids in a schoolyard! This motive is, one must admit, often stronger than the motive that aims at the general good. Certainly, Mill grants this. He also grants that we experience as a simple unity the sense that our duty demands that justice be served – and that serving justice as our duty is *not* the same as serving virtue, seeking after the general good. Indeed, Mill grants that justice as our duty is sufficiently strong, sufficiently demanding, as to call into question the utilitarian claim that the general good alone can justify any action. What he must do to defend utilitarianism is to take for granted that his 'proof' of his Principle of Utility (given in the preceding chapter of *Utilitarianism*) has succeeded, but then to establish on utilitarian grounds the *apparent* primacy of justice. As Mill sees it, the first step in this task is that of locating our ordinary or customary general concept or idea of justice. He assumes as the framework in which he is going to make his case the associationist psychology which he had defended and which pervades the whole argument of the essay on *Utilitarianism*.

Mill will take for granted that our idea of justice is an association of several ideas – including, since it is in fact a strong motive to act, feelings of pleasure – justice is something that pleases us, and injustice something that pains us. His task is to analyze the concept into its basic constituents. These constituents will be integrant parts, not clearly separable in the simple and unified idea of justice that moves us. But through analysis these parts, which remain present dispositionally, can be recovered and brought to consciousness. The concept will be a case where there is a felt sense of obligation: the just is obligatory. But, contrary to what Whewell claimed about the concept of justice, this concept, revealed by Mill's analysis, will have no *a priori* validity. It will indeed feel as if acts falling under this concept are unconditionally obligatory. That feeling of unconditional validity is precisely what makes it seem as if the Just is prior to the Principle of Utility. Since Mill has already, in the preceding chapter of the essay, given a 'proof' of the Principle of Utility, justice *cannot* be morally prior to utility. But his analysis will show, he hopes, why it seems *as if* justice is prior to utility. But the customary concept of justice cannot be one that is devoid of *all* moral force. Mill will go on to attempt to show that what the Principle of Justice justifies can be shown, for the most part at least, by the Principle of Utility to be morally justified, and indeed he will attempt to show that the morally prior Principle of Utility justifies the notion that our sense of justice *ought* to have – though in a suitably qualified way – the moral force of unconditional validity. In other words, he will attempt to show that the Principle of Utility justifies morally our having this concept – our customary concept of justice – which has the appearance of being a concept conformity which is felt to be prior to the Principle of Utility. Whewell claims that the concept of justice is simple and incapable of analysis; Mill aims to show, upon the principles of associationist psychology, that it is simple, a felt unity, but nonetheless capable of analysis. Whewell claims that the simplicity is not only the mark of the unconditional validity it is customarily felt to have; Mill aims to show that this felt unconditional validity, when suitably qualified, is in fact, by the principle of utility, morally justified.

He begins this task of analysis, asking what justice is, as Socrates began his similar tasks, by looking at examples, various kinds of act, each kind said to be a case of justice, to find what they have in common. These kinds that Mill notes are the following.

[1] It is commonly taken that it is contrary to what justice requires to deprive a person of something the possession of which they have by legal right;

[2] Some laws violate moral rules, and it is in that case taken that it is contrary to what justice requires to deprive a person of possession of something to which they have moral right, even if legally they may be deprived of it;

[3] It is commonly thought that persons deserve good if they do what is right, and that to deprive such a person of the deserved good is contrary to what justice requires, whereas a person who does something wrong or painful or evil deserves punishment;

[4] Violating a contract or failing to do something that was promised is commonly thought to be contrary to what justice requires;

[5] It is commonly thought that letting one's judgment be swayed by irrelevant factors such as race or class or sex is contrary to what justice requires;

[6] Some communists, like Robert Owen and his followers or the earlier Diggers, take impartiality to require equality in the distribution of goods – it is contrary to what justice requires, these persons hold, to distribute goods by any criterion other than need, for example, being a member of the aristocracy ought not to entitle one to a greater share of social goods than a servant or a slave.

Mill's problem is to determine what these various cases of justice have in common: what makes them all instances of justice?

7 Justice is rulish

First, it is necessary to note that each of the things we have (with Mill) noted involves a *rule*, a generalization or regularity about human behavior that *ought to be*: thus, for example, it ought to be that promises are kept, and if the world is as it ought to be then every act of promising results in a promise kept; or, more generally, if it ought to be that whenever A then B, then, if the moral injunction is successful, the regularity will in fact hold that whenever A then B. Since, in each case, it ought to be that the regularity holds, it follows that if one fulfills the antecedent then one ought to fulfill the consequent: it ought to be that promises are kept, so then, if one has made a promise then it ought to be that one keeps that promise, and if one does not here do as one ought to do then there will be a violation of the rule, the regularity the rule enjoins will be false and the world will not be as it ought to be; and, more generally, if it ought to be that whenever A then B, then, if one is in situation A then one ought to ensure that B occurs, for if one does not do that then the rule will be violated, the regularity that the rule enjoins is false, and the world is not as it ought to be.

For Mill, the basic rule is, of course, the Principle of Utility: it ought to be for everyone that whenever one acts then that act will (relative to possible alternatives) maximize utility. But there are, he argues, subsidiary moral rules – such as the rules he has listed when giving examples of just actions.

Mill argues that moral rules, including, in particular, the rules that come under the heading of Justice, *do in fact* play an important part in our lives as moral beings but also that they *ought* to play such a role – that is, *ought* according to the Principle of Utility. Mill makes out a case that living our lives by these rules, these 'secondary principles' as he calls them (CW X, p. 224), is conducive to maximizing happiness overall – that is, so acting makes the lot of all better than if we tried to live without such secondary principles as those of Justice and attempted to act as if securing the maximal happiness of humankind were our sole end. 'The proposition,' he declares, 'that happiness is the end of morality, does not mean that no road ought to be set down to that goal, or that persons going thither should not be advised to take one direction rather than another' (CW X, p. 224). Mill makes clear the connections, as he sees them, among rights or duty, rules, justice, and happiness, in a letter he wrote to George Grote:

> human happiness, including one's own, is in general more successfully pursued by acting on general rules, than by measuring the consequences of each act; and this is still more the case with the general happiness, since any other plan would not only leave everybody uncertain what to expect, but would involve perpetual quarreling: and hence general rules must be laid down for people's conduct to one another, or in other words, rights and obligations must ... be recognized; and people must, on the one hand, not be required to sacrifice even their own less good to another's greater, where no general rule has given the other a right to the sacrifice; while when a right *has* been recognized, they must, in most cases, yield to that right even at the sacrifice, in the particular case, of their own greater good to another's less. (CW XIV, p. 762)

We can see from this how Mill conceived that secondary rules, and the rules of justice in particular, can be justified by the Principle of Utility. The point is two-fold. First, there is the need for regularity of conduct: it is useful to know what others are going to do; the rules enjoin, and thereby bring about, regularity in behavior. Our own life, and the life of everyone else, is made happier if we can anticipate what everyone will do in certain situations. Second, in principle the Principle of Utility alone would do the job of rendering behavior regular and predictable – were we able clearly to apply it. But, as Butler argued, and as Whewell was to make much of (1862, pp. 216–27), we cannot, for the most part, know all the consequences of any human action. It follows that for the most part none of us can know whether the rule applies.

So everyone will do what he or she *suspects* the rule to require. The uncertainty in knowledge will mean that different persons will differ as to whether a certain action is required by the rule. So regularity in behavior, predictability, will not exist. But interaction with our fellows clearly requires that there be regularity and predictability in human behavior. Rules are useful and life is the better for having them. The Principle of Utility therefore requires that there be rules and that there be rules beyond the Principle of Utility. The Principle of Utility therefore enjoins that there be rules other than itself – in other words, that there be 'secondary principles' like the principles of justice. In fact, Mill adds, 'in this condition of the world, paradoxical as the assertion may be, the conscious ability to do without happiness gives the best prospect of realizing such happiness as is attainable' (CW X, p. 217).

The central point about the rules of morality, and of justice in particular, is that they form a *system*. This is a system of *duties*, things that we ought to do, and *rights*, things that we can morally expect will be done. This system of rules brings about a system of regularities in behavior: with the system of rules one can participate in one's community in security, knowing and relying upon what are the regular patterns of behavior of one's fellows. Given the utility of the security brought about by the system of rights and duties, minor violations, even if they can be justified by the Principle of Utility, would jeopardize the security of the system and therefore cannot be allowed: most of the violations which seem to be justified by the Principle of Utility turn out after all not to be justified by the Principle of Utility.

We can now see how the end defining morality, namely, of course, that of maximizing utility, therefore enjoins that one act for ends other than the maximization of utility, and that one act according to rules other than the Principle that Mill has argued is, or ought to be, the supreme or basic moral rule. Mill thus has a reply to Whewell's charge that utilitarianism is an impossible moral doctrine because it imposes upon any actor the impossible burden of knowing sufficient to determine what is one's own duty and what is the duty of others: the reply is that we can rely upon various rules, inductively justified by human experience, as secondary guides about what one ought oneself to do, and what we may reasonably expect others, as moral beings, to do and, indeed, may reasonably rely upon them doing, as these secondary rules enjoin (CW X, pp. 224–5).

Morality is thus rulish and its being rulish can be justified by the Principle of Utility.

8 But rulish is not enough

Being rulish is, however, only one mark of justice. As Mill goes on to point out (CW X, p. 246), this will not distinguish morality, or therefore justice, from the expedient. A rule is moral, and not merely expedient, if, Mill argues, we deem a violation of the rule to demand some sort of punishment. All the six instances of justice that Mill began by listing fit this pattern: they are rules, and we deem violations of any of these rules to be worthy of punishment.

However, Mill's task is not yet complete. Many other rules besides those of justice fit the pattern we have just delineated. We have now only this, namely, the separation of the moral, including the just, from the expedient, but we have not yet characterized the just as only one part of the moral. While any act which is merely inexpedient is never thought of as one worthy of some sort of punishment, this is not true of an act taken to be immoral – failing to do things that are charitable is morally wrong and is felt to be worthy of some sort of punishment, if only public disapprobation. But being uncharitable, while immoral, is not contrary to any rule of justice. So, the concept at which Mill has now arrived, of an act which violates a law and is worthy, therefore, of punishment, is still too broad, still too generic: it distinguishes the moral from the expedient, but there is much to morality beyond the requirements of justice. We have, therefore, arrived at a concept that distinguishes the moral from the expedient but does not pick out, within the concept of the moral, those acts which fall under the narrower concept of being just.

Mill has captured the concept of the genus moral. But that means his aim to define justice is only partially completed: he has defined the genus but has yet to define the species. On the traditional doctrine for the definition of a concept, one defines a species in terms of a genus and a specific difference. Mill has given the genus moral. Part of his aim at defining justice is complete, but more remains to be done. He still has the further task of determining the specific difference that picks out the species justice within the genus moral.

To this end, Mill draws a distinction between two distinct sorts of obligatory act, and argues that, while rules of both sorts are moral, the rules of justice, at least those in the six categories he has listed, fall under only one of these sorts.

Here are the two sorts.

First. Some kinds of action are obligatory, but are not directed, as it were, at any particular person. One has an obligation to be charitable, but it is not required that one be charitable to this or that particular person at this or that particular time. One is obliged to be charitable, but no particular person has a right to one's charity; one can choose who will receive one's charity. Obligations of this sort are said to be imperfect.

Second. In contrast to these acts of imperfect obligation, there are obligations, like that involved in promising, where another definite person has a definite right corresponding to the obligation. If one promises to return a book to person P, then one has an obligation to return the book to P, while P has the moral right to have the book returned. Obligations of this sort are said to be perfect.

Mill argues that just actions among moral actions are always cases of perfect obligation; that is true at least of the examples in the list given of things just. As Mill puts it, any case of injustice always involves both 'a wrong done, and some assignable person who is wronged,' and justice 'implies something which it is not only right to do and wrong not to do, but which some individual person can claim from us as his moral right' (CW X, p. 247).

This is the specific difference for which Mill was searching (or, as we shall see directly, part of the specific difference). Unjust acts are acts worthy of punishment – this makes them fall under the genus of acts that are immoral – but, further, unjust acts are acts by which some particular individual suffers harm – this is the specific difference that determines the species. To violate a right, to fail to do something which another has a moral right to expect, is to commit an injustice, and doing something unjust is doing something worthy of punishment. But, as it turns out, we still have not yet got the full definition for which Mill was searching.

9 Justice as serving our common interest in security

When a moral right is violated, we deem the act to be one worthy of punishment. With regard to the punishment, there are two possibilities. On the one hand, the motive to punishment may be the primitive urge to retaliate, to inflict pain on the person who has done you damage, taken what is rightfully yours, or has done wrong to someone close to you, one of your children, perhaps, or some other member of your family or perhaps of your clan. On the other hand, human sympathies go beyond the immediate group, extending, perhaps, to the whole of humankind. One sees someone else wronged, and one feels the harm the other feels as the other feels it, even where that person is a stranger – but that stranger is still a person and our human sympathies are broad enough, Mill suggests, to bring it about that one feels the pain the other feels at the wrong that has been done to that other. Think of the good Samaritan. In this sort of case, too, in which the wrong is done to a stranger, one is moved to punish the wrongdoer. In either case, where the wronged is close to one or where the wronged is a stranger, then the urge to punish is simply the urge to strike out at the person who has done the wrong, inflicted the pain. In either case, the motive is clear; the wrongdoer's pain becomes your pleasure.

This is true, and it explains why the idea of justice has a motivational or conative aspect as well as cognitive or descriptive content. This conative element has to be taken to be among the integrant parts of our idea of justice. But this feature is a conative element and, since each rule designated as moral involves the desire for punishment if the rule is violated, this conative element is common to all cases of moral rules. So the presence of a conative element does not distinguish the rules of justice within the genus of moral rule. Specifically, it does not explain the *apparent primacy* of justice in our customary moral code. There is a further integrant part of our idea of justice that remains to be uncovered.

It is part of our customary idea of justice that the just person is not moved by a desire for punishment for some more or less trivial or personal wrong. For example, the just person is not moved simply by some more or less trivial desire to inflict pain as punishment on one's brother who took the piece of cake that he had promised one. Here a rule, one of perfect obligation, has been violated – promises ought to be kept – and punishment is in fact deserved. Yet the brother's act is not really an injustice. It's a personal matter; we might admonish the wrongdoer ourselves, but the act, though wrong, is not one in which one expects or requires the community as such to intervene and do the punishing. Moreover, even when the harm is other than personal and has been done to others, if it is merely an incidental case of harm, though there is no doubt a desire to punish, one does not feel called upon to invoke the community. When we hear of some colleague P losing a book that a student promised to return but failed to do so, and in fact disappeared, then our sympathy is with our colleague – he has suffered a wrong and we feel with him the pain he feels at the failure of the student to do what is right. But, again, it is something merely personal, not something in which the community has an interest. These are cases of perfect obligation, to use Mill's term, and they are cases in which the failure to do what is right is worthy of punishment, and in fact we feel in both cases that the one who failed to do what is morally right deserves to be punished. These examples both fulfill the criterion of what is just, as we have so far defined it: the obligation gives a right, a moral expectation, to a definite individual, and a failure to do what is right ought in some way to be punished. But it is part of our customary notion of justice that neither of these kinds of act is an instance of something having been done that is contrary to what justice requires. One feels that the person who purloined the piece of cake should be given a smack or at least a good scolding. And one feels that the person who wrongly kept the book should also be scolded, and, perhaps, should have a negative opinion about his character circulated among those with whom he will perhaps have to live or work in the future.

But suppose the person who purloined the cake had, instead, deliberately purloined a loaf of bread that had been left on the table in a more or less public place for it to be picked up by an unemployed worker who expected to be able to pick it up. And suppose that the person who took the book and didn't return it had taken a book that the owner, a professor, had placed on a shelf where it would be available to all members of his or her class. Each of these new cases involves an act which is clearly unjust. Each involves an act violating an expectation of perfect obligation. Each involves an act worthy of punishment. What else is there that makes these instances of injustice?

The answer that Mill gives is that in each of these cases one feels that the act is not merely a minor thing, or something incidental to what else is going on, but that one feels in these cases a more general involvement with the being and workings of the broader social world. There is the moral sentiment that society as a whole or aggregate, each individual in it, feels the wrong – there is a common interest in preventing such acts, and society as a whole, everyone in that society, therefore feels that the wrongdoer deserves punishment, or, in other words, has an interest in punishing anyone who performs an act of either of these sorts.

It is here, where there is a *common interest in the preventing* of a sort of act, an interest that pervades society, and is an interest shared by all members of the aggregate; and where there is a *common interest in punishing* one who performs such an act, that one finds the final mark that picks out the just from among the moral: justice forbids, and the just person morally disapprobates, any harm 'of the kind in which society has a common interest...in the repression of' (CW X, p. 248). Where there is such a common interest spreading throughout the community as a whole, then there is a rule which makes a certain sort of act an act of perfect obligation. It is a rule that defines the rights of all, that is, of each person in the society – rights that deserve protection. So the relevant sort of act is one in which we, simply as members of a society, have a common interest in ensuring that it is done; the rule must secure rights which are rights of each and all. And, since it is a moral rule, those rights deserve protection by society, that is, protection by each individual person together with every other person, these taken together and recognizing one another as members of their society. The relevant rules are like this: 'Thou shalt not bear false witness,' 'Thou shalt not steal [anything possessed by another].' An act of a kind which violates one of these rules arouses the feeling – *in everyone* – that it is an act that deserves to be punished. 'When we call anything a person's right, we mean that he has a valid claim on society to protect him in the possession of it, either by the force of law, or by that of education and opinion' (CW X, p. 250).

We are almost there. When we look at the rules of justice, they are rules the violation of which deserves punishment, and they are rules of perfect obligation. But we find that they share a certain special feature. This is the last of the marks that serve to distinguish the just as a species within the genus moral. This special feature is that they all arise out of a common interest, an interest in each member of the social aggregate. Because they serve an interest common to all members of the society, they must confer, in one way or another, rights which protect us in our being as members of the society from predation, as it were, by any other member of the society. The interest which alone is felt by each member of a society (of any size) is that that member be secure in his or her own being. This is the common interest which motivates a certain set of rules. These are those rules which *render each and all of us secure as members of our community in the possession of the necessities of life*. It is these rules which, Mill argues, form the rules of justice: it is this feature – that of securing for each and all security in the possession of the necessities of life – which forms the final part of the specific difference in the definition of the concept of justice.

Mill has picked out the rules of justice by finding that interest which alone could render those rules so demanding; it is our common interest each has in the security of his or her being. Thus, the cognitive content of our sense of justice is a set of rules protecting for each the security of his or her being; while, because that interest which each has in the maintaining of these rules is such a strong interest, an interest which precedes all other interests, the concept of justice as motivating or conative is as strong, as demanding, as it is.

The point deserves a bit of elaboration. The crucial fact is that persons cannot survive in any decent way apart from a community of other persons. Community is a necessity of life. Security in the possession of, say, food is a necessity of life. Sharing equitably in the burdens and costs of living together is a necessity; why join the community or keep the peace if one is going continually to be oppressed by others? Being able to trade goods is also a necessity, at least for a society of any complexity. One achieves community through being able to trust one another. One can live together in peace with others only so long as the rules are applied equitably to all. To repeat, *the rules of justice are the rules that secure these necessities of life.* Thus, the rules of justice guarantee each of us possession of what we produce ourselves and a fair share of anything we jointly produce. They provide, too, for the equitable sharing of burdens living in a community requires and the equitable sharing of the costs arising in the joint production of goods. They provide, through the mechanism of promising, for the exchange of goods. Through rules like that of truth-telling they make it possible for people to live together in a community. And there are rules that provide for the equitable treatment of all in the application of the rules.

10 The analysis of the idea of justice also uncovers the fact of motivation

It is important to remember that to speak of morality and justice is not merely to speak of a set of propositions. By themselves, the propositions that one ought to be charitable or that one ought to keep one's promises are *inert.* But in fact our sense of justice *moves us: it is a motive.* Indeed, our sense of justice is *a motive that strongly demands* that one rest secure with, or defend with the help of others forming the aggregate which is society as a whole, what oneself has through one's own rights or what others have through their rights.[6] The existence of the rights of justice, and the motivated conformity of all to these norms, protects us in the possession of goods (property), and ensures a reasonable allocation of goods from among scarce resources (equity). The threat of punishment for violating someone's rights strengthens that protection.

Justice is among the strongest of the passions that move us; and this fact must be located among the (metaphysical) parts into which our idea of justice is analyzed, Mill argues as a psychologist and as a moral philosopher. When we analyze this motive, he proposes, that is, in other words, when we analyze our idea of justice, then we find that basically the parts which are the roots of this strength are, on the one hand, primitive animal urges we share with lower beasts – the urges for self-protection, vengeance and retaliation – as well as, on the other hand, our more human sympathies for the welfare of others – especially our friends and family, but also others only distantly connected to us. It is the duty of others to respect rights conferred by the rules of justice: those rights and those duties are assured, conformity to them made reliable and secure, through the threat of punishment; but this assurance is made yet more reliable and secure by the very strength as a motive of our idea of justice. The rules of justice ensure us of some minimum at least from among the scarce resources that nature yields up to us in our community; they provide us with security against threats by others. These rules we share with others; we are, moreover, all prepared to defend and prepared to punish the unjust; and this shared passion to protect and to punish is among the strongest that move us. Without such rules, strongly defended and enforced, there would be, and sometimes is, a war of all against all, and truly *Homo hominis lupus*. Such was the Hobbesian view of humanity, at least according to Whewell. But, while Mill shared with Hobbes the rejection of *a priori* principles which Whewell took to be the root of the view of people as amoral or immoral beings, Mill had a view of human beings in which people have, among the passions which move us, our more human sympathies that bind us to others, with their ends becoming our ends. It is these human sympathies that raise us above the merely animal, and which make possible the cooperative behavior embodied in the rules of justice: man, Mill makes clear, is not wolf to man, and he shows how it is possible to hold this view and to defend it against both the inhuman view of human being found in Hobbes – the view that persons lack any genuine higher qualities and motives – and the equally inhuman view of human being found in Whewell, which requires humans to reach out to a realm of transcendental forms which it is impossible for us as ordinary this-worldly beings to attain – which is, of course, precisely what makes it inhuman. *It is Mill's view, not that of Whewell or that of Hobbes, which is the genuinely human.*

It is worth noting that seeking justice is an end in itself, something done because it is the just thing to do: it is done for its own sake. To say this is to say that justice is part of our happiness. Since justice is not a primitive or instinctual motive, it has become one through a process of association. It is similar to the miser case that Mill used as an example. Accumulating money has become part of the miser's happiness; an act of accumulation has become something done for its own sake. Similarly, doing something for a friend, because he or she is a friend, has also become part of one's happiness and has become something done for its own sake: when one does something for a friend, doing that, whatever it is, is an end in itself. Similarly, doing something out of vengeance is part of one's happiness. Perhaps doing something like that, retaliating out of vengeance, may be a primitive, unlearned, or instinctual motive, or it may be learned – acting to preserve for oneself the necessities of life that one has accumulated is perhaps originally done as a means, and retaliating, seeking vengeance, is to seek the return of those possessions and to seek to inflict pain on the aggressor is to seek a sort of payment, whereby paying that price will deter such aggression in the future. Perhaps these things are learned, perhaps in their basic forms they are unlearned – it does not matter: whether primitive or learned, the motive of vengeance is there, as is the motive of preserving what one possesses of the things necessary for life, and acting on such a motive is to do something for its own sake: so acting is part of our happiness. It is similar for justice as a motive, except that doing something because it is the just thing to do is certainly learned. An act done because it is the just thing to do is done for its own sake: so acting has become part of one's happiness. That happiness is a fusion of other happinesses. Among these, Mill proposes, is certainly the happiness which is sought out of vengeance for challenging one's possession of certain necessities of life; and also the happiness that arises from sympathy for someone else who has had his or her possession of necessities of life challenged. These are strong motives, and the happinesses at which they aim are strongly felt: to achieve them is very satisfying. Seeking justice is to seek things out of a fusion of these motives and these happinesses. As a fusion it has become a different motive, but one that has the strength of the motives of which it is a fusion: the strength, in other words, of any motive aimed at preserving either oneself or another in possession of the necessities of life. The happiness at which it aims is also a fusion, different from the happinesses of which it is the fusion but retaining their strength as motivating powers.

11 The analysis of our idea of justice completed

Here, then, are the parts into which Mill analyzes our idea of justice. **First**, a just act is one somehow productive of a good, that is, something pleasurable for others, and such that, if it is. This makes it the right thing to do, and makes it something required by the art of living well. **Second**, a just act falls under a rule, and it follows from the first condition that the rule is such that acts falling under it maximize good, that is, utility. But this is true not only of acts which are moral but also of those that are expedient. **Third**, failure to do what is expedient may be foolish, but it is not punishable; however, if an act called for by a rule of justice is not done, then punishment is called for. But this characteristic, while a feature of acts which are just, distinguishes an act as moral, rather than more narrowly just. So here we have the genus moral under which justice is a species. **Fourth**, justice involves another definite person having the right to be protected in the possession of some good. As Mill puts it, a just act is an act of perfect obligation. **Fifth**, it is taken for granted from the second condition that the rules are accepted by, and apply to, one and all, and that, if a rule is violated, then the one whose rights are being violated can call on society as a whole to enforce the rule or, if that is not possible, then he or she can call upon society as a whole to punish the person who violated the rights conferred by the rule. We have, finally, a **sixth** condition. The rules of justice play a special role in our lives as social beings: these are rules that, if conformed to by all, ensure that any and each person is secure in his or her life and in the possessions of things that are essential to survival. Each person has a direct interest in his or her own life and in the possession of the necessities of life, and the mechanism of sympathy gives to each person a similar interest with regard to others. Without the rules of justice no one could trust anyone else; one would have Hobbes's war of all against all – which is in no one's interest. So each of us has the strongest interest in everyone conforming to these rules, and the general enforcement by all in securing this conformity and in punishing deviations.

12 Mill's conclusions

Mill has now given his analysis of the concept of justice. Justice, as Mill analyzes it, is a powerful motive, and, though an association of simpler ideas, is unique in its simplicity and feeling. This uniqueness and simplicity are not a matter of its metaphysical status as a transcendental entity, as Whewell claimed, but occur only by virtue of wholly natural and this-worldly processes of association in which the mode of association is chemical in nature and not mechanical. Mill has described how this powerful motive arises out of more primitive urges to act; he thus argues that it does not move us, as Whewell, following Plato and Aristotle, argued, because of its metaphysical status as a substantial form, and therefore an unanalyzable power, but rather moves us in more or less the same way as any naturalistic motive, from hunger to friendship, moves us. Justice is a wholly natural phenomenon.

Mill, in arguing for justice being something wholly natural, has thus argued that, unlike Whewellian forms, our ordinary concept of justice, we discover upon analysis, while it is strong and unique, nonetheless has no claim in itself to our unconditional assent. There is, therefore, contrary to claims by Whewell (or Frankena), nothing about justice that demands it be given priority over the principle of utility.

Mill has, in fact, argued that, given the naturalistic nature of justice, this concept has no intrinsic claim to be morally required: from naturalistic facts one cannot derive any claim that any principle is obligatory – 'is' does not imply 'ought.'[7]

Mill has, therefore, clearly established that there is nothing intrinsic to justice that could establish that it is an 'ought,' let alone an 'ought' that ought to take priority over the principle of utility. So, the 'proof' that Mill earlier gave for the principle of utility is unchallenged after all.

But, for all that, justice clearly does in any ordinary way make strong moral demands on us.

Mill makes two points.

One: Being just requires conformity to a number of different principles. (We, following Mill, listed six, above; one could think of more that satisfy Mill's criterion for a principle to be a principle of justice.) Mill points out that these can come into conflict. Thus, one ought not to steal, but, if one is unemployed with no public assistance, then the theft of a loaf of bread might well be justified; while it is a principle of justice that theft is wrong, in the context described that action of theft can be justified by the further principle of justice that one has a right to life, and this implies that one has a right to ensure that one's hunger receives at least minimal satisfaction. One finds this sort of conflict very often in social contexts: ought there to be a minimum wage? and, if so, then at what level ought it to be set? Or taxation: ought there to be a flat tax? or a graduated income tax? One can argue from equity to both of these alternatives, which nonetheless conflict! Or, again, one ought to obey the law, and therefore in particular the law that one ought not to sleep under bridges; this law applies equitably to the rich and the poor, yet inequitably affects the poor. Another conflict in applying the rules of justice. The point is, of course, this: that, when its rules come into conflict, justice provides no way to adjudicate.[8] How, then, can such disputes be resolved?[9] Mill points out that some rule is needed to effect a decision when rules of justice conflict and that what one finds is that, as a matter of fact, generally the appeal that is made is that one do what the overall social good requires, that is, to the Principle of Utility. One finds such an appeal even among those who claim justice is *a priori*, though they so appeal only at the cost of some consistency. (Mill has little trouble in finding such appeals and such inconsistencies in Whewell.) But Mill has established that the rules of justice are not *a priori*. And what he has argued is that his principle of utility *alone* has *any sort of 'proof'* that it defines what *ought to be* and therefore what we *ought to do*, that is, it alone defines the end at which we *ought* to aim. It follows directly that this principle alone can serve as adjudicator. So, this has to be the principle to which one appeals to resolve such conflicts: 'Social utility alone can decide the preference' (CW X, p. 254). Or, as he also puts the point, 'From these confusions there is no other mode of extrication than the utilitarian' (CW X, p. 255).

Two: Utility not only decides when principles of justice come into conflict; it justifies the whole practice of justice. Why *ought* one, why *ought* we be just? Justice cannot justify itself: contrary to Whewell, justice is not valid *a priori*; it is not self-evidently correct. So, one needs another principle, one which *can* be defended as defining what ought to be. Utility alone satisfies this condition. It cannot be established *a priori*, by intuition or by some deductive proof. But it does have a sort of 'proof,' the only 'sort of proof to which the principle of utility is susceptible' (CW X, p. 237): this 'proof' justifying the principle of utility as defining what *ought to be* is the 'proof' presented in Chapter IV of *Utilitarianism*, the chapter preceding Chapter V on justice. It is this principle, then, to which we appeal to justify the whole system or practice of justice.

The Principle of Utility justifies the various rules which constitute the system of justice: these are the rules that guarantee that each of us has those things which are essential to his or her existence, as an individual and as a member of his or her society. Each and every individual has the strongest interest in securing universal conformity to these rules. Universal conformity serves the general interest.

Since these rules define what is necessary to our existence and to our existence as social beings, utility justifies their enforcement through the threat of punishment for anyone who violates a principle of justice.

Indeed, it is to utility that one must appeal when deciding the mode of punishment that is appropriate to different violations of different rules of justice.

The sentiment or passion of justice is – Mill agrees with Whewell on this point – one of the strongest of motives. Its strength – Mill argues against Whewell – derives from the desire for vengeance or retaliation, on the one hand, and, on the other hand, our social sympathies with others. 'The sentiment of justice, in that one of its elements which consists of the desire to punish, is...the natural feeling of retaliation or vengeance, rendered by intellect and sympathy applicable to those injuries, that is, to those hurts that wound us through, or in common with, society at large' (CW X, pp. 248–9). The motive to conform to, and to secure conformity to, the rules of justice is thus very strong; and its having this strength is itself of great utility, given the importance of such conformity. Thus, *the strength of the motive is itself also justified by the Principle of Utility.*

The motive has its genetic origins in primitive urges. These are strong, but, when associated with similar feelings consequent upon our social sympathies, a stronger motive results. Whewell is correct that our sense of justice cannot, because it does not, consist of these basic urges added together; our sense of justice is altogether unique, different in kind from these basic urges from our animal nature. But Whewell is wrong to conclude that therefore this idea, this motive, cannot be accounted for by associationist principles, that justice must therefore be known not out of our sense experience of the world but *a priori*, by rational intuition, as a metaphysical form guaranteeing the objective ontological grounding to the principles of justice to which we are innately moved to conform. It is hard to see how principles that come into conflict, as do the principles of justice, could all be grounded *a priori* in the ontological structure of the universe. Would a good God really have created a universe so ontologically in conflict with itself? one so ambiguous in its demands on human beings? But the unique concept of justice can have its origins in animal nature, because the laws of association do not generate their products by mere mechanical or additive connections in which the parts are all integrant parts but, rather, generate their products by processes that are chemical in kind. In particular, the idea of justice, as the product of an association of simpler ideas, can be unique and different in kind from the animal impulses which are its genetic antecedents. So Mill can agree with Whewell on the special nature of the sense of justice, its uniqueness, its unity, and its distinctive and demanding quality, while insisting both on its naturalistic origin and also on the social utility of our having these stronger motives which are parts (that is, metaphysical parts) of our idea of justice. And Mill can, in thus arguing, allow that the idea of justice includes principles that at some times come into conflict. Such are the vagaries of association – vagaries can allow for principles that are at times inconsistent, whereas the ontological structures proposed by Whewell cannot.

Mill can, therefore, reasonably conclude that justice and its stern demands constitute no challenge to utilitarian ethics. On the one hand, we can understand in a naturalistic way why we feel so strongly about justice when we recognize that it is a very human mechanism for securing and protecting very important and general human interests, with its genetic origins in primitive impulses to retaliation and vengeance. On the other hand, these interests are so important that the principle of utility itself requires that we continue with this strongly motivated discourse of justice and rights. So utility recognizes justice and its major features, but, contrary to what Whewell argued and what many more recent commentators and moral theorists have maintained, rights established by justice are not absolute and certainly do not, as we have come to say, trump utility. They are not absolute and certainly are not grounded in the ontological structure of the universe, but they do constitute – as we would expect – a central and important part in utilitarian ethics. As Mill puts it in his concluding statement,

> Justice remains the appropriate name for certain social utilities which are vastly more important, and therefore more absolute and imperative, than any others as a class... and which, therefore, ought to be guarded by a sentiment not only different in degree, but also in kind; distinguished from the milder feeling which attaches to the mere idea of promoting human pleasure or convenience, at once by the more definite nature of its commands, and by the sterner character of its sanctions. (CW X, p. 259)

13 Conclusion

Mill aimed in the final chapter of his *Utilitarianism* to establish that the common criticism of the utilitarian system of ethics that this system is not to be on a secure foundation because it presupposes as more basic, as more strongly felt as a motive than, and as more central to our ordinary or customary morality, some Principle of Justice. We have tried to explain Mill's Principle as he intended it, and have attempted to show that many of the common criticisms of Mill's principle, and of the moral stances that he takes up on it as providing sound moral grounds, are unsound: they do not succeed. This is not to say that everything has been said that needs to be said about these matters: there are many criticisms that we have not addressed. But we have at least established that Mill is not the tissue of confusions he is portrayed to be in the learned papers and in the textbooks of many commentators. We have, in other words, at least established that both students and scholars deserve better than this usual fare.

Notes

1. For a general overview of Mill's philosophy, see Wilson (2007). For Mill's logic, see Wilson (2008) and Wilson (forthcoming). See also Fumerton (2009).
2. For general discussion of Mill's utilitarianism, see W. Donner (1998) and Donner (2009). But see the detailed discussion of this proof in Wilson (1982) and Wilson (1983).
3. Mill later in the essay explains how things originally not pleasures come to be part of pleasure or have pleasure 'inherent in them' (CW X, p. 210).
4. See Whewell (1837), Whewell (1845), and Whewell (1862).
5. For other aspects of the Mill–Whewell confrontation, see Wilson (2008).
6. Thus, Frankena (1973) and Audi (2004) make ethics a matter of intuiting moral principles; morality and justice are, for these philosophers, merely sets of propositions, inert with no intrinsic connection to action. They miss the fact that Mill grasps, that justice places demands on us which, in themselves, *are* strong motives to action. Whewell grasps the same point, though he differs from Mill in giving it a metaphysical basis as an active form, an entity that moves in the direction required of us by the form.

   Mill is often said to be an act utilitarian, applying the principle of utility to individual acts, and equally often said to be a rule utilitarian, applying the principle of utility first to determine a set of rules that are moral (Mill's 'secondary principles'), and only then determining whether an act is moral, not by seeing whether it conforms directly to the principle of utility, but by seeing whether is falls under one of the set of secondary moral rules. They both have their points, but both are wrong. They both read Mill as making moral judgment as essentially propositional in form, merely a matter of cognitive content. They miss the point that, as Mill convincingly argues, and as Whewell takes for granted, a moral judgment is essentially motivating, that is, conative in form. Those who characterize Mill instead as a 'motive utilitarian' are as near to the truth as such chapter-heading terms will allow.

   Crisp (2007) has criticized Audi's moral theory as being essentially cognitive and therefore not really a theory about morality as it really is, insofar as it misses the conative nature of moral judgment. There is good reason to adopt as our label for Mill's utilitarianism the term 'motive utilitarianism.' This welcome way of putting things can be found in Railton (1997).
7. See also Mill's essay on 'Nature' in CW X.

8. This is the problem that Ross (1930) faced when what he called *'prima facie* duties,' which we know to obtain by our moral intuition, come into conflict.
9. Again, see Ross (1930). Audi (2004) follows him in the suggestion that one is dealing with actions as organic wholes; that the conflicting *prima facie* rules apply to parts of a whole, but that the whole is organic and not the mere sum of its parts; and that the whole has an intrinsic value that is unique and knowable by our moral intuition (cf. Audi 2004, pp. 136ff). There is no reason, however, why there cannot be conflicting intuitions about whether one ought to have this organic whole or instead that other one: intuition provides no criterion. The further suggestion that we can settle differences by resorting to the technique of finding a 'reflective equilibrium' (Audi 2004, pp. 74ff), that is, that we reflect on the differing intuitions until we reach an equilibrium, is spurious; it is a mere expression of a *pious hope*, but no guarantee, that reflecting on the conflicting intuitions will – eventually – lead to one's having a single, and therefore nonconflicting, intuition. In any case, there is still the problem of figuring out why some 'intuitive' or 'self-evident' principle *ought* to be accepted – why the intuition or feeling of self-evidence should be taken to be anything more than an expression of one's feelings – strongly held feelings, no doubt, but, as Bentham and Mill argued, that does not constitute a justification. One might attempt an ontological justification after the fashion of Plato and Whewell, but Bentham and the Mills, cogently, argue that such a metaphysics is an illusion. Intuitions and intuitions of forms are basically nothing more than conservative ideology, expressions of one's preference for the *status quo*. (Whewell never has an intuition that women, as a matter of right, should have the vote; no one has ever felt that it is *prima facie* obligatory to support the right to strike, let alone a *prima facie* right to support a workers' revolution.)

References

Audi, Robert (2004) *The Good in the Right: A Theory of Intuition and Intrinsic Value* (Princeton, NJ: Princeton University Press).

Bentham, Jeremy ([1789] 1970) *An Introduction to the Principles of Morals and Legislation*, J. Burns and H.L.A. Hart (eds) (London: Athlone Press).

Crisp, Roger (2007) 'Intuitionism and Disagreement,' in *Rationality and the Good: Critical Essays on the Ethics and Epistemology of Robert Audi*, M. Timmons, J. Greco, and A.R. Mele (eds) (Oxford: Oxford University Press).

Donner, W. (1998) 'Mill's Utilitarianism,' in *The Cambridge Companion to John Stuart Mill*, John Skorupski (ed.) (Cambridge: Cambridge University Press).

Donner, W. (2009) 'Mill's Moral and Political Philosophy,' *Mill*, W. Donner and R. Fumerton (Oxford: Blackwell).

Frankena, William (1973) *Ethics*, 2nd edn (Englewood, Cliffs, NJ: Prentice-Hall).

Fumerton, R. (2009) 'Mill's Logic, Metaphysics, and Epistemology,' *Mill*, W. Donner and R. Fumerton (Oxford: Blackwell).

Railton, Peter (1997) 'How Thinking about Character and Utilitarianism Might Lead to Rethinking the Character of Utilitarianism,' in *Mill's Utilitarianism: Critical Essays*, David Lyons (ed.) (Lanham, Maryland: Rowan and Littlefield).

Robson, J.M. (ed.) (1969) *The Collected Works of John Stuart Mill: Essays on Ethics, Religion, and Society*, Vol. X (Toronto: University of Toronto Press).

Robson, J.M. (ed.) (1972) *The Collected Works of John Stuart Mill: The Later Letters*, Vol. XIV (Toronto: University of Toronto Press).

Ross, W.D. (1930) *The Right and the Good* (Oxford: Oxford University Press).

Whewell, William (1837) 'Preface,' in *Dissertation on the Progress of Ethical Philosophy during the Seventeenth and Eighteenth Centuries*, 2nd edn, James Mackintosh (Edinburgh: Adam and Charles Black).

Whewell, William (1845) *The Elements of Morality and Polity* (New York: Harper and Brothers).

Whewell, William (1862) *Lectures on the History of Moral Philosophy*, 2nd edn (Cambridge: Deighton, Bell & Co.).

Wilson, F. (1982) 'Mill's Proof that Happiness Is the Criterion of Morality,' *Journal of Business Ethics* 1, 59–72.

Wilson, F. (1983) 'Mill's "Proof" of Utility and the Composition of Causes,' *Journal of Business Ethics* 2, 135–58.

Wilson, F. (2007) 'John Stuart Mill,' *The Stanford Encyclopedia of Philosophy*, G.N. Zalta (ed.) http://plato.stanford.edu/entries/mill/, date first published Thursday January 3, 2002, substantive revision Tuesday July 10, 2007.

Wilson, F. (2008) 'The Logic of John Stuart Mill,' *Handbook of the History of Logic. Volume 4: British Logic in the Nineteenth Century*, Dov Gabbay and John Woods (eds) (Amsterdam: Elsevier North Holland).

Wilson, F. (forthcoming) 'Mill: Logic and Metaphysics,' *Routledge Companion to Nineteenth Century Philosophy*, Dean Moyar (ed.) (London: Routledge).

Part II

Mill and Others on Justice

5
Mill and Rawls

Henry R. West

No collection of writings on Mill and justice would be complete without a comparison of Mill's account of justice with that of John Rawls. Rawls's *A Theory of Justice* attracted more attention than any writing on justice in the twentieth century. It bred a substantial volume of secondary literature – interpretation, criticism, and efforts to apply the theory in other areas. Rawls himself, in later writings, expanded – or contracted, some commentators would say – it to more general questions of political philosophy and to justice among nations. In this chapter I will focus on the original statement of his position in *A Theory of Justice*. The basic model on which the theory is constructed seems very simple, but the limitations of its scope and the supporting arguments for it are very complex. In the first place, Rawls is presenting an ideal theory for a well-ordered society, with strict compliance. He thinks that this helps to provide principles to criticize the injustice in our own society. But he goes on to provide argument for institutional arrangements in nonideal societies in light of the ideal. Secondly, the scenario by which he argues for his principles of justice is subject to controversial assumptions.

In *A Theory of Justice*, John Rawls says that his aim is to work out a theory of justice that represents an alternative to utilitarian thought generally (1971, p. 22). Rawls not only presents an alternative theory; he has criticisms of utilitarianism. In this chapter, I want to discuss the similarities and differences between Rawls's theory and Mill's. I want to argue that Mill's theory of justice is very close to that of Rawls and that some of Rawls's criticisms do not apply to Mill's version of utilitarianism. Which theory is the better of the two will be up to the reader's judgment.

The alternative to a utilitarian theory of justice that Rawls presents consists of two principles, with priority given to the first:

> First: Each person is to have an equal right to the most extensive basic liberty compatible with a similar liberty for others.
>
> Second: Social and economic inequalities are to be arranged so that they are both (a) reasonably expected to be to everyone's advantage, and (b) attached to positions and offices open to all. (1971, p. 60)

Later in the work, Rawls restates the second principle with important revisions. He says that inequalities are to be '(a) to the greatest benefit of the least advantaged and (b) attached to offices and positions open to all under conditions of fair equality of opportunity' (1971, p. 83). These are major revisions, as will be seen in the discussion of the second principle.

The basic liberties that Rawls is referring to here are equal liberties of citizenship, 'political liberty (the right to vote and to be eligible for public office) together with freedom of speech and assembly; liberty of conscience and freedom of thought; freedom of the person ... the right to hold (personal) property; and freedom from arbitrary arrest and seizure as defined by the concept of the rule of law' (1971, p. 61). Mill strongly believed in all of these liberties, argued for some of them in *On Liberty* and *The Subjection of Women*, and worked for them as a political activist.

Rawls claims that these two principles, although in many cases they would result in the same substantive judgments regarding justice and injustice as utilitarianism, would not make such judgments subject to the contingencies of circumstances and calculations. Rawls does not give his detailed argument for the priority of the first principle until Section 82, 'The Grounds for the Priority of Liberty,' but in Section 39, 'Priority of Liberty Defined,' Rawls discusses cases in which the priority of liberty may be limited. Here he splits the theory of justice into two parts. The first or ideal part assumes strict compliance and works out the principles that characterize a well-ordered society under favorable circumstances. Nonideal theory, the second part, is worked out after an ideal conception of justice has been chosen. Under ideal circumstances the two principles that Rawls proposes have a 'lexical' ordering – the second principle is to be applied only after the first principle has been fulfilled. But he gives two kinds of circumstances that justify or excuse a restriction of liberty. First, a restriction can derive from the natural limitations and accidents of human life, or from historical and social contingencies. Even in a well-ordered society, the existence of effective penal machinery serves as men's security against one another, and there need to be limitations upon the freedom of children, the mentally ill, and so on. The second kind of case is one occurring in nonideal theory – injustice already exists. Examples are how to deal with the intolerant and with the violence of rival sects. Curbing the liberties of the intolerant and restraining the violence of rival sects may be justified. He also says that in many historical situations a lesser political liberty may have been justified. Here one may recall Mill's concern that extending the franchise to the working class before there is universal education is a problem, which he thought of attempting to solve by giving multiple votes to those with more education. These remarks by Rawls show that he shares with Mill concern about the consequences of liberty. Rawls's discussion of paternalism in this section is also in line with Mill's discussion in *On Liberty*.

In Section 82 Rawls presents 'The Grounds for the Priority of Liberty.' Although Rawls thinks that his two principles have superiority over the principle of utility because they do not depend upon the principle of diminishing marginal utility, his argument in the original edition is basically diminishing marginal utility. Here it is:

> Now the basis for the priority of liberty is roughly as follows: as the conditions of civilization improve, the marginal significance for our good of further economic and social advantages diminishes relative to the interests of liberty, which become stronger as the conditions for the exercise of the equal freedoms are more fully realized. Beyond some point it becomes and then remains irrational from the standpoint of the original position to acknowledge a lesser liberty for the sake of greater material means and amenities of office. (1971, p. 542)

As the general level of well-being rises, only the less urgent wants remain to be satisfied by further advances. At the same time, 'a growing insistence upon the right to pursue our spiritual and cultural interests asserts itself... Until the basic wants of individuals can be fulfilled, the relative urgency of their interest in liberty cannot be firmly decided in advance... But under favorable circumstances the fundamental interest in determining our plan of life eventually assumes a prior place' (Rawls, 1971, p. 543). In the revised edition (Rawls, 1999), this explicit reference to diminishing marginal utility is replaced by references to a hierarchy of interests, changing under different circumstances, and under favorable circumstances liberty becoming a higher-order interest, becoming regulative from then on. In a footnote he says that the view he expresses in the text is essentially Mill's. I think that we may conclude that Rawls and Mill do not differ over the priority of liberty. It can be derived as a principle subordinate to the principle of utility as well as an outcome from a hypothetical social contract.

Rawls also makes empirical generalizations about the basis for self-esteem. 'The basis of self-esteem in a just society is not then one's income share but the publicly affirmed distribution of fundamental rights and liberties' (1971, p. 544). Again, this is an empirical claim that a utilitarian would take into account in arguing for fundamental rights and liberties. Self-esteem is certainly an important, perhaps essential, ingredient in happiness.

There are differences with regard to the social conditions in which Mill is discussing a theory of justice and those in which Rawls is comparing utilitarianism and his theory. Rawls assumes a well-ordered society. A well-ordered society is one designed to advance the good of its members and effectively regulated by a public conception of justice. It is a society 'in which [1] everyone accepts and knows that the others accept the same principles of justice, and [2] the basic social institutions generally satisfy and are generally known to satisfy these principles. In this case while men may put forth excessive demands on one another, they nevertheless acknowledge a common point of view from which their claims may be adjudicated... Among individuals with disparate aims and purposes a shared conception of justice establishes the bonds of civic friendship; the general desire for justice limits the pursuit of other ends' (Rawls, 1971, p. 5). He recognizes that no existing societies are well-ordered in this sense. So Rawls is presenting an ideal case. He is giving us an ideal system of justice, an ideal against which we may measure and critique our own society. Mill includes in his analysis of justice a theory that would apply to penal justice as well as to distributive justice, and he does not limit his analysis to a well-ordered society. Mill recognizes that there are differing conceptions of justice in his own society, and he is arguing that utility provides a way of adjudicating these differences. Another difference between the theories of Rawls and Mill is the scope of the theories. Rawls is considering only the justice of the 'basic structure' of society – the basic rights and duties of citizens. Mill's theory is more general. He analyzes the concept of justice in general, and then he argues that the most essential elements in that concept are rights and duties based on the principle of utility.

In what follows, I am primarily concerned with contrasting Rawls and Mill with regard to the limited scope of Rawls's theory. But, just as Rawls makes some comments on such issues as taxation in a society that is not well ordered, I shall extend the contrast between Rawls and Mill to include those comments.

As mentioned, Rawls has a way of arguing for principles of justice based on a hypothetical 'social contract.' The basic idea is that principles of justice are to be chosen as a hypothetical social contract between free, rational, and equal individuals under conditions of fairness, such that the conditions are not to give any advantage to those who have undeserved superiority due to status based on inherited wealth or talent or social privilege. To achieve these conditions, Rawls imagines that principles of justice are chosen from an 'original position' behind what he calls a 'veil of ignorance.' He claims that the conditions embodied in the description of the original position are ones that we are ready to accept upon due consideration to regard as reasonable. Rawls here appeals to intuition as to whether they are reasonable.

In choosing the principles of justice, the choosers are not to know their place in society – class position or social status – or fortune in the distribution of natural assets and abilities – intelligence, strength, or the like. Nor are they to know their 'conception of the good' – what they value in life – or their psychological propensities – such as whether they are risk takers or risk averse. Thus they are unable to choose principles that would give themselves any advantages over others.

Rawls recognizes that no one is able to be ignorant of these personal features. His point is that they are irrelevant with regard to appropriate arguments for what is just; so he provides this imaginative scenario to call attention to what would be fair or unfair in a conception of justice.

Because the people in the original position are not to know their own individual desires, Rawls, for motivation in choosing, postulates that they are self-interested, with a desire to maximize what he calls 'primary goods,' goods that one would want whatever else one might want. His list of these primary goods varies from one place to another in the text of *A Theory of Justice*, but it usually includes wealth and income, powers and opportunities, rights and liberties, and the bases of self-respect. Rawls also postulates that the people are mutually disinterested, not motivated by envy or altruism, not motivated by the desire that others have more or less than themselves. Rawls admits that this motivational structure is not that of real persons in real life, but he thinks that it provides a model of a fair procedure for constructing principles of justice that would be impartial. Everyone is alike and not able to give any special privilege to themselves or anyone else. He contrasts this with motivation to accept the principle of utility as the principle of justice. Utilitarianism, he says, requires that people's motivation be universal benevolence, or it requires that people – using the original situation as a procedure – base their life expectations on having an equal chance of being anyone in a society. The claim that people should not regard themselves as having an equal chance of being anyone in the society seems an arbitrary restriction to prevent the choice from being a utilitarian one. If one does not know one's place in society, why not choose that with the highest expected utility? Rawls claims that the choosers do not know whether or not they are risk averse, but he assumes that they are. They are not willing to risk the worst outcome. He also assumes that they are not envious. But they must know that real people are envious or benevolent, and it is not intuitively obvious that these emotions should play no role in their decisions.

The people in the original position are to have up-to-date information concerning psychological, social, economic, and political sciences. They are to know the general consequences of their choices of principles of justice, but they are not to know how they themselves would be affected. They are not to know anything about their own individual characteristics – their individual status or membership in any groups that might give them special advantages. What Rawls is trying to do is to give an argument that the reader might accept. Suppose you didn't know your place in society – whether you were wealthy or poor, religious or secular, belonging to an oppressed minority or the majority, male or female, interested in political activism or not, conservative or progressive, biologically disabled or physically superior, intellectually talented or not, energetic or not, descended from an advantaged family or not, wanting to speak out or publish or not, wanting to participate in the political process or not, and on and on – Rawls wants you to discount any of those differences, and to ask you what principles of justice you would endorse if you did not know all of those things. This is what Rawls calls 'justice as fairness.' It is what justice would be from an impartial point of view. Mill says that utilitarianism requires that agents be impartial. 'As between his own happiness and that of others, utilitarianism requires him to be as strictly impartial as a disinterested and benevolent spectator' (CW X p. 218). But this is Mill on what the *theory* of utilitarianism requires as a first principle. He does not, as Rawls does not, expect individuals not to be self-centered. Thus there is a great similarity between the two positions on procedural grounds.

Rawls says that under these conditions it is possible that the principle of utility would be chosen as the principle of justice. Why wouldn't one want the best probability of the greatest happiness? His opposition to this is that the principle of utility would allow it as just if the lesser life prospects for some were required simply for the sake of a greater sum of advantages enjoyed by others. 'In the absence of strong and lasting benevolent impulses, a rational man would not accept a basic structure merely because it maximized the algebraic sum of advantages irrespective of its permanent effects on his own rights and interests' (1971, p. 14). But one does not know, behind the veil of ignorance, that it would have permanent effects on *his* (or her) rights and interests. The *expected* utility of the utilitarian structure for the hypothetical individual would be increased. Rawls says that the people in the original position do not know if they are risk averse, but he seems to build in that they are. The strategy that Rawls argues for is called a 'maximin' strategy – raising the expectations of the worst off, rather than the expectations of the average. It is a strategy highly criticized in the secondary literature on Rawls's book, and he downplayed it in the revised edition. I shall argue that, to the extent that it can be defended, it requires utilitarian arguments.

In the section on 'Classical Utilitarianism' (1971, pp. 22–7), Rawls says that the 'strict classical doctrine' receives perhaps its clearest and most accessible formulation in Henry Sidgwick, but in a footnote he includes J.S. Mill, represented by *Utilitarianism*, as among those who hold a utilitarian view. Rawls states the classical view as follows: 'The main idea is that society is rightly ordered, and therefore just, when its major institutions are arranged so as to achieve the greatest net balance of satisfaction summed over all the individuals belonging to it' (1971, p. 22).

This is a fair statement of the goal of a utilitarian theory of justice, but Rawls uses a model of its implementation that is unfair to utilitarianism, or at least to the utilitarianism of J.S. Mill. Rawls says that, just as the well-being of a person is constructed from a series of satisfactions which are experienced at different moments in time and which constitute the life of the individual, so the utilitarian theory is that the well-being of society is to be constructed from the fulfillment of the systems of desires of the many individuals who belong to it. 'Just as an individual balances present and future gains against present and future losses, so a society may balance satisfactions and dissatisfactions between different individuals' (1971, p. 24). The utilitarian, Rawls says, adopts for society as a whole the principle of rational choice for one man. The nature of the decision made by the ideal legislator is essentially a question of efficient administration, conflating all persons into one. 'Utilitarianism does not take seriously the distinction between persons' (1971, p. 27). I shall later challenge this as a claim against John Stuart Mill. Rawls, however, in the original position, has conflated all persons into one. He calls it a 'contract' theory, but it is really a choice theory. The so-called individuals in the original position, because they do not know anything about themselves, are really one person. In the original position, Rawls does not take seriously the distinction between persons.

In succeeding pages Rawls draws other contrasts between his theory and utilitarianism. His theory gives a priority, if not absolute weight, to the claims of liberty and right against the desirability of increasing aggregate social welfare. I have pointed out that the priority of liberty depends on the Principle of Diminishing Marginal Utility, and I shall argue that his arguments for the importance of rights to protect the security of individuals are also utilitarian. Another contrast is that in utilitarianism the satisfaction of any desire has some value in itself; it does not matter, except indirectly, what the desires are for. In Rawls's theory of justice, the principles of right, and so of justice, put limits on what satisfactions have value: interests requiring the violation of justice have no value. 'Having no merit in the first place, they cannot override its claims' (1971, p. 31). Rawls says that, because his theory of justice imposes certain criteria on the design of the basic structure of society, it follows that initial bounds are placed upon what kinds of persons men and women should be. Utilitarianism, on the other hand, he says, relies upon the natural facts and contingencies of human life in determining what forms of moral character are to be encouraged in a just society (Rawls, 1971, p. 32). Rawls concludes his section on utilitarianism by saying that his theory thinks of a well-ordered society as a scheme of cooperation for reciprocal advantage regulated by principles that persons would choose in an initial situation that is fair; utilitarianism thinks of a well-ordered society as the efficient administration of social resources to maximize the satisfaction of the many individual systems of desires accepted as given (1971, p. 33). But this characterization of utilitarianism is unfair to Mill's version of utilitarianism. For Mill, desires are not accepted as given. Mill's conception of utility is of happiness and unhappiness, not satisfaction of given desires. The satisfaction of given desires may not result in the greatest happiness. The point of education and of legislation is largely to modify desires so that people get pleasure from socially beneficial activities. Furthermore, for Mill, there are qualitatively higher and lower pleasures. Only those who have developed their intellects, their aesthetic appreciation, and their moral sentiments can attain the greatest happiness. Only those who have developed an interest in one another, resulting in benevolent social feelings, and their sense of duty to do what is right (and refrain from doing what is wrong) can know the higher pleasures of the moral sentiments. Furthermore, Mill is very much concerned with what sort of persons men and women should be. It is contrary to greatest happiness for people to be selfish and insensitive to the needs of others. Mill does not depend upon the 'natural facts and contingencies of human life' in determining what sorts of moral character are to be encouraged in a just society. To think otherwise is to ignore Mill's insistence that the greatest happiness principle is to determine all of what he calls the 'Art of Life,' which includes character development. The virtues have a prominent place in Mill's philosophy, based upon what character traits will produce the greatest happiness and the least unhappiness.

It is true that on the utilitarian scheme pleasure based on antisocial attitudes and motives is regarded as intrinsically good. But it does not follow that it is to be encouraged. Rawls attempts to ignore envy by ruling it out of court in the determination of the principles of justice. Mill would recognize it as a psychologically realistic phenomenon and attempt to eliminate it by realistic social policies that make people feel at one with one another. Thus Mill espoused cooperative economic structures in which workers would feel association rather than competition with one another and cooperative ownership structures in which there would not be the invidious resentment of employers' exploitation of workers. Rawls says that 'the acceptance of the two principles constitutes an understanding to discard as irrelevant as a matter of social justice much of the information and many of the complications of everyday life' (1971, p. 88). Is this to the advantage of the two principles, or to the advantage of the utilitarian principle?

In Section 29, Rawls gives the main grounds for the two principles of justice. One of these is what he calls the strains of commitment. 'Not only do the parties protect their basic rights but they insure themselves against the worst eventualities' (1971, p. 174). Should a person gamble with his liberties and substantive interests, hoping that the application of the principle of utility might secure him a greater well-being, he may have difficulty abiding by his undertaking. This argument can be turned around and applied against Rawls's 'maximin' strategy. Should a person accept the two principles, he may find that he has natural talents and advantages that cannot be used except insofar as they benefit the least advantaged. Because such persons have more power in actual life, if they are selfish they will find that the maximin principle has strains that they cannot accept. If there is any good argument for the maximin strategy, it would appear to be a utilitarian one: the worst eventualities are so severe that no probability of greater well-being from unequal distribution of rights and liberties and satisfaction of substantive interests can outweigh the losses from the worst eventualities. In that case a utilitarian would argue that it is unjust on utilitarian grounds for those who are worst off to be made still worse off for the benefit of the more prosperous.

The other ground that Rawls discusses in this section is publicity. A conception of justice is stable when the public recognition of its realization by the social system tends to bring about the corresponding sense of justice. When the two principles are satisfied, each person's liberties are secured and everyone is benefited by social cooperation. When the principle of utility is satisfied, he claims, there is no such assurance that everyone benefits. The social system may demand that some should forgo advantages for the sake of the greater good of the whole. In this comparison, Rawls fails to admit that his principles require that those who would benefit from greater inequality that is not for the benefit of everyone are forced to forgo these advantages. Rawls's principles, to the extent that they differ from the utilitarian principle, require even greater sacrifices of those who would *benefit* from inequality. Under his principles, everyone benefits by social cooperation compared with non-cooperation, but not obviously when compared with alternative forms of cooperation. This will become apparent as we examine how radical his second principle is.

First, let us consider Rawls's analysis of fair equality of opportunity. Rawls recognizes that liberal theory, including that of utilitarianism, seeks to achieve equality of opportunity. Those with similar abilities and skills and the same willingness to use them should have similar life chances, regardless of their initial place in the social system, that is, irrespective of the income class into which they are born. This requires preventing excessive accumulations of property and wealth and of maintaining equal opportunities of education for all. 'Chances to acquire cultural knowledge and skills should not depend upon one's class position, and so the school system, whether public or private, should be designed to even out class barriers' (1971, p. 73). To the extent that there are differences in wealth and income, they must not provide a way in which those with greater wealth and income can provide better education for their children than those who are in the class with the least wealth and income. The children of Bill Gates, if there is a Bill

Gates in the society, cannot buy better education than that provided for the poorest citizen, whether in public school or funded by vouchers for private schools. The worst schools must be as good as the best. This is a Utopian proposal, but it is one that utilitarians also strive for. John Stuart Mill wanted parents to be coerced into providing education for their children, by vouchers if they could not afford it, and his ideal would, no doubt, have been that the schools of poor children be as good as those of the wealthy, even if unrealistic in his time. Mill lived in a time when there were hardly any public schools. He was advocating a practical objective – that all children have enough education to be able to read and write and do the calculations for home economy. If he were living today, he would no doubt have higher ideals.

Rawls recognizes that so far his analysis of fair equality of opportunity is radical in eliminating the influence of social contingencies, but he thinks that it does not go far enough. It still permits the distribution of wealth and income to be determined by the natural distribution of abilities and talents, by the outcome of the 'natural lottery,' and this outcome is arbitrary from a moral perspective. Furthermore, the principle of fair opportunity can be only imperfectly carried out, at least as long as some form of the family exists. 'The extent to which natural capacities develop and reach fruition is affected by all kinds of social conditions and class attitudes. Even the willingness to make an effort, to try, and so to be deserving in the ordinary sense is itself dependent upon happy family and social circumstances' (Rawls, 1971, p. 74). Here, I think, we can see a contrast between Mill and Rawls. Rawls has more egalitarian ideals than Mill. Rawls has a baseline of absolute equality. The two principles 'are a special case of a more general conception of justice that can be expressed as follows. All social values – liberty and opportunity, income and wealth, and the bases of self-respect – are to be distributed equally unless an unequal distribution of any, or of all, of these values is to everyone's advantage. Injustice, then, is simply inequalities that are not to the benefit of all' (Rawls, 1971, p. 62).

Mill, in the first place, has a more limited conception of justice. Justice is the name for certain classes of moral rules, which concern the essentials of human well-being more nearly, and are therefore of more absolute obligation, than any other rules for the guidance of life:

> The moral rules which forbid mankind to hurt one another (in which we must never forget to include wrongful interference with each other's freedom) are more vital to human well-being than any maxims, however important, which only point to the managing of

> some department of human affairs... It is their observance which alone preserves peace among human beings: ... a person may possibly not need the benefits of others; but he always needs that they should not do him hurt. (CW X, pp. 255–6)

Justice is limited to rights, and it is not clear that Mill would regard any inequality that is not to the benefit of all as an injustice. Mill's example of the justice of wages is an example. Is it just or not that talent and skill should give title to superior remuneration? One side argues against it on the ground that all who do the best they can deserve equally well. The other side argues that society receives more from the more efficient laborers. Mill says that any choice between them, on grounds of justice, is perfectly arbitrary. 'Social utility alone can decide the preference' (CW X, p. 254). Mill is not saying that equality trumps inequality in the absence of inequality being to the advantage of everyone. He is saying that there is a utilitarian argument for equal wages for equal effort and a utilitarian argument for rewarding efficiency of labor due to talent and skill. Another example is justice of taxation. One opinion is that justice demands that those with most ability to pay should pay more, perhaps at a graduated rate. Another opinion is to disregard means and take the same sum from each person on the grounds that each receives equal benefit. It could be argued that each does not receive equal benefit, but between the two claims of justice in taxation, whether it should be proportional to benefit or proportional to ability to pay, Mill says 'there is no other extrication than the utilitarian' (CW X, p. 255).

It is interesting to see what Rawls says about taxation. He distinguishes two functions of taxation. One is to prevent inequalities in wealth beyond a certain limit through taxes on inheritance and gifts and to set limits on the rights of bequests in order to maintain fair equality of opportunity and to prevent the role of wealth from corrupting the political process. The other is to raise revenue to provide for public goods and to make transfer payments necessary for inequalities to be for the well-being of the worst off. He thinks that in a well-ordered society a proportional expenditure tax is better than a tax on income. But it does not follow that, given the injustice of existing institutions, even steeply progressive income taxes are not unjustified. He says that no mention has been made at any point of the traditional criteria of taxation, such as that taxes are to be levied according to benefits received or the ability to pay. He insists that inheritance and progressive income taxes are not predicated on the idea that individuals have similar utility functions satisfying the diminishing marginal principle. 'This problem is one for the utilitarian, not for contract theory' (1971, p. 280).

Mill distinguishes duties of justice from other moral duties. Mill thinks that the idea of a penal sanction is the generating idea of the notion of justice, but it does not distinguish justice from moral obligation in general. 'Justice implies something which it is not only right to do, and wrong not to do, but which some individual can claim from us as his moral right. No one has a moral right to our generosity or beneficence, because we are not bound to practice those virtues towards any given individual' (CW X, p. 247). Mill says that this corresponds to the distinction between perfect and imperfect duties, but this correlation won't stand up. Perfect duties are those that can be completely fulfilled, as are the negative duties such as not to kill, not to enslave, not to lie. But there are positive duties involving rights that cannot be completely fulfilled. A child may have a right to a parent's care, but there may be no limit to what that care entails. Is that a perfect obligation that can be completely fulfilled? Child neglect would be a case of injustice, but a parent's obligation to care for a child is open-ended. There are also what are called 'welfare' rights: a right to a decent job, to decent housing, to healthcare and so on. In these cases, there are assignable people who are claimed to have the rights, but it is not clear what assignable people have the correlative duties to provide the services to meet the needs. Welfare rights could be accommodated by saying that *society* has the obligation. Perhaps Mill has focused on unjust *acts*, without giving adequate attention to unjust *states of affairs*. There are unjust laws and traditions, unjust political systems, unjust economic systems, unjust status systems and so on that do not point to agents who deserve punishment, unless one points to those in power who could but do not change the system – and they perhaps deserve to be replaced with responsible agents rather than punished. In this respect, the approach that Rawls takes to the basic structure of society is superior to Mill's. Rawls's two principles make abstract statements about the justice or injustice of the rights and obligations that constitute justice and injustice without the detailed assignment of responsibility to individuals for the justice or injustice. Details are to be worked out after the 'veil of ignorance' is lifted and national and local constitutions are drawn up, branches of government are assigned duties, and officials are appointed to carry out these duties. The two principles are only to govern background conditions for the justice or injustice of these institutions. But utilitarianism can address the basic structure of society, even if Mill's conceptual analysis in *Utilitarianism* is too focused on individual acts. In other writings and his political activities Mill does address the justice and injustices of alternative systems of property, inequalities in education and living conditions, and so on.

In the *Autobiography*, Mill says that it is injustice 'that some are born to riches and the vast majority born to poverty' (CW I, p. 239). He says that his and Harriet Taylor's ideal of ultimate improvement went far beyond democracy and would class them under the general designation of Socialists: 'We looked forward to a time when society will no longer be divided into the idle and the industrious ... when the division of the produce of labor, instead of depending, as in so great a degree it now does, on the accident of birth, will be made by concert, on an acknowledged principle of justice; and when it will no longer either be, or thought to be, impossible for human beings to exert themselves strenuously in procuring benefits which are not to be exclusively their own but to be shared with the society they belong to. The social problem of the future we considered to be, how to unite the greatest liberty of action, with a common ownership of the raw material of the globe, and an equal participation of all in the benefits of combined labor' (CW I, p. 239). Mill advocated nationalization of all land. In *Principles of Political Economy*, he said, 'The essential principle of property being to assure to all persons what they have produced by their labor and accumulated by their abstinence, this principle cannot apply to what is not the produce of labor, the raw material of the earth. If the land derived its productive power wholly from nature, and not at all from industry, or if there were any means of discriminating what is derived from each source, it not only would not be necessary, but it would be the height of injustice, to let the gift of nature be engrossed by individuals ... the State might be the universal landlord, and the cultivators tenants under it, either on lease or at will' (CW II, p. 227). 'When private property in land is not expedient, it is unjust' (CW II, p. 230).

Mill reflects Rawls's description of a sense of justice in a well-ordered society in *Chapters on Socialism*. There he says that, in the economy of society, 'if there be any who suffer physical or moral degradation, whose bodily necessities are either not satisfied or satisfied in a manner, which only brutish creatures can be content with, this ... [is] a failure of the social arrangements ... If the minds and feelings of the prosperous were in a right state, would they accept their prosperity if for the sake of it even one person near to them was, for any other cause than voluntary fault, excluded from a desirable existence?' (CW

V, p. 713). He, more than Rawls, justifies inequality on grounds of lack of exertion and improvidence. But he is critical of present society as not rewarding exertion and abstinence. Because enjoyable existence derives, he says, from labor and abstinence, society might be relieved of responsibility if 'every one who was willing to undergo a fair share of this labor and abstinence could attain a fair share of the fruit' (CW V, p. 714). But, instead of being proportional to labor and abstinence, it is the reverse. Those who receive the least are those who labor and abstain the most: 'the very idea of distributive justice, or of any proportionality between success and merit, or between success and exertion, is in the present state of society... chimerical' (CW V, p. 714). And it is not only that the individual should get what he or she deserves. He agrees with Rawls: 'In a well-constituted community every one would be a gainer by every other person's successful exertions...' (CW V, pp. 715–16).

In summary, the substantive principles of justice are very similar according to the theories of Rawls and of Mill. Both give priority to liberty under normal circumstances, and both allow flexibility under unusual circumstances. Rawls has a lexical ordering giving priority to liberty in a well-ordered society with strict adherence, but not in partial compliance conditions with intolerance and threat of violence. Mill gives the example in Chapter V of *Utilitarianism* of the necessity of overriding the liberty of a physician in order to save a life. Both are concerned with equality of opportunity, especially concerning the need to avoid advantage of inheritance. Both are concerned with promoting the welfare of the least advantaged class in society. Rawls attempts to avoid the calculations and contingencies in having the principle of utility the foundation for these priorities. But an examination of the arguments for Rawls's two principles indicates that they are founded on utilitarian considerations. The people in his initial condition would accept the priority of liberty only because they believe in the diminishing marginal utility of other values. They would accept the principle that inequalities are just only if they benefit the worst off only because they believe that the disutility of the worst off outweighs any advantages of the prosperous. And Mill does not assume that people in real life are completely benevolent. His analysis of justice as a system of rights to protect the self-interest of people in situations of conflict does not fail to take seriously the difference between individuals. There may be a difference between the intuitions of Rawls and Mill regarding the justice of rewarding exertion and abstinence, with Mill placing greater weight on these as useful than Rawls would allow with his theory. But, in general, there is a convergence between Rawls's system of justice and that of Mill.

References

Rawls, John (1971) *A Theory of Justice* (Cambridge, MA: Harvard Belknap).

Rawls, John (1999) *A Theory of Justice*, Revised Edition (Cambridge, MA: Harvard Belknap).

Robson, J.M. (ed.) (1965) *The Collected Works of John Stuart Mill: Principles of Political Economy Part 1*, Vol. II (Toronto: University of Toronto Press).

Robson, J.M. (ed.) (1967) *The Collected Works of John Stuart Mill: Essays on Economics and Society Part 2*, Vol. V (Toronto: University of Toronto Press).

Robson, J.M. (ed.) (1969) *The Collected Works of John Stuart Mill: Essays on Ethics, Religion, and Society*, Vol. X (Toronto: University of Toronto Press).

Robson, J.M. (ed.) (1977) *The Collected Works of John Stuart Mill: Essays on Politics and Society Part 1*, Vol. XVIII (Toronto: University of Toronto Press).

Robson, J.M. and Stillinger, Jack (eds) (1981) *The Collected Works of John Stuart Mill: Autobiography and Literary Essays*, Vol. I (Toronto: University of Toronto Press).

6
Mill's Justice and Political Liberalism

D. G. Brown

In recent work Martha Nussbaum takes on central issues about the limits of just coercion by law, and about the stability of a liberal state in the face of cultural pluralism. In her very valuable book *Hiding from Humanity: Disgust, Shame, and the Law,* she says that she comes to many of the same practical conclusions as Mill, in rough agreement with his Harm Principle, but argues that Mill's position is defective in rationale; she hopes to provide a better account, along with a diagnosis of some of the dangers to liberal societies, in a way which provides better support for her version of political liberalism (2004, pp. 16–17). In 'Millean Liberty and Sexual Orientation' she explores further the merits of the Harm Principle, and its vicissitudes in American jurisprudence, and in 'Radical Evil in the Lockean State: The Neglect of the Political Emotions' she gives a deeper account of the underlying threat; in the course of considering remedies she revisits Mill's response. Along the way she refers to relevant passages in other works of hers.[1]

In this chapter, Section I considers her interpretation of Mill, which, despite her acute attentions to his text, seems to me to need significant revision. Section II tries to summarize and assess the respects in which Nussbaum finds that Mill provides a deficient rationale for his conceptions of liberty and coercion. Section III compares Nussbaum's and Mill's resources for meeting the many threats to liberalism. Section IV argues that Mill's account of justice is the key to his conception of the relation between morality and liberty, and that Millean liberalism offers a more respectful, more realistic, and more coherent response to cultural pluralism than does political liberalism. Mill preserves the sound core of the Enlightenment in a way which makes political liberalism seem a failure of nerve.

1 Interpretation of Mill's text

It would not matter if minor differences appeared in the responses of Nussbaum and Mill to such issues as private sexual practices, gang loitering, possession of drugs, minority rights, prostitution, or the regulation of pornography. One merit of the Harm Principle is that its application requires the ongoing empirical study of current circumstances. It does matter, I think, that Nussbaum finds in Mill a significant limitation on the range of harms intended.

> Mill believed that the harm, to fall under his principle, had to be both imminent and very likely, and that it had to be harm with regard to certain antecedently demarcated areas of fundamental 'constituted rights'. (2004, p. 65)

A note attached to this claim refers us to her (2002), where we find:

> What should our ethical and legal approach be to questions of sexual orientation? I believe, and have argued repeatedly, [5] that it ought to be that of John Stuart Mill: conduct that does not harm other people, in the very specific sense of violating their 'constituted rights', is never a fit object of legal interference, or even of the coercive sort of moral sanction. It is, instead, an appropriate object of reasoned persuasion. Mill's 'harm principle' has been the subject of much dispute, and if one thinks that the category of harm is totally unspecified in his text it would not be a terribly helpful category. However, I believe that it is adequately specified: Mill defines the relevant class of harms as those that violate 'constituted rights', that special class of human interests he identifies in chapter V of *Utilitarianism*, which give rise to strict duties to assignable individuals. These rights lie in the general area of security and safety of the person and property. (2002, p. 322)

Such a line of interpretation, which makes the content of the Harm Principle depend on the theory of rights, goes back to John Rees in the 1960s, and I still claim to have nipped it in the bud (Brown, 1978). But, without rehearsing that history, a digital search tells us that the only place in Mill's entire corpus where he uses the phrase 'constituted rights' is in chapter IV, paragraph 3 of *On Liberty* (CW XVIII, p. 276). The preceding sentences make it clear that the rights referred to as *constituted* are those which 'either by express legal provision or by tacit understanding, ought to be considered as rights.' This first category of harms people may be required to avoid is 'injuring the interests of one another' when the interests meet this qualification. So far from making explicit the kind of harm which the Harm Principle says is a necessary condition of legitimate restriction, this passage remarks that some harms do rise to the level of justifying the most severe restrictions. Then it at once asserts that lesser harms may legitimately be punished by opinion but not by law, and these are characterized in very broad terms, merely as being among the things which 'affect prejudicially the interests of others.' I find some obscurity in just how 'tacit understanding' adds to 'express legal provision' to complete the category of 'constituted rights;' perhaps he is thinking of conventions. But, in any case, this very sentence extends the applicability of the Harm Principle beyond constituted rights, and this precludes the interpretation of the principle as restricted to the one class of harms.

The wider importance of this point is that it preserves the structure of Mill's moral theory. The Harm Principle, however appropriate the custom is of calling it the Principle of Liberty, does not purport to say what conduct may and may not be restricted. That can be the role only of Mill's theory of liberty as a whole, and, as Mill remarks in chapter V, paragraph 3 of *On Liberty*, 'it must by no means be supposed, because damage, or the probability of damage, to the interests of others, can alone justify the interference of society, that therefore it always does justify such interference' (CW XVIII, p. 292). Only a necessary condition is laid down, and thus a restriction on the kind of legitimate justification, for restriction of liberty. Attempts to introduce rights into the interpretation of 'harm' have usually amounted to attempts to make the Harm Principle do more of the work of the complete theory of liberty. The connection between that theory and moral conclusions about rights, justice, and duties is guaranteed by the moral theory, since 'We do not call anything wrong, unless we mean to imply that a person ought to be punished in some way or other for doing it' (CW X, p. 246). Mill says in that same paragraph that the distinction between deserving and not deserving punishment lies at the bottom of the notions of right and wrong, and offers the distinction between *moral requirement* and *desirability* as corresponding to that between '*compelled*, or only *persuaded and exhorted*.' What we need, then, once the harmfulness of conduct, of whatever kind, has come in accordance with the Harm Principle to satisfy the necessary condition for compulsion, are the further considerations which determine whether the conduct ought actually to be subject to compulsion of this or that kind and degree. By Mill's moral theory, this amounts to the determination of, first, what punishment, if any, is deserved, thereby fulfilling a necessary condition of moral wrongness; and, second, of whether in various circumstances a deserved punishment should, all things considered, be inflicted. So the completion of the theory of liberty is provided by the moral theory of the justice of punishment. Only when the moral assessment of the harm is carried out can we identify individual rights, and, among them, the relative importances of preserving them. Mill is enough of a 'philosophical utilitarian' to insist that conclusions about rights are downstream from the assessment of utilities, especially the assessment of harms of any kind.[2]

The interpretation which counts all sizes and shapes of harms as harm is faithful to Mill's acceptance of the harms in competition and in any social regulation. It also allows fine tuning of the Harm Principle, by which protection from the harms of offensive behavior is one of the Millean ways of respecting persons.

There is indeed a problem about Mill's use of the term 'harm,' but it concerns not any limitation on what he counts as harm, but rather his conspicuous enlargement of its extension. It seems clear that he thinks it unnecessary to offer a general account of what harm is, and assumes that a speaker of English can accept his specific claims of the harmfulness of various types of conduct. In fact, however, even though his Harm Principle seems to hold admirably for the justification of the criminal law, taken as an unrestricted principle, and read as ordinary English, it is simply false. As I have argued elsewhere,[3] it is unacceptably libertarian, and only by counting as harmful conduct large ranges of indifference, unfairness, self-preference, free riding, and unsociability is he able to arrive at his overall sensible and congenial substantive view of moral requirement. The implications for our present discussion are minimal, since the central concern is the criminal law. But when it comes to the adequacy of Millean morality to the problems addressed by political liberalism one must move beyond the literal statement of the Harm Principle, and address as well the full substance of his moral position.

It speaks well for Nussbaum's attention to Mill's text that she is sensitive to a Kantian aspect of his moral theory. In a discussion of harm entailed in punishment itself, she writes:

> Mill seems to assume that everyone has an equal claim to the conditions of self-development, and that it is therefore unfair of some to claim a greater liberty at the expense of the liberty and development of others. This argument is plausible enough, but (as we shall shortly see) not easily reconciled with the ideas of Utilitarianism. It has a Kantian flavor. (2004, pp. 330–1)

What is shortly referred to is a just claim to liberty, to the effect that

> there is something about a person, and a person's inviolability, that requires liberty. Thus, put in this way, the argument for liberty appeals not to the dubious notion of overall social good, but to the idea of what it is to treat each person as an end. (2004, p. 333)

This helps to explain the terms of an earlier remark:

> It is not terribly clear how such a consideration fits with the general Utilitarian framework of Mill's analysis. (2004, p. 330)

Even more specifically, in the course of discussing women's right to self-development, we are told:

> But he seems to have no clear way to rule out the permanent subordination of a small group (let's say, a group of enforced nurses and childcare workers) if that would be useful to the greater number. His own notion of the 'just claim' to self-development rebels against such an idea, and, similarly, his arguments in favor of women's emancipation do not depend entirely upon Utilitarian considerations. Insofar as they depart from those, however, Mill is veering round to a different sort of theory, more Kantian in spirit, in which each person is inviolable, and an end. (2004, p. 334)

It is now essential to ask exactly what it is in Mill's Utilitarianism that drives him toward unacceptable conclusions. It would be ironic if Mill were under suspicion of inconsistency for holding sound views, when actually nothing in his 'general Utilitarian framework' clashed with them.

But exactly this is what seems to be the case. With respect to the subordination of a group, imagined above, I see no ground for saying that Mill's utilitarianism would commit him to it, other than the attribution to him of a moral requirement to maximize utility. In fact, the most explicit phrasing I have found for Nussbaum's idea of Mill's Utilitarianism had already been given:

> Mill was a Utilitarian philosopher. Though in many ways critical of Bentham's version of Utilitarianism, he remained convinced that the best way to defend a social principle was to show that it conduced to the greatest happiness of the greatest number. (2004, p. 323)

This language conforms to the studious indeterminacy of formulation which pervades much present-day debate, for and against utilitarianism, but it is hard to see how this Utilitarianism generates a problem for Mill unless it sets a standard not merely for desirable or advisable principles but for principles of moral requirement. But there is demonstrably no such principle in Mill. He is simply not a maximizing consequentialist. The 'philosophical utilitarianism' which his Principle of Utility commits him to is silent on any ultimate distribution of utilities. If some other part of his utilitarianism is claimed to yield such unacceptable consequences, the textual evidence needs to be provided.

2 Rationales for coercion

Mill and Nussbaum both have problems about the justification of social coercion, the central occasion for the problems being the criminal law, and as liberals they share the characteristic liberal problem of working out the use of coercion to ensure the rights of individuals and groups to freedom from coercion. Their differences arise from their shared need to understand and defend against threats to liberty.

Historical change has given rise to new threats from cultural pluralism both within national states and in international relations, and, although in the long run international conflicts are bound to have critical effects within states, it is surely a sensible first approximation to think about the justification of law within current liberal jurisdictions. Within this limitation it remains instructive, I think, to keep in mind the relation between old and new threats, and the bearing of old and new rationales on each of these. To the extent that Nussbaum can provide deeper insight into the motives which endanger liberty, that may be at least as relevant to Mill's situation as to our own.

Nussbaum's discontent with Mill seems to have two main sources: one the inadequacy of his arguments in support of extensive individual liberty, the other his imperfect awareness of the deeper sources of danger to liberty. As to the arguments, she divides them (2004, p. 325) into the oddly named 'truth-based justification of liberty' and the 'person-based justification,' matched roughly to Chapters II and III of *On Liberty*.

The oddity of that name given to the first line of argument reflects the misconceived basis of her most serious argument against a Millean 'truth-based justification of liberty: that it is the *wrong sort* of justification, in the sense that it treats the individual citizens as means to the general well-being, and indeed one generation as the means to the next generation's progress' (2004, p. 327). One would never guess from this *either* [1] that Mill's argument is not an argument for the Harm Principle, since it assumes that the principle applies and yields strong reasons for restriction of expression, from the grievous damage that speech can do both personally and politically; *or* [2] that the conclusion of the argument concerns not liberty of action generally, but liberty of thought and discussion. The criticism neglects Mill's always clear sense of his intended audience. He claims that audience in the first sentence of Chapter II as accepting the importance of 'liberty of the press' as one of the securities against corrupt or tyrannical government; so one of his most powerful considerations is taken to be conceded. He has also eloquently reminded them, in the Introduction, of two of his main themes, the ability of a democratic government to impose a tyranny of the majority, and the power of the informal sanctions of public opinion. Evidently he now hopes to persuade optimists about the coming democracy and complacent right-thinking traditionalists that they gravely underestimate the necessity of freedom of thought and discussion. He then canvasses and rebuts the sorts of arguments that impress such people. His project requires convincing them that in modern society repression in the name of truth can be as pernicious as concealing truth by violence. That such an argument, from the danger tyranny poses for the welfare of the individual to the need for freedom of thought and discussion, should be classified as an argument *from* truth and *from* the importance of general welfare is a double travesty.

The argument along the way is a strong example of diagnosing and trying to defend against one kind of harm, a social threat to one kind of liberty. Nussbaum concedes as much in saying that she has been led to the conclusion defended long ago by Mill:

> The dignity and freedom of the individual person need constant and vigilant protection against the tyranny of majorities who define their own ways of doing things as right and normal, and who then set about inflicting damage on others. (2004, p. 278)

The interesting part of her criticism lies, rather, in the matter of diagnosis of the dangers:

> What our analysis in terms of shame and stigma has added is a deeper account of why we should expect this to be a permanent feature of most or all societies.

This is a familiar pattern of her relation to Mill's conclusions (2004, p. 278).

Before leaving the 'truth-based justification' of freedom of thought and discussion, however, I cannot ignore some points of detail. (Compare Nussbaum, 2004, pp. 326–7.) Lifelong engagement in debates about civil liberties leaves me with no squeamishness about Mill's insistence that absolutely all opinions must be accessible in a public forum, subject to the restrictions which any sane theory keeps in place. We are in the arena where the damage that expression can certainly do has to be balanced against the damage that restricting it can do, and on Mill's theory of liberty these are questions of the justice of using coercion. His absoluteness properly conceived is consistent with a normal array of restrictions connected with defamation; incitement to riot; fraud; confidential relations; disturbing the peace; time, place, and manner of public deliberation; military secrets – and advertising. Controlling dishonest or misleading market transactions, however tricky, does not require new fundamental principles for commercial speech. Granting that we must respect the very special experiences of German society, a prohibition of anti-Semitic speech is nevertheless unfortunate, and it is clear to me that on Millean principles Canada's laws against hate speech should be repealed. If Mill did not confront many issues current now, his view is clear enough that Milleans can do him that service. Much concern about the clarity or consistency of Mill on freedom of thought and discussion reflects an assumption that he shared the obsessions of present-day maximizing utilitarians.

Some remaining objections to Mill's views on freedom of discussion amount to arguing that they are not consistent with political liberalism, and are best dealt with in Sections III and IV below.

Turning now to what Nussbaum calls the 'person-based justification of liberty,' she is uncomfortable with what she calls a 'perfectionist' strand in the argument that 'conditions of liberty are necessary for the development of human potential' (2004, p. 330). She candidly acknowledges that 'Mill seems to assume that everyone has an equal claim to the conditions of self-development, and that it is therefore unfair of some to claim a greater liberty at the expense of the liberty and development of others' (2004, pp. 330–1). She comments that this 'has a Kantian flavor,' and wonders if it can be reconciled with 'the ideas of Utilitarianism' (2004, p. 331), but in Section I we have already seen the need to discount this problem. She nevertheless goes on to say:

> At various points in his argument, Mill shows a special interest in the person of genius, whose benefits to the human race may be lost

> through forced adherence to conventional norms. This is the perfectionist strand in Mill's person-based justification. (2004, p. 331)

In this same paragraph Nussbaum quotes bits from Chapter III, paragraph 9 of Mill's *On Liberty*, which offers a grand vision:

> It is not by wearing down into uniformity all that is individual in themselves, but by cultivating it, and calling it forth, within the limits imposed by the rights and interests of others, that human beings become a noble and beautiful object of contemplation; and as the works partake of the character of those who do them, by the same process human life also becomes rich, diversified, and animating, furnishing more abundant aliment to high thoughts and elevating feelings, and strengthening the tie which binds every individual to the race, by making the race infinitely better worth belonging to. (CW XVIII, p. 266)

She also notices Mill's concerns for the current conditions which tend to make 'mediocrity the ascendant power among mankind' (CW XVIII, p. 268). Commenting, she refers to 'such perfectionist and inegalitarian considerations,' and says: 'Such remarks suggest that liberty is of use primarily because it fosters the development of a small number of outstanding people who make contributions that benefit others.' But clearly such remarks do no such thing, and this aspersion on them, I think, flows from an indeterminacy in the phrase 'person-based justification of liberty.' We need to ask: justification of what claim about liberty? The assumption seems to be that Mill is throughout arguing in support of the claim that individuals have certain moral rights to liberty, which it is the duty of the state to protect by force. But, as the phrase omitted from the quotation above implies – 'within the limits imposed by the rights and interests of others' – he often takes those rights as given, and goes on to argue for a quite distinct claim, that liberty is both a condition of and an ingredient in the highest value that the development of the human individual can achieve. For a variety of argumentative purposes, he has both a moral justification of liberty and an aesthetic justification of liberty.

> It really is of importance, not only what men do, but also what manner of men they are that do it. Among the works of man, which human life is rightly employed in perfecting and beautifying, the first in importance surely is man himself. (CW XVIII, p. 263)

Our whole literature is discolored by the preoccupation of present-day utilitarians with a theory of moral requirement, which encourages us all to read right past Mill's firm distinction between the morality and the aesthetics of conduct. It seems common to forget that Mill's Principle of Utility, the principle that the only thing which is desirable as an end in itself is happiness,[4] governs ultimate desirability equally in all the arts of the aesthetically admirable, the morally required, and the personally and socially prudent. No doubt his account of individuality and self-development is important as part of his quasi-Aristotelian conception of happiness, and so of his conception of utility in general. But to take his impassioned account of human perfectibility in any individual as in some inegalitarian tension with his arguments for individual rights is a misunderstanding. I am not aware of a clear sense of the term 'perfectionist' which can serve to blur this distinction.

I conclude that little damage has been done to Mill's justifications of liberty, and that the important questions concern the need for a deeper understanding of the threats to liberty. It is hard to believe that Mill's own sense of them would not have deepened during the past century and a half of bitter historical experience. But Nussbaum provides an impressive psychological perspective on the perennial problems of political philosophy, one as applicable to Mill's time as to ours. In her 'Radical Evil in the Lockean State' she gives depth to her interest in the political emotions by a historical reminder of the place in liberal political theory of notions like Kant's of radical evil, as a feature of the human condition. When our basic needs, in driving us to social cooperation, expose us to conflict over resources, we are forced to notice our vulnerabilities of all kinds.

> Thus my account of prejudice and hatred, whether religious or ethnic or sex-based, is more complicated than Kant's, invoking not only mere plurality but also the hatred of weakness, helplessness, and (ultimately) death that is omnipresent in our relationship to our humanity. (2006, p. 164)
>
> Thus, unlike Kant, I think that radical evil is not a bare disposition to behave badly in certain circumstances. It has an underlying content and a narrative history. Radical evil concerns the pursuit of transcendence and the hatred of finitude: it is about narcissism, we might say, and the fear of death that is a powerful prop to narcissism. Thus the remedy for radical evil will have to address this deeper problem—not curing it, for life is too painful for human beings ever to accept it as it is, but mitigating the role of narcissism in social life. (2006, p. 165)

One must simply acknowledge that this account, worked out in rich detail, brings to bear substantial insight new to the discussion. Given our present concern with the adequacy of Mill's liberalism to meet the threats from cultural pluralism, I think the question which calls for thoughtful reflection is this. To what extent does the absence of such considerations undermine Mill's straightforward hopes for the improvement of humankind? This question divides into two. One is the question of whether his estimate of the dangers to liberalism was inadequate even to the situation he believed to be that of the mid-nineteenth century; the other is whether it has been overtaken by the new problems of more pluralistic cultures. In both cases the answer will bear on our ultimate question, that of the relative merits of Millean liberalism and political liberalism.

It seems to me that the very distinctive substance of Nussbaum's challenge to both Kant and Mill, as it directs us to the working out of powerful emotions, may be less important than its location in a more general enterprise to which she is recalling us: I mean the diagnosis of intolerance, group hostility, and organized violence as rooted in the personal vulnerability of individuals. Most of the problems Mill faced have not gone away, and, while his arguments could no doubt have been improved by psychological insights largely unavailable to him, as ours now can be, in the wider perspective of individual vulnerability I argue that his awareness of it governed the whole shape of his conceptions of morality and liberty.

On Liberty begins with the remark that historically 'By liberty, was meant protection against the tyranny of the political rulers' (CW XVIII, p. 217). Whatever checks to power were raised,

> To prevent the weaker members of the community from being preyed upon by innumerable vultures, it was needful that there should be an animal of prey stronger than the rest, commissioned to keep them down. But as the king of the vultures would be no less bent upon preying on the flock than any of the minor harpies, it was indispensable to be in a perpetual attitude of defense against his beak and claws. (CW XVIII, p. 217)

I have mentioned his introductions to liberty of thought and discussion, reminding us of liberty of the press as defense against tyranny, and warning of the new tyranny of the majority. Nussbaum, as quoted above on rights, alludes to the central role in his account of justice of *security*, which is said there to be 'to everyone's feelings the most vital of all interests' (CW XVIII, p. 251). And again: 'but security no human being can possibly do without...' (CW XVIII, pp. 255–6). Yet the most striking evidence of Mill's sense of human vulnerability is hiding in plain view. It consists in the central role he has given to his conception of morality as the art of collective self-defense.

Mill's originality is evident in his transformation of the Principle of Utility into a first principle of practical reason, governing the aesthetics of conduct and prudence as well as morality, but even more in conceiving moral requirement in a way which links it conceptually with his other great concern, individual liberty. As I have tried to argue fully elsewhere,[5] the enforceability of moral requirement becomes a defining characteristic of it, and once conduct meets the Harm Principle's necessary condition, harmfulness to nonconsenting others, the actual deservingness of punishment depends upon the justice of practices of punishment, which in turn is a matter of the justice of self-defense. In this way the art of morality becomes the art of collective self-defense. The theory of morality and the theory of liberty are two facets of a single conception, as they determine respectively what conduct can in principle be subject to coercion and what in principle must be left free. Mill can accordingly say: 'Whenever, in short, there is a definite damage, or a definite risk of damage, either to an individual or to the public, the case is taken out of the province of liberty, and placed in that of morality or law' (CW XVIII, p. 282).

This overall structure of his view is some evidence of his degree of awareness of the vulnerability of individuals, but it will also be relevant to consider the resources he would rely on to assure the stability of a liberal regime.

3 The challenges to the liberal state

However deep their understanding of the vulnerability of individuals, and with or without Nussbaum's psychological insights, she and Mill both concern themselves with preserving and developing those 'social feelings of mankind' that a liberal society depends on. Comparison of their resources bears on both the perennial dangers to liberalism and the special challenges of modern cultural pluralism.

The completely general question of the stability of liberal states is quite beyond my wisdom. I do not know how to assess the dangers arising from climate change and world poverty through immigration problems and national security, or the internal dangers arising from the dominance of global corporations over national governments and the deep financial corruption of democratic processes. That puts me even more at a loss to judge the relative importance of internal measures, from defense of legal rights, to reform of democratic processes, to relief of poverty and unemployment, to cultural accommodation, to defense of the integrity of the educational system, to diversification of the media, to the promotion of the arts. Such measures, in addition to functioning in the shadow of the global issues, have many dimensions, from the educational effects of simply living under the legal regime, to the sociology of media biases, to the political impact of religious movements. Such daunting complexity prompts me to restrict this discussion mainly to the large similarities between Nussbaum's proposals for the emotional health of the body politic and Mill's, which she acknowledges in some detail, and to which she contributes her particular insights.

Having rejected Rousseau's conception of a 'civil religion' on Kantian grounds of its incompatibility with basic liberal freedoms, she is remarkably sympathetic toward Mill's conception of a 'religion of humanity,' having at its center a moral ideal of caring deeply about humanity generally, 'that could be promulgated through public education.' She makes what I take to be a sensible observation:

> I have argued that a liberal society, without offending against respect for pluralism, can still employ a moral ideal of this sort, and promote a moral education aimed at underwriting it. This ideal would serve as a basis for public political culture, in connection with public norms of equality and respect. (2006, p. 169)

Then her next paragraph raises the issues which I think are hardest to resolve in assessing the relative importance of defensive measures of various kinds, so I quote it in full:

> How, more precisely, would this moral education be institutionalized? A good part of it, I argue, would in fact take the form of developing institutions that express the views of equal respect and due attention to the needs of all: a just tax system, a just healthcare system, a just welfare system. But institutions remain stable only when human beings have the will to sustain them, a fact that the collapse of social democracy in the United States, since the Reagan era, has made an all too vivid reality. Therefore, I argue, public education at all levels should focus on putting forward something like Mill's religion of humanity, conveying the sense that all human lives are of

> equal worth, and all worthy of being lived with dignity and a decent minimum level of well-being. (2006, p. 169)

My own suspicion is that the month-to-month experience of living under a just and liberal regime is the most potent form of education. It works on two levels: one simply the direct knowledge of the security and respect provided, the other the practical effects on poverty, health, opportunity, and whatever else which make vulnerable people less vulnerable and more receptive.

There are several kinds of evidence that Mill thought on such lines. In the opening sections of *Considerations on Representative Government*, he refers to the first of two modes of operation by which a form of government or a set of political institutions affects the welfare of the community as 'its operation as an agency of national education' (CW XVIII, p. 393). More generally, Colin Heydt, in his interesting book *Rethinking Mill's Ethics: Character and Aesthetic Education*, not only notices the importance to Mill of his conception of the aesthetics of conduct and his interest in the formation of character, but usefully directs attention to two areas where Mill attended to the continuous educational effects of institutional structures. In the absence of his wished-for science of ethology, Mill attended with what resources he had to the art of character formation in the family (as well known in *The Subjection of Women*) and in the workplace (in the less commonly noticed *Principles of Political Economy*).

In the middle of this same Nussbaum paragraph, the expression of dismay not only reminds us why it is not accidental that American writers have been especially concerned with the stability of liberal institutions, but also provides justification for any liberal regime to concern itself with education in the narrower sense. It also gives point to the idea that her analysis of the roots of toxic emotions calls for artists to contribute to public education. It is charming that both she and Mill turn to poetry as wholesome for emotional and moral development. It can be a measure of her contribution that among prescriptions for emotional health Whitman is surely a more potent draught than Wordsworth.

In the area of education, conceived broadly, it may be encouraging to note, we have a curious advantage over Mill in grounds for optimism. It is hard to remember the extent to which Mill seems to have believed that everything civilized, and in particular moral, was acquired by conditioning, in accordance with associationist psychology. That makes progress contingent on maintaining a historical continuity. In our world of general opinion, we have emerged from the ascendancy of behaviorism to fall under the ascendancy of evolutionary psychology; but it is indeed reasonable for us to count on greater innate resources for the cultivation of both a willingness to cooperate and a sense of justice.

At the same time, we should retain Mill's vivid awareness of the distinction between fundamental and derivative moral disagreements. We have a tendency to forget the extent to which moral conclusions clash because of their derivation from differing views of the world, so that they are no more (or less) intractable than matters of economics, history, psychology, or divergent personal experiences.

On the whole, it seems that Mill's interest in the art of character development and Nussbaum's interest in the growth of well grounded emotion are not as disparate as they might appear to be, and that the ideas they have of the threats to a liberal regime and of their defensive resources are remarkably similar. To the considerable extent that Nussbaum provides a deeper analysis of the socially ominous emotions, that insight seems to bear on the perennial problems of liberal societies. If it is also the case that her insights allow a wiser and more promising approach to the new challenges of cultural pluralism, that should emerge from a direct confrontation between a predictable Millean response and the response of political liberalism.

4 Justice and political liberalisms

Political liberalism comes in a range of flavors, from the most astringent to the bland, but that inconvenience for the literature invites this discussion to show that Mill provides a convincing alternative to the whole range.

A difficulty that has beset attempts simply to define political liberalism, at least from Rawls onward, has been the obscurity of the distinction between core doctrines, or free-standing conceptions of justice, or liberal essentials, on the one hand, and comprehensive doctrines on the other. The distinction seems sometimes to be developed retroactively, from the distinction between what one can and cannot legitimately appeal to in the exercise of a legal or political role, perhaps right down to the political role of citizen. Sometimes 'comprehensive doctrines' seems to be code for 'religious beliefs and conceptions of the good life,' the core being what's left when these are excluded. Sometimes a richly specified notion of 'public reason' becomes the core, and comprehensive doctrines everything else. At times it even seems that the core principles are simply read off from the structure of existing liberal democratic constitutions taken to be desirable historical outcomes. Such confusion stands in the way of a principled account of the limits of legitimate coercion.

In its best forms, political liberalism is explicitly a moral doctrine whose deepest level is respect for persons, meaning respect for their rights, needs, beliefs, commitments, and loyalties, including, in short, their reasonable 'comprehensive doctrines.' Such respect entails a commitment to maintaining the *legitimacy* of any coercive regime, in the classical liberal form of requiring the consent of the governed. But then, when the problem becomes that of maintaining the *stability* of a liberal society, it is characteristic of political liberalisms to argue that respect entails a further constraint, a restriction on justifications of the liberal constitution, namely a restriction to considerations appropriately addressed to all reasonable persons, including those who do not share the liberal valuation of autonomy and individuality.

In fact, I suggest that the most straightforward kind of defense of the legitimacy of coercion also suggests the most practical political strategy for promoting the stability of a constitutional democracy. For the least principled-looking version of political liberalism, which elicits its core principles from the *de facto* practices of the heritage of classical liberalism, suggests simply, for stability, the defense of a constitution in which a scheme of rights, limiting the powers of democratic majorities, has become legally difficult to amend.

Such deflation of the supposed demands of proper respect does involve dismissing as a futile exercise the classifications of doctrines as core or comprehensive, freestanding or derived, and so on, with attendant traffic laws governing the flow of discussion. However, a couple of reminders may soften the curtness of such dismissal. First, it is clear that legitimacy, in the sense in which it respects the right of people not to be coerced in ways that cannot be reasonably justified to them, has always been understood to concern the constitution of the legal regime they are subject to, and not each particular of requirement on them. We mean not the absurdity of justifying this restriction or that tax, but showing the constitutionality of a given law, its reflection of majority support, the availability of tribunals of redress, and the like. Legitimacy coexists with vigorous political struggle, bad social policy, and unfairness to many, and so tends to be a large-scale seldom revisited issue. But such seems to be precisely the occasion for the anxiety, understandably felt acutely in the United States, over the safety of constitutional guarantees of individual rights and freedoms. (The threat of pluralism to democratic process seems less pointed, as well as overshadowed by worse threats.) Such an approach to the matter of legitimacy focuses the issues sharply enough to suggest that respect for illiberal attitudes had better not go so far as to impede *whatever* justifications of the constitution are available. Justifications need to be articulated, for the support of movements in other parts of the world struggling to create liberal regimes, but also for the simplest support to stability, namely defense of the legal constitution.

A second reminder that the classification of doctrines is no great loss comes from the reason why the favorite distinctions, even when they are locally intelligible, fail to shape the whole field of debate in any usable way. That reason is the inextricable tangle of the debate itself. A moral duty to avoid harm may derive validly from a judgment of ultimate desirability; a judgment on merit may rest fallaciously on biological claims; a moral prohibition may rest on a metaphysical conception or on historical and literary authority; a dispute over fairness may turn on scientific fact. The question of 'what is really at stake here' often has several defensible answers. Nor has the sorting terminology helped. The fuzziness of the notion of 'comprehensive doctrines' is partly the pernicious effect of multiple ambiguity in the word 'moral.' Sometimes the moral contrasts with Mill's 'aesthetic' and implies requirement, obligation, duty, wrongness, and rights, in short 'the distinctively moral' or 'morality in the narrow sense.' In this sense we must insist that any defensible form of political liberalism has a moral basis, and that its core doctrines are moral doctrines, as Charles Larmore has argued all along,[6] and as Nussbaum agrees.[7] It would be incoherent to regard moral doctrines as somehow the property of comprehensive doctrines, though the latter will, of course, include antiliberal and nonpolitical moral doctrines. At the same time established usages extend the term moral not just to the whole scope of the ethical in Aristotle's sense, but beyond conduct and character to overall conceptions of the good life. It serves clarity to avoid such use of the word.

In our liberal societies, then, awash with such differences, we are looking for a principled account of the legitimacy with which our legal system uses coercion in the defense of individual liberty, and for a strategy of engagement with those in our pluralist society who find that the liberal neutrality embodied in the drawn legal lines fails to respect their ways of life. The account of legitimacy is surely something liberals automatically need, for their own satisfaction. The strategy is the point at which political liberalism introduces its distinctive restriction of discourse to the political, in some sense to be specified. For both enterprises I am happy to accept that the solution must be embodied in moral principles founded on respect for persons. Let us set up for comparison a Millean alternative to political liberalism.

It will be simplest now just to set out my interpretation of Mill's moral theory, on which the realm of liberty is the complement to that of morality, and morality is delimited through the justice of coercion, which rests in turn on the fairness of punishment. His justification of the liberal state rests, ultimately, not indeed on Justice as Fairness, but on one conception of justice as fairness. Having defended the interpretation at length elsewhere,[8] I keep here to bare statement.

Morality is the art of collective self-defense. Conduct is wrong only if it is harmful to others, and thereby deserves punishment either legally or informally. Such deservingness depends on the principles defining practices of punishment, the justification of which, while it typically corresponds to utility, depends really on the social analogue of the justice of personal self-defense. The criterion of moral wrongness rests finally on the fairness of using coercion of given severity against the infliction of given harms. Its central cases are violations of the rights of others. The business of the state includes the enforcement of morality (critical, not positive morality); its liberal neutrality consists in its defense of any and all morally permissible conduct from interference by others. So Mill's answer to the question of what moral justification can be given for the coercive action of the state is itself his theory of what morality is all about. That theory includes 'philosophical utilitarianism' but no maximizing requirement, and rests finally on a deontic principle of the fairness of self-defensive coercion.

Mill has assimilated the evolving conception of 'morality in the narrow sense.' In this way he presents the defender of the liberal state with a formally simple schema for justification. Ideals of the good life for the individual or the merely aesthetic excellences of character are no longer part of morality. The realm of the political has as its center whatever affects the power of the state to impose legal requirements. The theory of what coercive requirements can be morally justified is just the theory of moral requirement. Morality being the judge of legitimate coercion, moral principle supplies a justification of the state which is in one sense 'freestanding.' It is up to the theory of moral requirement to take account of security and vulnerability, harm and help, desire and aversion, aspiration and indifference, in whatever ways its principles imply. Conceptions of the good life will take their moral chances, by a route which is independent of the possible direct appeal to them as justifying liberal ways.

It is essential, however, to understand the limitations of being 'freestanding' in this limited sense, which is that of resting on moral principles, including principles of justice, and not on the appeal to the desirability of a kind of life, of individuality, autonomy, self-realization or whatever. Any morality we need to consider will be concerned to protect people from some forms of harm or disrespect. The deprivation of any highly valued aspect of a way of life will be a candidate for grounding a moral requirement. So morality itself must engage in the evaluation of aspects of ways of life and of the relative importance of those aspects. It is a strength of negative substantive moralities, like Mill's very negative utilitarianism, that their main currency is aspects of the bad life, since the undesirability of disease, hunger, and violent death is more widely agreed upon. Indeed, the most relevant and promising area of 'overlapping consensus' is this lowest end of conceptions of the good life. In fairness, Rawls might be entitled to claim, though he can hardly be said to have made the point, that his notion of a set of primary goods recognized the spectrum of un/desirabilities. In any case, I am not aware of any conception of justice or morality offered as 'freestanding' which escapes such structured dependence on judgments of the good.

At this late stage I offer with diffidence a couple of points which, though controversial, seem obvious to me, about the top end of the range of ultimate goods in a life. What it is for an individual to thrive, or to be counted at death as having been happy in his or her life, depends on many things, such as the individual's talents, temperament, opportunities, cultural background, and accidents of experience. Equally important, for many individuals several possible ways of life are open to them, and yet the alternatives are incompatible. If reason tells us anything, it is that, just as individuals make overall career choices whose wisdom or unwisdom will forever remain unclear, it makes no sense to try to rank order the types of life thus chosen.

Section I above noted the tension in Mill's moral theory between the Harm Principle as stated and the extending of the notion of harm to reach his full moral position. When we reject that extension for harm we must choose among further possible rejections. It seems clear to me that the amended Mill must supplement the positive side of the Harm Principle with further wrong-making characteristics, thereby abandoning the extremely negative utilitarianism which the principle embodies. That would leave room to recognize as a major contribution his insight that the evolution of our conception of morality has brought us to its enforceability in principle. This is what enables him to offer *morality as such* as the core set of doctrines which political liberalism unsuccessfully looks for. The cost to Mill is opening up the range of possible fundamental moral principles. But he is already engaged in helping himself to deontic principles from his commonsense moral beliefs, comforted by his conviction that such morality proves to be philosophically utilitarian. It is small cost to most of us who are already back to the drawing board about substantive moral theory.

The amended Millean solution to the problem of a respectful justification of the liberal state, accordingly, offers morality itself, with a fairness account of justice at its core, as the freestanding defense of the constitution. Political discourse retains its old-fashioned status as the application of moral principle to political situations, and moral debate is clearly as open-endedly controversial as ever. The Millean solution to the second problem, that of respectful engagement with illiberal cultures and beliefs, which takes on the full range of reasonable disagreement, turns essentially on the nature of that respect which its moral basis requires. I now argue that his solution provides the decisive case against the notions of restraint which I see as central to political liberalism.

The attitudes which imbue Mill's account of the liberty of thought and discussion are so well captured in an unpublished paper by Julia Skorupska that I wish I could simply refer the reader to that source to begin my argument. She has kindly permitted me to use some quotation along with descriptive comment of my own. She writes:

> I will argue that Rawls was mistaken when he grouped Mill with Kant and classified him as a traditional liberal theorist unable to respond to the problems of pluralism. While Mill did insist that the considerations and values which we could appeal to in political life could not be limited, he accepted that pluralism would be a permanent feature of social life and denied that reason could be used to conclusively determine what is of value. Rather he believed that the only way to approach better answers to this question was through an on-going broad and passionate conversation. (Skorupska, 2006)

She gives wide-ranging textual evidence to support the final conclusion about Mill, that

> rather his work offers an alternative response to the problems of pluralism that gives a central role to substantive engagement instead of searching for areas of agreement. (Skorupska, 2006)

I find that this last contrast is a good fit for the distinction I want to draw between two ways of showing respect for persons. Confronted with disagreement or incomprehension, it can, of course, be a measure of respect to change the subject or to look for some area of agreement, but that is consistent with a measure of contempt, indifference, or despair of change. A more robust respect addresses the issues, willing to understand an opposing attitude, allowing that it might have merit, and prepared to offer reasons. Hope lies not in the topics to be avoided, but in the spirit in which any topic is addressed, and there is no disagreement that cannot be addressed respectfully. Various aspects of Mill's approach embody his reliance on the form of engagement rather than the choice of ground.

The most thoroughgoing of all empiricists, Mill forcefully reminds us of our fallibility. Not only may the belief we think dangerously false turn out to be true; he enunciates clearly the Popperian principle that rational assurance in any claim depends on its continued openness to challenge. Disengagement is out of place, on the ground, among others, that liberal conceptions of human flourishing, varied and complex as they are, could profit from continuing reconsideration. Since the pursuit of an ultimate ideal is an experiment in living, Mill is free of suspicion that he might think reason could settle *a priori* the nature of the good life. (This seems to me to support another view of Skorupska's, which I should report, that the ongoing conversation needs on Mill's view to be passionate, and that the arts of rhetoric are appropriate to it.) Mill, Nussbaum, and the rest of us can perhaps agree on the relevance of the arts to the growth of mutual understanding.

Mutual understanding, from mutual familiarity, from in turn mutual accessibility, seems to be the path forward provided by Mill's commitment to the freedom of thought and discussion. Proper respect for radical disagreement calls for a maxim of rhetoric of which Mill was master: Know your audience. At the level of common debate, are you speaking to secular liberals, or to fundamentalist Christians, or to Muslim traditionalists? The answer must be: To each, on appropriate occasions, with appropriate manner and manners. It is desirable that everyone have access to everything, the Muslim jihadist to liberal opinion addressed to Christians, the liberal Christian to comment by secular conservatives, and so on. Not everyone will endure, or even overhear, everything. But some faith in the power of osmosis is even more in place on the more mundane level of personal acquaintance, business dealings, and common media. To fall silent for fear of causing offense is to show a deep disrespect. I am content to rest the whole project on the faith that reasonableness can eventually prevail.

Such considerations are more directly relevant to the impact on moral disagreement of religious beliefs than to the impact of disparate conceptions of the good life, partly because religious beliefs are commonly stated as doctrines, providing the moral debate with explicit premises and conclusions. The common attitude that moral issues are essentially intractable is doubly misguided. On the one hand, many liberal conclusions about the rights and freedoms of individuals are well defended and tested, and, as Mill insisted, available without apology as the basis for action. It is consistent to be respectful of creationist religious convictions and to enforce educational standards, including competent teaching of biology, in public schools, as neatly captured in a remark I have heard: 'We must debate with these believers; and we must prevail.' On the other hand, most moral disagreement is *borrowed* from nonmoral disagreement, in the sense of being derivative from the empirical or metaphysical disagreements about the subsidiary premises by which the respective moral positions become applications of more fundamental moral attitudes. The present-day exponential surge in communication, inquiry, and everyday contact, at the same time as it multiples live options for the individual's way of life, generates the materials for resolution of derivative moral disagreement.

In sum, Mill's empiricist version of practical reason preserves the universalism, individualism, and compassion of the Enlightenment, while moderating its political pretensions to those of a work in progress. Yet his liberalism keeps that 'sense of importance which nerves all civilized effort.' In comparison, the forms of disengagement which I have taken to be the fruit of political liberalism seem like a failure of nerve.[9]

Notes

1. These include Nussbaum (2001) and Nussbaum (1994).
2. I have set out and defended this interpretation in Brown (2010, Sections 6–8); and see Sections 3 and 4 on the term 'philosophical utilitarianism,' introduced by Scanlon (1982, p. 108) for the 'thesis about the nature of morality' on which 'all that counts morally is the well-being of individuals, no one of whom is singled out as counting for more than the others.'
3. Brown (1972), Brown (1982), Brown (2010), and Brown (forthcoming).
4. Brown (1973). See, for example, the 'theory of life' at the end of *Utilitarianism* II 2 and the statement of the Greatest Happiness Principle (CW X, pp. 210 and 214).
5. In Brown (1972) and Brown (1982), but most fully in Brown (2010, Sections 5–8).
6. Larmore (1987, Chapter 3), Larmore (1990), and Larmore (1999), revised as Larmore (2008, Chapter 6). I regard Larmore's version of political liberalism as the most thoughtful and well worked out, but on matters of whether respect calls for restraint or engagement still 180 degrees from Mill's direction.

7. Nussbaum (2004, p. 60), and see references to mutual respect, human dignity, reciprocity, inviolability of the person, and so on as at its core (Nussbaum, 2004, pp. 321, 328, and 334).
8. Brown (2010, especially Sections 5 to 8).
9. As so often, I am much indebted to Alister Browne for his critical comments.

References

Brown, D.G. 1972 'Mill on Liberty and Morality', *Philosophical Review* 81(2), 133–158.

—— 1973 'What is Mill's Principle of Utility?', *Canadian Journal of Philosophy* 3, 1–12.

—— 1978 'Mill on Harm to Others' Interests', *Political Studies* 26(3), 395–399.

—— 1982 'Mill's Criterion of Wrong Conduct', *Dialogue* 12(1), 27–44.

—— 2010 'Mill's Moral Theory: Ongoing Revisionism', *Politics, Philosophy and Economics* 9(1), 5–45.

—— 2010 'Mill on the harm in not voting', *Utilitas* 22(2), 126–133.

Larmore, Charles 1987 *Patterns of Moral Complexity* (Cambridge:Cambridge University Press).

—— 1990 'Political Liberalism', *Political Theory* 18, 339–360.

—— 1999 'The Moral Basis of Political Liberalism', *Journal of Philosophy* 96, 599–625.

—— 2008 *The Autonomy of Morality* (Cambridge: Cambridge University Press).

Heydt, Colin 2006 *Rethinking Mill's Ethics: Character and Aesthetic Education* (London: Continuum).

Nussbaum, Martha C. 2006 'Radical Evil in the Lockean State: The Neglect of the Political Emotions', *Journal of Moral Philosophy* 3(2), 159–178.

—— 2004 *Hiding from Humanity: Disgust, Shame, and the Law* (Princeton and Oxford: Princeton University Press).

—— 2002 'Millean Liberty and Sexual Orientation', *Law and Philosophy* 21, 317–334.

—— 2001 *Upheavals of Thought: The Intelligence of Emotions* (Cambridge: Cambridge University Press).

—— 1994 *The Therapy of Desire: Theory and Practice in Hellenistic Ethics* (Princeton: Princeton University Press).

Scanlon, T.M. 1982 'Contractualism and Utilitatianism', in *Utilitarianism and Beyond*, ed. Amartya Sen and Bernard Williams (Cambridge: Cambridge University Press), 103–128.

Skorupska, Julia 2006 'Liberalism and Politics: Reading Mill as a "Political" Theorist', unpublished paper read to the Ninth Conference of the International Society for Utilitarian Studies.

7
Happiness and the Moral Sentiment of Justice

Jonathan Riley

1 Introduction

Human happiness consists of feelings of pleasure, including relief from pain, John Stuart Mill insists, but it must be distinguished from mere physical gratification as well as from mere subjective contentment.[1] Human beings, besides having physical senses, instincts, and appetites also possessed by other animals, 'have faculties more elevated than the animal appetites, and, when once made conscious of them, do not regard anything as happiness which does not include their gratification' (CW X, pp. 210–11). These 'more elevated' human faculties, though they require to be developed, enable humans to experience higher kinds of pleasant feelings than beasts can experience, namely, 'the pleasures of the intellect, of the feelings and the imagination, and of the moral sentiments' (CW X, p. 211). The more elevated faculties apparently include mental capacities to form and recall complex ideas, embody them in propositions, and reason about them, capacities to imagine novel and more perfect things and feel the aesthetic emotions associated with them, and capacities to form ideas of right and wrong and experience the moral sentiments associated with them.

Mill claims that the kinds of pleasant feelings that gratify these mental capacities have 'a much greater value as pleasures than ... those of mere sensation' for most, if not all, people who have been 'made conscious' of their elevated faculties. Mere physical *sensations* of pleasure are elementary feelings experienced by the body, 'disjoined from the higher faculties' (CW X, p. 213). Unlike simple sensations, the higher pleasures are complex feelings or emotions that are inseparable from the higher faculties. These complex feelings have various ingredients, including simple sensations of pleasure (or their traces in memory or imagination) but also various products of the higher faculties such as complex ideas, reasons, and judgments. As Mill puts it, higher pleasures are superior in quality to lower pleasures, where 'a superiority in quality... so far outweigh[s] quantity as to render it, in comparison, of small account' (CW X, p. 211). Qualitative superiority effectively means infinite superiority.

Mill emphasizes that most people who have exercised and developed their higher faculties, and who are thus 'equally capable of appreciating and enjoying' higher and lower kinds of pleasures, 'do give a most marked preference to the manner of existence which employs their higher faculties,' and their 'marked preference' is so profound, he stresses, that they would not give up the 'manner of existence which employs their higher faculties' (CW X, p. 210) for a lower grade of existence which only employs their animal senses and appetites, no matter how large an amount of bodily sensation of pleasure could be enjoyed in the lower grade of existence.

Humans have common desires for things such as food, shelter, and sex that satisfy their bodily needs, as well as common desires for employment, income, and leisure that permit them to engage in everyday activities. But the highly endowed being will not consent to satisfy these physical cravings and merely expedient sorts of desires by means of foolish, degrading, or immoral actions. In particular, he will not consent to satisfy his desires by violating others' recognized rights.

This extreme 'unwillingness' of a being of higher faculties to 'sink into what he feels to be a lower grade of existence' is best called 'a sense of dignity,' Mill suggests, 'which all human beings possess in one form or other, and in some, though by no means in exact, proportion to their higher faculties,' and he argues that the sense of dignity 'is so essential a part of the happiness of those in whom it is strong, that *nothing* which conflicts with it could be, otherwise than momentarily, an object of desire to them' (CW X, p. 212).[2] Since the sense of dignity tends to grow stronger as the individual develops his higher faculties, 'highly endowed beings' – or at least most of them – prefer never to give up intellectual, aesthetic, or moral kinds of pleasures for any competing kinds: 'Whoever supposes that this preference takes place at a sacrifice of happiness – that the superior being, in anything like equal circumstances, is not happier than the inferior – confounds the two very different ideas, of happiness, and content' (CW X, p. 211).

True, a pig or a fool may be content with physical gratifications or base pleasures, whereas a highly endowed being will always feel discontent because, 'as the world is constituted,' the gratification of his elevated faculties is 'imperfect' (CW X, p. 211). But the pleasures of the elevated faculties, though never so perfect as to satisfy the highly endowed person, have a much higher value as pleasures than those of mere physical sensation or those of mediocre or abused mental faculties: 'It is better to be a human being dissatisfied than a pig satisfied; better to be Socrates dissatisfied than a fool satisfied. And if the fool, or the pig, is of a different opinion, it is because they only know their own side of the question' (CW X, p. 212).

People capable of higher pleasures may sometimes choose to postpone them to lower pleasures 'from infirmity of character,' Mill admits. But such weakness of will 'is quite compatible with a full appreciation of the intrinsic superiority of the higher' (CW X, p. 212). These people continue to recognize the qualitative superiority of the higher pleasures and regret choosing to defer them to the lower. Another familiar observation is that 'many who begin with youthful enthusiasm for everything noble, as they advance in years sink into indolence and selfishness' (CW X, p. 212). But Mill insists that they do not voluntarily choose foolish, base, and selfish pleasures in preference to the higher. Rather, their higher faculties have been crushed and atrophied by hostile influences or mere lack of exercise. They sink into foolish, base, and selfish enjoyments because they have lost the capacity to enjoy pleasures of the intellect, of the creative imagination, and of the moral sentiments.

Mill's doctrine of higher pleasures deserves a much more extended treatment than can be given here.[3] I shall confine attention to his analysis of the higher pleasures of the moral sentiments, including his view of how conflicts between moral pleasures and other sorts of higher pleasures – that is, nonmoral intellectual pleasures and nonmoral aesthetic ones – should be resolved. As I read him, he conceives of human happiness such that moral pleasures – pleasant feelings that gratify the elevated capacities involved in production of the moral sentiments – are of a kind that is superior in quality to all conflicting kinds of pleasant feelings. Pleasures of justice are the epitome of this moral kind.[4] A pleasant feeling of justice is a complex feeling that grows up around the complex idea of justice, which, as Mill understands it, amounts to the idea of a social code that impartially distributes equal rights and correlative duties enforced by a sentiment that anyone who infringes the social rules deserves some form of punishment. I shall soon be discussing the nature of the pleasant feeling of justice in more detail. But the point I wish to stress at the moment is that it is qualitatively superior to all competing kinds of pleasures. Thus, even a bit of the pleasure of justice is more valuable as pleasure than any finite amount of a nonmoral 'merely expedient' kind of mental pleasure, that is, a feeling of pleasure that is inseparable from the idea of some useful everyday object or activity but distinct from the idea of justice. *A fortiori*, the pleasure of justice is infinitely more valuable as pleasure than simple physical sensations of pleasure arising from the body.

Mill indicates that higher pleasures of justice are feelings of 'security' enjoyed in common with one's fellows (CW X, pp. 250–1).[5] This pleasant feeling of security can only arise under binding general rules that distribute equal rights and correlative duties for all, backed by sanctions. There are no other sources for this kind of pleasure. Given the absolute superiority of the feeling of security over all competing kinds of pleasures, it follows that, for reasonable individuals who are competently acquainted with the different kinds of enjoyments, a social code of equal rights, duties, and sanctions has absolute priority over all competing sources of happiness.

But, at least for the foreseeable future, reasonable people must be expected to disagree about which particular rules and rights ought to be recognized in their society to promote the pleasant feeling of security. To remove the disagreement, society needs a decision procedure to select a particular code that shall be recognized as authoritative for everyone in the community. No individual can complete the formation of his idea of justice, or enjoy the pleasant feeling of security associated with justice, until such an authoritative code of rights, duties, and sanctions has been decided upon by society, or by those who have succeeded in making themselves society's representatives. Thus, the social decision procedure is properly an *internal* component of every person's idea and pleasure of justice.

In this regard, Mill shows no inclination to recommend a traditional utilitarian decision procedure that relies on incredibly rich utility information to calculate an authoritative code that maximizes the sum total of security. Rather, he seems to have in mind a democratic social decision procedure that aggregates over the diverse preference orderings which reasonable yet fallible individuals seeking security may be expected to form and express with respect to alternative possible codes. Moreover, he never presumes that an optimal code can be selected in its entirety all at once by some ideal impartial observer. Rather, he apparently takes for granted that the code must be constructed in a gradual and piecemeal manner by flawed human beings who exercise and develop their elevated faculties and learn to correct their mistakes. Indeed, this gradual process of construction may be of indefinite duration, characterized by continuing disagreement at virtually every step of the way. Thus, a truly optimal code may remain an elusive ideal, approached but perhaps never actually realized. The code actually selected as authoritative by society at any given moment of time may well be highly imperfect from the ideal perspective, given the limited development of human faculties and the poor information currently available about the best rules and rights for maximizing security.

The higher pleasure of security is only made possible by an authoritative social code of justice that distributes equal individual rights and correlative duties. This pleasant feeling of security is a variable that can only be maximized under a particular social code that, in the estimation of competent majorities, gives the most protection for vital personal concerns shared by all members of the community. To experience the pleasure of security in this moral sense, an individual must be capable of imagining himself in other people's positions and inferring that, no matter which position he occupies, he receives the same protection for the vital personal concerns which he shares with everyone else, an inference that is warranted if equal rights and duties for all are recognized and enforced. His moral feeling of security is compromised when he knows either that some members of society are excluded from the system of equal rights, or that some people are able to escape due punishment even though they refuse to fulfill their duties to others. Even if equal rights and duties are distributed to everyone and there is full compliance with the rules, the moral pleasure of security varies in quantity across different possible social codes. The amount of it experienced by any individual capable of experiencing it depends upon the nature of the rights and duties distributed by the code. Roughly, the moral pleasure of security increases as more complete protection is provided by the rights-assignment for any of the vital personal concerns shared by all members of the community.

For ease of exposition, I shall assume that an authoritative moral code is also a legal code, and that legal rules are invariably also moral rules. These assumptions can and must be relaxed for a more adequate treatment of Mill's moral and political philosophy. But I emphasize that this is a gross simplification. Mill is quite aware that moral rules cannot always be expediently enforced as positive laws, and that morality is the product of a far more complex social decision process than a formal lawmaking procedure. Moreover, there is no doubt that legal rules may be enacted for merely expedient purposes as opposed to the distribution and enforcement of moral rights.

It follows that, as long as he fulfills his moral and legal duties distributed by an optimal social code, any individual has capacious freedom to pursue in his own way all kinds of pleasant feelings besides the pleasure of security. He is free to act in accord with his own equal rights because by acting thus he does not cause others to experience any painful feelings of insecurity, in other words, any harms that have been deemed wrongful and unjust by competent majorities because they damage vital personal concerns. This capacious individual freedom is a remarkable feature of Mill's extraordinary version of utilitarianism as I interpret it.

With these introductory remarks as background, I propose to look more closely at Mill's psychological account of the 'peculiar energy and assertiveness' of the moral sentiment of justice. He suggests that the sentiment's peculiar force can be traced to the qualitative superiority of the pleasant feeling of security that is inseparable from it and that ultimately motivates it. In this regard, there is no dispute that moral agents who possess a sentiment of justice are aware of its peculiar impressiveness in comparison to, say, pleasant feelings of a merely expedient kind. Mill's dispute is instead with those who claim that the sentiment of justice is '*sui generis* like our sensations of colour and taste' (CW X, p. 240). Recall that pleasure is defined to include relief from pain, that is, security from pain. The higher kind of moral pleasure which I am identifying as the pleasant feeling of 'security' can also be depicted as a feeling of relief or security from a higher kind of pain or harm that is classified as immoral or unjust. He brands such thinkers as 'intuitive' moralists because they claim that the moral sentiments are simple instinctive feelings that are produced in an ultimately mysterious way by a special 'natural faculty' (CW X, p. 206). He actually divides the intuitive school into two camps. One camp conceives of the special moral faculty as a 'sensitive' faculty, roughly analogous to our physical senses, that 'discerns what is right or wrong in the particular case in hand, as our other senses discern the sight or sound actually present.' He quickly dismisses this camp, and asserts that intuitive moralists must abandon it if they have 'any pretensions to philosophy' (CW X, p. 206). The quick dismissal is potentially misleading, however, because this camp seems to be the one that he is mainly concerned to rebut.

The other camp, which he appears to take more seriously yet also decisively rejects, conceives of the moral faculty as an 'intellectual instinct, leading us to judge in a particular way' (CW X, p. 240). According to intuitionists of this stripe, the moral instinct is a 'branch of our reason' that discerns principles of right and wrong and prompts us to make moral judgments in accord with them independently of our physical sensations and appetites, and thus independently of any supposed *a posteriori* form of reasoning based on experience of pleasure and pain. In short, the moral instinct is an instinct of pure *a priori* reason that discovers or constructs its own ideas of morality, and that moves us to take a practical interest in these ideas independently of any natural inclinations to enjoy pleasure and avoid pain. Unlike a sense akin to our other senses, this rational instinct 'supplies us only with the general principles of moral judgments' instead of perceiving virtuous and vicious characters, or right and wrong actions, 'in the concrete' (CW X, p. 206). The general principles of morality and justice are 'evident *a priori*' to this rational instinct, 'requiring nothing to command assent, except that the meaning of the terms be understood' (CW X, p. 206).

Mill expressly mentions Kant as a leading figure of the second camp of intuitive moralists. Despite his admiration for 'this remarkable man,' he argues that Kant's *a priori* rationalist approach to justice and right is fatally flawed (CW X, p. 206). Kant insists that pure reason can construct general moral principles without reference to utility consequences, and that it can also cause a moral feeling in us that freely determines the will to give priority to these principles of conduct despite any conflicting natural desires and passions. According to Mill, this Kantian approach needs to be abandoned, or at least suitably modified so that moral principles are inferred by reason from our experience of the pleasures and pains caused by different actions and characters in various types of situations. Any adequate approach to justice must rely on *a posteriori* reasoning about the probable utility consequences of distinct feasible social codes that distribute and sanction different bundles of equal rights and duties that are designed to give protection to vital personal interests or needs shared by all. More specifically, the distinct possible codes must be ranked against one another, by estimating and comparing how much of the pleasant feeling of security is likely to be enjoyed under each of them. This moral kind of pleasure is a crucial ingredient of every fully reasonable person's conception of happiness.

Although Mill never says so, Francis Hutcheson, David Hume, and even Adam Smith are leading figures of the first camp of intuitive moralists, which Mill so abruptly dismisses. These great British sentimentalists are, like Mill himself, opponents of any *a priori* rationalist ethics. Unlike him, however, they treat the moral sentiments as simple feelings that are produced in a mysterious way by the human frame and constitution under certain conditions. Just as it is ultimately mysterious how sensations of color are produced in us upon the view of various external objects, they argue, it is ultimately inexplicable how sensations of right and wrong are generated upon the contemplation of various passions, characters, and actions. As they see things, reason, whether conceived strictly, as purely *a priori* deductive reasoning, or generously, as also including *a posteriori* inductive reasoning, does not create, and cannot explain, the moral feelings of virtue and vice, praiseworthiness and blameworthiness, which are said to be a peculiar kind of pleasures and pains. Nature has not left the production of these distinctive feelings to reason, which is seen as a quite weak faculty of limited scope. Rather, the moral feelings are triggered automatically by the perception of virtuous or vicious qualities in desires, emotions, and associated characters and actions. Yet the sentimentalists concede that the moral feelings may be misguided, just as sensations of color are misplaced when an illusory oasis is perceived in the desert. Reason helps to correct and guide the projection of these peculiar moral pleasures or pains onto the passions, characters, and other objects that, after due reflection, are perceived to have virtuous or vicious qualities. This role for reason is allowed whether the moral feelings are said to be produced by a special moral sense (as both Hutcheson and Hume assert) or to arise instead from a general capacity for sympathy that does not presuppose any special moral sense (as Smith maintains). Reasoning about the probable pleasant and painful effects of various characters and actions, based on experience of the effects, is needed to direct and refine the instinctive moral sentiments.

Mill shares the conviction of the British sentimentalists that moral judgment is ultimately a matter of sentiment. But he also argues that the moral sentiments are complex feelings whose very formation depends on reasoning about utility consequences. The moral sentiment of justice or injustice is not a simple instinctive feeling, he argues, but rather 'a derivative feeling, formed by a combination of others' (CW X, pp. 240–1). Thus, whereas the sentimentalists insist that the moral sentiments are *sui generis* and cannot be further analyzed although the conditions under which they emerge can be clarified, Mill disagrees and follows an alternative British approach, namely, the approach pioneered by Hartley and notably developed by James Mill and Bain as well as by Mill himself.[6] According to this latter form of empiricist moral psychology, which, like the sentimentalist brand of intuitionism, is a distinctive offshoot from Locke's theory of human understanding, the moral sentiments are complex feelings that are derived – that is, inferred, caused, produced – by reason from various ingredients, including instincts, ideas, and sensations of pleasure and pain. By implication, such derivative feelings can be analyzed in terms of their ingredients. In particular, given that it is composed of various elements, the sentiment of justice can be analyzed in terms of psychological theorems that explain how these elements become inseparably associated to form a complex whole that exhibits its own distinctive properties or qualities.

To help us grasp how a reasonable individual who ultimately desires only happiness can not only understand the moral feelings of right and wrong, virtue and vice, but also be motivated to assign overriding importance to them for his conduct, Mill aims to show that these moral sentiments are complex pleasures and pains that are produced by the intellect from various ingredients, and that a peculiar qualitative superiority attaches to such moral pleasures and pains as compared with competing kinds of pleasures and pains. If this can be done, it constitutes an important step in his argument that the utilitarian standard as he understands it can be proved, keeping in mind that he is using 'a larger meaning of the word proof' such that it covers not only logically necessary conclusions derived by deductive reasoning from admittedly valid premises but also highly probable – that is, virtually certain – conclusions derived by inductive reasoning on the basis of experience. I shall return to this important claim in my conclusion, after we have considered his psychological explanation of the peculiar force of the moral sentiment of justice and injustice.

2 The idea of justice

According to Mill, the sentiment of justice grows up around a 'universal or widely spread' idea of justice. The idea is at the core of the sentiment, as it were, and so the idea requires clarification before the sentiment can be understood. Indeed, if we can determine what the idea of justice is, he says, 'we shall...have resolved also the main problem,' namely, the problem whether such an idea 'would be capable of gathering round it a sentiment of that peculiar character and intensity by virtue of the general laws of our emotional constitution, or whether the sentiment is inexplicable, and requires to be regarded as a special provision of Nature' (CW X, p. 242). He insists that the sentiment is explicable in terms of 'the general laws' of a hedonistic psychology.

Mill emphasizes that the idea of justice is very complex, with many different and competing applications. All things considered, however, it boils down to common code that distributes equal rights and correlative duties for all, guarded by a sentiment that demands punishment of those who refuse to respect others' rights.

Moreover, justice is 'the chief part, and incomparably the most sacred and binding part, of all morality' (CW X, p. 255). This idea of justice, as consisting of a social code of equal rights and duties that has supreme moral importance and thus ought to be enforced in the face of any competing considerations, does appear to be widely recognized, even if some philosophers suggest that other elements are properly added. Two points in particular deserve emphasis.

First, he suggests that the idea of justice, insofar as it demands equal rights for all, is a beautiful ideal that is latent in the inegalitarian laws and cultures of observed civil societies. In practice, most members of even our most advanced societies distort the idea of justice with mistaken notions of expediency. As a result, majorities mistakenly consider it both expedient and just to distribute and enforce unequal rights. Although we are gradually learning to condemn all such inequalities, we still tolerate some injustices under the illusion that they are expedient. A long and arduous struggle has already occurred to persuade majorities to correct some of the erroneous notions of expediency that cloud their ideas of justice. And the struggle must still go on to persuade them to correct their remaining mistakes, even if Mill seems optimistic that the corrections will eventually be made: 'and so it will be, and in part already is, with the aristocracies of colour, race, and sex' (CW X, p. 259). In any case, majorities must keep learning to correct their false notions of expediency if societies are ever to attain a genuine morality of justice, such that the same bundles of equal rights and duties are distributed and sanctioned for all persons.

A second point worth emphasizing is that, as indicated earlier, Mill does not suppose that the rules of justice must always be positive laws but instead allows that they can be authoritative social customs or common dictates of conscience. Indeed, he argues that expediency may call in some situations for the rules to be left as customs or even as mere self-imposed commands to do right. As a result, he recognizes different ways of punishing or blaming those who infringe the rules of justice, depending on the forms in which the rules are clothed: 'We do not call anything wrong, unless we mean to imply that a person ought to be punished in some way or other for doing it; if not by law, by the opinion of his fellow creatures; if not by opinion, by the reproaches of his own conscience' (CW X, p. 242). Legal sanctions may be expedient ways of delivering punishment in some situations, for instance, but not in others. In any case, he clearly uses the term 'punishment' to cover internal as well as external sanctions against wrongdoing. External sanctions include legal penalties as well as social stigma and other coercive forms of public expression of resentment such as organized boycotts and demonstrations. Internal sanctions include the pangs of guilt inflicted by one's own conscience or desire to do right, which may be weak or non-existent in some individuals (CW X, pp. 227–33).[7] I shall say a bit more about both of these points before discussing Mill's explanation of the sentiment that grows up around the idea of justice.

3 The ideal of equal rights for all

To get a handle on the idea of justice, Mill reviews 'the various modes of action and arrangements of human affairs which are classed, by universal or widely spread opinion, as just or as unjust' to discover whether 'some one common attribute or collection of attributes is always present' (CW X, p. 245). He isolates at least six popular maxims of justice, briefly stated as follows: [1] respect any person's legal rights, except when the other maxims intervene, for example, the person may have forfeited his rights or they may be assigned by bad laws; [2] respect his moral rights, even if they are not recognized by the existing laws; [3] show due reciprocity, that is, promote a distribution of goods and evils that accords with moral desert in the sense that an individual receives good if he does right but receives evil if he does wrong; [4] keep one's promises or, more generally, do not disappoint others' reasonable expectations 'raised by our own conduct, at least if we have raised those expectations knowingly and voluntarily;' [5] display impartiality or, in other words, follow procedures that treat everyone equally in accordance with standards set by the other maxims – for example, impartiality can simply mean 'giving to every one his right;' and [6] respect equality, a maxim that means very different things to different people and 'always conforms in its variations to their notion of utility' such that they think inequality is permissible if expediency requires it. The common element in these diverse maxims, he suggests, is the idea of a personal right.

Moreover, he suggests that this idea of a personal claim, which he has derived from widespread popular opinion, is the germ of a reasonable idea of justice that can withstand philosophical criticism. In his view, philosophers must agree that morality is the part of life which is distinguished by the notion of duty or obligation, 'a thing which may be exacted from a person' and failure to perform which deserves punishment; and justice is 'incomparably the most sacred and binding part' of morality which is distinguished by the notion of 'a right in some person, correlative to the moral obligation.' The other part of morality, in which personal rights are not involved, is charity or beneficence: 'No one has a moral right to our generosity or beneficence, because we are not morally bound to practice those virtues towards any given individual' (CW X, pp. 246–7).

Popular opinion has advanced to the stage, then, that justice is conceived by most in terms of social rules that impartially provide equal protection for what are supposed to be the moral rights of individuals. But up to now, Mill says, opinion has still not recognized that justice implies equality in the rights themselves. Equality and the 'nearly allied' idea of impartiality have been commonly regarded as obligatory only as instruments for implementing the other four popular maxims, he insists. Impartiality and equality are accepted as part of the meaning of 'the more general obligation of giving to everyone his right.' But this is compatible with maintaining inequality in the rights themselves. Even in advanced societies, equality of rights for all has not yet been consistently recognized as essential to the idea of justice: 'each person maintains that equality is the dictate of justice, except where he thinks that expediency requires inequality' (CW X, p. 244).[8]

Despite the fact that unequal rights are commonly embodied in social laws and conventions, Mill argues that an ideal of equal rights for all is lurking within existing social practices. Moral rights have not yet been commonly regarded as universal equal rights, he says in *The Subjection of Women*, because most people in civil societies have had, and still do have, a distorted view of morality. Civil societies have been predominantly hierarchical. Even now, with increasing social and economic equality and the rise of democracy, the effects of hierarchy persist.

He goes on to explain that civil societies in their earliest stages featured a 'morality of submission' involving 'the obligation to submit to power.' Now, with increasing equality of social conditions and the slow and gradual dissipation of the effects of hierarchy, civil societies seem to be struggling toward an authentic morality of justice. Even though most people may not feel or acknowledge this true morality for generations to come, so that an enlightened minority is left to fight in the meantime for its achievement, Mill is hopeful that civil societies will eventually achieve such an ideal morality of equal rights for all. In short, authentic moral rights are equal rights for all, distributed and sanctioned by an authoritative code of social rules.

4 Forms of social rules

According to Mill's idea of justice, the social rules that confer universal equal rights and correlative obligations may take any of several forms, including positive laws, social customs, or dictates of conscience. This point emerges fairly clearly when he turns to discussing the etymology of the word corresponding to 'just' in 'most, if not all, languages.' After recognizing that 'etymology is slight evidence of what the idea now signified is, but the very best evidence of how it sprang up,' he suggests that 'the *idée mere*, the primitive element, in the formation of the notion of justice, was conformity to law' (CW X, p. 245). But this root idea of conformity to law has undergone crucial transformations, he points out, as civil societies have advanced. First, it was gradually transformed from the idea of conformity to existing positive law into the idea of conformity to 'such laws as *ought* to exist, including such as ought to exist but do not.' As a result, positive laws themselves came to be seen as unjust, 'if supposed to be contrary to what ought to be law.' Nevertheless, 'the idea of law and of its injunctions was still predominant in the notion of justice, even when the laws actually in force ceased to be accepted as the standard of it' (CW X, p. 245).[9]

Second, the root idea evolved further into the idea of conformity to what ought to be law, even if legal sanctions must be foregone as inexpedient in comparison with other ways of punishing infringements of the law that ought to exist. An obligation of justice ought to be compelled and violations of it ought to be punished, we think, by expedient means. Expressions of disapproval by ourselves and others are seen to be more effective instruments than legal sanctions for punishing violations of moral obligations in some cases.

It is also possible to imagine that the root idea of conformity to law might eventually be transformed yet again, at an ideal stage of advancement far beyond the practices of civil societies hitherto observed, a stage in which all individuals have developed such high intellectual, moral, and aesthetic capacities that they always voluntarily satisfy their obligations to others. In such an ideal civil society, the root idea may be transformed into the idea of conformity to nothing but shared dictates of conscience since everyone is a moral agent and coercive sanctions (legal and customary) have become unnecessary. At our relatively early stage of advancement, we cannot say whether human beings will ever prove capable of such a social utopia, in which universal equal rights and correlative obligations are distributed by a public code yet enforced entirely by shared dictates of conscience.

5 The sentiment of justice

Recall that Mill says the complex idea of justice is constituted in part by a sentiment that guards the social code: the sentiment is 'a desire that punishment may be suffered by those who infringe the rule' (CW X,

p. 250). Evidently, the idea of justice includes the desire for retribution, or due retaliation, against anyone who violates another's rights.

It should not be thought that any person who understands the idea of justice will automatically have a desire for justice. An individual might understand the idea, including its sentimental component, and yet reject it as undesirable in terms of his selfish material interests. The moral individual is more reasonable than the selfish one, in Mill's view, because the pleasant feeling of the moral sentiment is superior in quality to any competing pleasures, and a rational person always prefers to maximize his happiness 'both in point of quantity and quality' (CW X, p. 214).

A fully rational individual is a moral agent who desires justice as part of his happiness and makes moral judgments by expressing his feelings that those who break the rules must be punished in some way for their wrongdoing. If he himself violates others' rights, for instance, he feels that he ought to be punished by the reproaches of his own conscience, and that others are justified in feeling resentment and retaliating against him. Similarly, if others violate his rights or those of third parties, he feels that the wrongdoers deserve to feel guilty and have no cause for complaint if they suffer external sanctions of one sort or another. Indeed, such a moral agent is willing to incur considerable costs to support legal sanctions or organized public expressions of resentment whenever they are expedient ways of delivering punishment.

Recall as well that, according to Mill, once the idea of justice has been identified, it is not especially difficult to explain how the desire for justice can grow up around the idea 'by virtue of the general laws of our emotional constitution' (CW X, p. 242). In contrast to both British sentimentalists like Hume and *a priori* rationalists like Kant, he maintains that this moral feeling is not instinctive, nor is there any mystery to its mode of production. Rather, the desire for justice is a desire to realize the idea of justice as essential to happiness: the ingredients of the sentiment can be derived by reason with reference to the idea. As I understand him, Mill maintains that the sentiment of justice is a complex desire that can be broken up into two aspects or phases, namely: a desire for social unity on terms that all reasonable individuals can accept to their collective benefit; and a desire to retaliate against anyone who intentionally, recklessly, or negligently ignores these reasonable terms and thereby wrongfully harms others. These two aspects have different origins, and each can be traced to various more elementary causal ingredients. The desire for social unity, for instance, is a complex desire to achieve a complex idea of social harmony produced by the higher mental faculties of imagination and reasoning: it is a desire for mutual cooperation in terms of a social code that distributes the particular equal rights and duties judged by competent majorities as most likely to provide the best protection for vital personal concerns that everyone is perceived to have. The desire to retaliate against those who refuse to cooperate is a complex desire that originates not in the intellect but in an animal instinct to attack whatever threatens harm to oneself or one's kin. Once this instinct is blended with the desire for social unity, it is transformed into a desire that suitable punishment ought to be inflicted on wrongdoers, but only on wrongdoers. In other words, vengeance is desirable against anyone who violates others' rights under the code, but not against anyone who merely causes some other kinds of harms.

Among the ingredients of the complex desire for justice are the feelings of pleasure, including relief from pain, that, for a hedonist like Mill, ultimately motivate it. Even a narrowly selfish rational agent feels pleasure at the thought that his vital personal concerns are protected under a social code that distributes equal rights and duties for all, for instance, provided he feels assured that others like himself will follow the rules. And he has such assurance to the extent that external sanctions are enforced against infringements of the rules. Indeed, if wrongdoers could always be detected and punished by others at virtually no cost, then there might well be no need for anything but rational self-interest to underpin a stable social system of justice.

But the costs of eradicating wrongdoing through detection and punishment by others are prohibitive. Rather, if wrongdoing is ever to be stamped out in an expedient way – a way that does not turn society into a totalitarian state in which a person's every move is monitored and scrutinized by the state – then the individual must develop a powerful desire to do right, that is, a conscience whose frustration brings him the peculiar kinds of pain involved in guilt and shame. Reasonable people with sentiments of justice can feel a higher kind of pleasure at *anyone's* (not just their own) voluntary compliance with the social rules, and they can experience a higher kind of suffering at *anyone's* infringement of the rules. Such moral agents do not need external sanctions to motivate them to do right. Their mutual cooperation under the social rules is not contingent on further calculations of material self-interest. The internal sanctions of conscience are a sufficiently powerful motivation for them. The higher quality of this pleasure of security apparently emerges as a result of a quasi-chemical reaction among the various causal ingredients, including lower kinds of pleasures, of the complex desire for justice, none of which considered alone exhibits the same quality. As mentioned earlier, Mill indicates that reasonable people who competently experience this moral pleasure judge that it is infinitely more valuable than any conflicting kinds of pleasures.

6 Talk of rights is not essential

When considering his psychological analysis of the sentiment of justice, it is important to keep in mind that Mill treats the idea of a right as a mere form in which other ingredients of the complex feeling 'clothe themselves' (CW X, p. 250) These 'ingredients in the sentiment of justice are, the desire to punish a person who has done harm, and the knowledge or belief that there is some definite individual or individuals to whom harm has been done' (CW X, p. 248). A right is a claim on other people to help secure or protect some vital personal interest of the right-holder, where violation of the claim is recognized as a kind of harm that is wrongful and thus deserving of punishment. Mill is taking for granted yet another ingredient that he thinks is found in any genuine moral sentiment, including the sentiment of justice. That ingredient is the desire for social unity, in particular, for the members of society to be treated alike under social rules 'which all rational beings might adopt *with benefit to their collective interest*' (CW X, p. 249). Equal rights are distributed and sanctioned for all by the rules so that every individual has an equal claim for protection of vital personal concerns shared by everyone.

For Mill, talk of rights can be dropped altogether in the analysis of the sentiment of justice, even if such talk remains convenient as a substitute for tedious reference to the various ingredients of the sentiment. Thus, he makes no mention of rights when summarizing his understanding of the sentiment.

In his view, the sentiment is a quasi-chemical compound in which the animal impulse to retaliate against harm is blended with, and modified by, the distinctively human desire for social unity on terms that every reasonable individual can endorse with a view to his enlightened self-interest – that is, his self-interest conceived not in narrowly materialistic terms but in terms of vital personal interests that everyone shares and that ought to be protected by equal right. The 'peculiar' force of the sentiment is produced by the animal desire, he suggests, whereas whatever is moral in the sentiment is derived from the desire for social unity. When blended together to make up the complex desire for justice, these component desires become inseparably associated with a complex kind of pleasure that is qualitatively superior to all competing kinds of pleasure.

7 Psychological analysis

According to Mill, the sentiment of justice is a complex moral desire for equal rights which is generated by a quasi-chemical reaction between the animal impulse to retaliate and the reasoned desire for social unity. Consider the animal desire to punish anyone who has done, or is threatening to do, what the animal perceives as an injury to itself or its kin. This desire seems to Mill to be 'a spontaneous outgrowth from two sentiments, both in the highest degree natural, and which either are or resemble instincts; the impulse of self-protection and the feeling of sympathy' (CW X, p. 248). Although he admits that the animal desire might not be a pure instinct but, rather, the product of intelligence to some extent, he ignores this issue because there is no question that the desire is 'common to all animal nature; for every animal tries to hurt those who have hurt, or who it thinks are about to hurt, itself or its young.' Every animal feels gratified by its 'retaliation or vengeance' in these situations, he insists, whether the gratification is correctly classified as merely a physical sensation or as a mental feeling of pleasure associated with some more or less crude idea of the object which the animal desires to punish. Even if a crude idea of the object of punishment is involved, the idea has nothing to do with a social decision to inflict punishment only in accord with general social rules. As a result, Mill agrees with Hume that the sentiment of justice does not originate in considerations of public utility. Nevertheless, the sentiment only acquires its moral character, he says, because the animal desire to punish becomes inseparably associated with an idea of utility: 'I conceive that the sentiment itself does not arise from anything which would commonly, or correctly, be termed an idea of expediency; but that though the sentiment does not, whatever is moral in it does' (CW X, p. 248).

Mill argues that the animal feeling is only a part of the sentiment of justice. The sentiment also involves a separate 'desire to be in unity with our fellow-creatures' (CW X, p. 231). Such a desire, and the associated pleasure a person takes at the idea of his attachment to some collectivity, is the product of distinctively human capacities of intellect and sympathetic imagination. As he explains:

> Human beings, on this point, only differ from other animals in two particulars. First, in being capable of sympathizing, not solely with

> their offspring, or, like some of the more noble animals, with some superior animal who is kind to them, but with all human, and even with all sentient, beings. Secondly, in having a more developed intelligence, which..., even apart from his superior range of sympathy, [renders] a human being...capable of apprehending a community of interest between himself and the human society of which he forms a part, such that any conduct which threatens the security of the society generally, is threatening to his own [security], and calls forth his instinct (if instinct it be) of self-defence. (CW X, p. 248)

Together, superiority of intelligence and enlarged sympathetic capacity enable a human being to 'attach himself to the collective idea of his tribe, his country, or mankind, in such a manner that any act hurtful to them, raises his instinct of sympathy, and urges him to resistance' (CW X, p. 248). This feeling of social attachment or desire for social unity, a product of man's superior mental capacities, is what 'moralizes' his sentiment of justice.

A person's amoral animal feeling of resentment is moralized by his 'social feeling' to act in conformity with social rules which all rational individuals might adopt to their mutual benefit. '[W]hat is moral [in the sentiment of justice] is the exclusive subordination of it to the social sympathies, so as to wait on and obey their call' (CW X, p. 249). Without the moral ingredient, the sentiment of justice would reduce to the animal feeling that 'tends to make us resent indiscriminately whatever anyone does that is disagreeable to us' as individuals. '[B]ut when moralized by the social feeling,' the sentiment of justice 'only acts in the directions conformable to the general good: just persons resenting a hurt to society though not otherwise a hurt to themselves, and not resenting a hurt to themselves, however painful, unless it be of the kind which society has a common-interest with them in the repression of' (CW X, p. 249). More specifically, just persons direct their resentment at harms that the members of society have a recognized equal right not to suffer, where the rights are established by majorities for the common good. Just persons do not resent harms to themselves which others have no recognized duties to refrain from causing. They understand that they have no rights to be protected from suffering losses in a competition conducted without force or fraud, for instance, even though such competitive harms may be intensely painful.[10] Nor do they have any rights to be protected from suffering 'mere dislike' or disgust at others' activities that otherwise do not 'directly and immediately' affect them in any perceptible way.[11]

The desire for social attachment, Mill emphasizes, is a natural feeling that is capable of providing a 'firm foundation' for any morality, including the utilitarian (CW X, p. 231). He admits that 'this feeling in most individuals is [currently] much inferior in strength to their selfish feelings, and is often wanting altogether' (CW X, p. 233). But it tends to become more powerful and intense 'as civilization goes on,' that is, as mutual cooperation grows more widespread: 'In an improving state of the human mind, the influences are constantly on the increase which tend to generate in each individual a feeling of unity with all the rest; which, if perfect, would make him never think of, or desire, any beneficial condition for himself, in the benefits of which they are not included' (CW X, p. 232). Even without artificial cultivation, this natural desire for social unity tends to gain in strength relative to the selfish feelings, he suggests, so that predominantly selfish individuals who may cooperate with each other only for prudent reasons of mutual advantage might eventually evolve into social and moral beings who feel so much sympathy for each other that each feels the others' vital personal interests as his own. If it were 'taught as a religion' and encouraged by education, he insists, there is no doubt that the feeling of unity could be made so powerful that everybody would 'feel that entireness of sympathy with all others, which would make any real discordance in the general direction of their conduct in life impossible' (CW X, p. 233). Ideally, everybody would feel that his personal happiness is inseparably associated with equal rights and duties for all: 'it will be impossible to live permanently on other terms with anybody' (CW X, p. 231).

Every member of such an ideal 'society of equals' would be a just person who knows that his fellows are also just. In this ideal context, each individual will voluntarily comply with a code of equal rights and duties even in the absence of material rewards for compliance or of external sanctions for noncompliance: his regard for others' rights is enforced by his highly developed conscience that threatens him with severe punishment in the form of overwhelming feelings of guilt for any deviation from the rules. Indeed, each person will be prepared to incur considerable personal inconvenience and material loss to inflict punishment on himself for any wrongdoing. Selfish rational agents, in contrast, will not incur personal costs to inflict punishment, but instead will free ride on the efforts of the just to punish anyone who violates others' rights.

Even though such an ideal 'society of equals' remains as yet imperfectly realized, 'the desire to be in unity... is already a powerful principle in human nature,' Mill says, and it is sufficiently powerful in some individuals to make them care for others' vital personal concerns independently of any threat of external sanctions: 'already a person in whom the social feeling is at all developed, cannot bring himself to think of the rest of his fellow creatures as struggling rivals with him for the means of happiness, whom he must desire to see defeated in their object in order that he may succeed in his' (CW X, p. 233). True, selfish feelings still remain superior in strength to the desire for social unity in most people. Most must, therefore, be duly threatened with legal penalties and organized public expressions of resentment so that they will find it in their material self-interest to pay due regard to others' rights. But these predominantly selfish individuals also can see that it is expedient for them and others to comply with a code of justice, provided that external sanctions are in place to enforce mutual cooperation. Any intelligent member of a civil society understands that his cooperation brings him material advantages if he has assurance that others will cooperate, even though he lacks the powerful desire for unity that would make him respect others' rights in the absence of external sanctions. Thus, even selfish individuals have reason to applaud the presence of just persons who firmly desire a social code of equal rights for all and are prepared to punish wrongdoers at considerable personal cost. Just individuals are needed to design, run, and maintain the political and legal institutions that construct and enforce the code. Indeed, some people must do these things willingly, without the need for external incentives, so that external sanctions can be applied against selfish agents who would otherwise infringe the rules and refuse to pay their fair share of taxes to support the institutions of justice.

The moral sentiment of justice, Mill argues, is a complex desire whose process of causation resembles a chemical reaction between the animal desire to retaliate and the distinctively human desire for social unity conceived in terms of social rules that all rational persons might adopt to their collective benefit. Any person who develops this moral sentiment reorients and channels his animal resentment in accord with social rules, including laws, customs, and shared dictates of conscience, that distribute and sanction equal rights and duties for all. The 'peculiar energy' of the sentiment results 'because there goes to the composition of the sentiment, not a rational only, but also an animal element, the thirst for retaliation; and this thirst derives its intensity, as well as its moral justification, from the extraordinarily important and impressive kind of utility which is concerned' (CW X, pp. 250–1). The higher kind of utility which is concerned is generated by the interaction of the various elements that enter into the sentiment. The animal pleasure which a person feels at indiscriminate punishment of those who do things disagreeable to him or his kin is transformed by its quasi-chemical reaction with the pleasure he takes in social unity to become an infinitely more valuable kind of pleasure, namely, the feeling of security which he associates with punishment of those who violate the recognized equal rights of others in his society. Such rights protect certain vital personal interests which most people (or their political representatives) agree are shared by all members of society and are so important that they ought to be protected by right. Punishment of wrongdoers is administered in accord with the social rules, and includes legal sanctions, public stigma, and feelings of guilt.

In short, the pleasure of the moral sentiment of justice is a higher kind of pleasure that an intelligent and sympathetic person takes in a secure existence enjoyed in common with the fellow members of his society, the group with which he identifies. As Mill affirms:

> All conduct which we class as wrong or criminal is, or we suppose it to be, an attack upon some vital interest of ourselves or of those we care for, (a category which may include the public, or the whole human race): conduct which, if allowed to be repeated, would destroy or impair the security and comfort of our lives. We are prompted to defend these paramount interests by repelling the attack, and guarding against its renewal; and our earliest experience gives us a feeling, which acts with the rapidity of an instinct, that the most direct and efficacious protection is retaliation. We are therefore prompted to retaliate by inflicting pain on the person who has inflicted or tried to inflict it upon ourselves. We endeavour, as far as possible, that our social institutions shall render us this service. We are gratified when, by that or other means, the pain is inflicted, and dissatisfied if from any cause it is not. (CW XXXI, p. 242)
>
> ... It would always give us pleasure, and chime in with our feelings of fitness, that acts which we deem unjust should be punished, though we do not always think it expedient that this should be done by the tribunals. (CW X, p. 245)

This higher pleasure of 'security [is] to everyone's feelings the most vital of all interests' (CW X, p. 251). But any person's own security in this moral sense is bound up with the equal security of his fellows. It is the security of equal rights and duties conferred on all under impartial rules.

8 Conclusion: justice and the proof of utility

To recapitulate: according to Mill, a just person possesses a powerful moral desire to respect equal rights for all. A democratic process of public reasoning enters into the very composition of this complex sentiment of justice: a just individual cannot know what justice requires of him in his society until competent majorities, after due deliberation, select a social code that distributes and sanctions the particular rights which, in their judgment, are most likely to provide maximum security for the vital personal interests shared by everyone. This complex desire is inseparably associated with, and ultimately motivated by, a higher pleasure of security. The higher pleasure is produced by a quasi-chemical reaction among the various ingredients of the sentiment. The reaction may require the ingredients to be repeatedly conjoined and thus it may take some time to unfold. But the ingredients are repeatedly experienced together by rational individuals who grow up in a civil society and observe the workings of its system of justice, even if such individuals must also imagine the system free of mistaken notions of expediency that distort the idea of equal rights for all.

The ingredients of the moral sentiment of justice include an animal instinct to retaliate against harm as well as a distinctively human 'social feeling' of being in unity with one's fellows by interacting with them under social rules that all rational members of the community can adopt for their mutual benefit. Any person becomes 'competently acquainted' with the higher pleasure of security only after he develops the intellectual and sympathetic capacities required to form the sentiment of justice and is thereby able to experience its pleasant quality. Its peculiar intrinsic value – its infinite superiority as pleasure to any competing kinds of enjoyments – is only discovered as it is experienced. Even so, a just person of confirmed moral character may not be conscious of the various ingredients of his desire for justice. He may never be aware of them, even though it can be validly inferred that they exist and that their quasi-chemical combination is what ultimately motivates his habitual respect for equal rights. He may see his moral commitment to equal rights as an irreducible end in itself, which has nothing to do with any feelings of pleasure, including relief from pain. This just person then acts *as if* his habitual disposition to do right were independent of pleasure. But the process of habit formation, whereby rights and other objects of pleasure replace pleasure itself as motives for action and thus become concrete parts of the otherwise abstract idea of happiness, is, for Mill, readily explicable in terms of the laws of association.

In light of his explanation of the connection between happiness and the sentiment of justice, Mill argues that the utilitarian theory of morals as he understands it is proved:

> It has always been evident that all cases of justice are also cases of expediency: the difference is in the peculiar sentiment which attaches to the former, as contradistinguished from the latter. If this characteristic sentiment has been sufficiently accounted for; if there is no necessity to assume for it any peculiarity of origin; if it is simply the natural feeling of resentment, moralized by being made coextensive with the demands of social good; and if this feeling not only does but ought to exist in all the classes of cases to which the idea of justice corresponds; that idea no longer presents itself as a stumbling-block to the utilitarian ethics. (CW X, p. 259)

As mentioned earlier, he makes clear that he is using the word proof with 'a larger meaning' than usual: 'It is evident that this cannot be proof in the ordinary and popular meaning of the term' (CW X, p. 206). We cannot directly prove that happiness is the sole ultimate end of morality by deducing that general conclusion from other more basic and admittedly valid premises: no such premises are available. Rather, the proof must be an indirect one: the conclusion must be an induction by simple enumeration, that is, a general proposition inferred on the basis that genuine counterexamples have never been observed in any particular cases to date. By accounting for the sentiment of justice in terms of the theorems of a hedonistic psychology, Mill believes that he has removed the only important source of potential counterexamples. In his view, the account 'resolve[s] ... the only real difficulty in the utilitarian theory of morals' and constitutes a key step in the indirect proof of utility (CW X, p. 259).

Remarkably, Mill is following Hume in enlarging the meaning of the word proof to include ways besides logical demonstration of arriving at conclusions that reason is incapable of doubting. Although his language is not always entirely clear, Hume appears to use the word proof as a synonym for certainty, and he refers to 'different kinds of Certainty' that are 'as satisfactory to the Mind, tho perhaps not so regular, as the demonstrative kind.'[12] For example, he uses 'intuitive proof' to refer to our certainty of the contents of our own sensations and passions: a proposition stating that we are experiencing a sensation of red or an impression of vice when we are in fact experiencing them is not doubted by the rational faculty and is regarded by it as intuitively proved. He also uses the term proof to refer to our certainty of the universal relation of cause and effect: the proposition that every phenomenon has a cause is not doubted by reason because, according to Hume, an overwhelming natural belief in the proposition is created in us by imagination and custom after our repeated experience of the constant and invariable sequences of particular causes and effects. Reason does not itself produce the belief, which is produced instead by our merely imagining an idea of causal necessity that is subsequently enlivened by the power of habit into a strong impression or feeling of causal necessity despite the fact that we never really perceive such a necessary relation. Yet reason accepts the belief and regards the law of universal causation as proved. Thus, as Hume says, he uses the term 'proofs' to include 'those arguments, which are deriv'd from the relation of cause and effect, and which are entirely free from doubt and uncertainty' ([1739/40] 1978, p. 124).

Mill follows Hume in expanding the meaning of the word proof. But he rejects Hume's psychological account of our robust belief in universal causation as well as Hume's moral intuitionism. Whereas Hume seems to think that we are instinctively inclined to believe in universal causation in the sense that imagination and habit together automatically lead us to adopt such a belief without the need for reasoning, Mill argues that the belief in universal causation is not formed in this way but instead is one of the last conclusions a reasonable person reaches, being an induction by simple enumeration based on the widest possible experience. This induction does not depend on any idea or feeling of causal necessity but instead merely reflects the fact that inexplicable counterexamples to the relation of cause and effect have never yet been observed across the widest possible range of experience to date.

And, whereas Hume insists that moral sentiments are simple instinctive feelings of virtue and vice that are a peculiar kind of pleasures and pains, Mill argues that the sentiment of justice is neither simple nor instinctive but instead is a complex desire constructed by the rational faculty and ultimately motivated by a higher kind of pleasure including relief from pain. Again, Mill thinks that a rational belief in the principle of utility is justified by a complete induction by simple enumeration, one based on the widest possible experience to date. In his view, there are no plausible counterexamples to the hypothesis that 'human nature is so constituted as to desire nothing which is not either a part of happiness or a means of happiness' (CW X, p. 237). As a result, the greatest happiness principle has the only proof it needs or can possibly have. All reasonable desires, including moral desires, reflect judgments that the object desired is pleasant – either a source of happiness or a concrete part of happiness insofar as what was once only a source has replaced pleasure itself in our consciousness. But thinking of an object as pleasant is the same thing as thinking of it as desirable.

Notes

1. According to Mill, 'human nature is so constituted as to desire nothing which is not either a part of happiness or a means of happiness,' where 'by "happiness" is intended pleasure, and the absence of pain' (CW X, p. 210).
2. Emphasis added.
3. Riley (unpublished working paper).
4. Riley (2010).
5. Recall that pleasure is defined to include relief from pain, that is, security from pain. The higher kind of moral pleasure which I am identifying as the pleasant feeling of 'security' can also be depicted as a feeling of relief or security from a higher kind of pain or harm that is classified as immoral or unjust.
6. See Hartley ([1749] 2010), James Mill ([1822] 1869), Bain ([1855] 1868), Bain ([1859] 1875), and J.S. Mill (CW VIII, pp. 842–83 and 852–60). See also J.S. Mill's 'Bain's Psychology' (CW XI; pp. 339–74) and 'James Mill's *Analysis*' (CW XXXI, pp. 93–253).
7. For further discussion of Mill's conception of punishment and its implications for his moral theory, see Riley (2009, pp. 93–9).
8. See also Mill (CW X, pp. 258–9).
9. For further discussion of this transformation, see Mill, 'Austin on Jurisprudence' (CW XXI, esp. pp. 182–8).
10. Mill argues that rights to be protected from fair competitive losses do not promote the common happiness. See Mill's *On Liberty* (CW XVIII, pp. 292–3).
11. This is a central implication of Mill's doctrine of individual liberty as outlined in *On Liberty*. See Riley (1998).
12. Hume makes these remarks in a 1754 letter addressed to John Stewart, quoted by Kemp Smith ([1941] 2005, p. 409).

References

Bain, Alexander ([1855] 1868) *The Senses and the Intellect*, 3rd ed. (London: Longmans and Green).

Bain, Alexander ([1859] 1875) *The Emotions and the Will*, 3rd ed. (London: Longmans and Green).

Hartley, David ([1749] 2010) *Observations on Man, His Frame, His Duty, and His Expectations* (London: British Library Reprint).

Hume, David ([1739/1740] 1978) *A Treatise of Human Nature*, 2nd ed., L.A. Selby-Bigge (ed.), with text revised and notes by P.H. Nidditch (Oxford: Clarendon Press.

Kemp Smith, Norman ([1941] 2005) *The Philosophy of David Hume*, intr. Don Garrett (Basingstoke: Palgrave Macmillan).
Mill, James ([1822] 1869) *Analysis of the Phenomena of the Human Mind*, 2nd ed., J.S. Mill (ed.) with added critical notes by Alexander Bain, Andrew Findlater, and George Grote (London: Longmans, Green, Reader & Dyer).
Riley, Jonathan (1998) *Mill on Liberty* (London: Routledge).
Riley, Jonathan (2009) 'Mill's Extraordinary Utilitarian Moral Theory,' *Politics, Philosophy, and Economics* 9(1), 67–116.
Riley, Jonathan (2010) 'Justice as Higher Pleasure,' *J.S. Mill: Thought and Influence: A Bicentennial Reappraisal*, P.J. Kelly and G. Varouxakis (eds) (London: Routledge).
Riley, Jonathan (unpublished working paper) 'Higher Pleasures and Rational Agency.'
Robson, J.M. (ed.) (1969) *The Collected Works of John Stuart Mill: Essays on Ethics, Religion, and Society*, Vol. X (Toronto: University of Toronto Press).
Robson, J.M. (ed.) (1974b) *The Collected Works of John Stuart Mill: A System of Logic Ratiocinative and Inductive Part 2*, Vol. VIII (Toronto: University of Toronto Press).
Robson, J.M. (ed.) (1977) *The Collected Works of John Stuart Mill: Essays on Politics and Society Part 1*, Vol. XVIII (Toronto: University of Toronto Press).
Robson, J.M. (ed.) (1978) *The Collected Works of John Stuart Mill: Essays on Philosophy and the Classics*, Vol. XI (Toronto: University of Toronto Press).
Robson, J.M. (ed.) (1989) *The Collected Works of John Stuart Mill: Miscellaneous Writings*, Vol. XXXI (Toronto: University of Toronto Press).

8
Justice for Barbarians

Chin Liew Ten

In his essay *On Liberty*, Mill famously argued for a restriction in the type of reasons that may be invoked in order to justify coercive social or legal intervention with the conduct of individuals: 'That the only purpose for which power can be rightfully exercised over any member of a civilized community, against his will, is to prevent harm to others' (CW XVIII, p. 223). He immediately specifies the scope of his view by maintaining that 'this doctrine is meant to apply only to human beings in the maturity of their faculties,' and not to children or 'young persons below the age which the law may fix as that of manhood or womanhood' (CW XVIII, p. 224). He further excludes, for the same reason, the application of the doctrine from 'those backward states of society in which the race itself may be considered in its nonage' (CW XVIII, p. 224).

How exactly are backward states of society like children? Since Mill is comparing such *states of society* with children, the relevant comparison is not between the capacities of *individuals* in those states and children as individuals. Within the same society, there could, of course, be individuals with different capacities and at different stages of development. That Mill was focusing on the state of society is confirmed by his remark: 'The early difficulties in the way of spontaneous progress are so great that there is seldom any choice of means for overcoming; and a ruler full of the spirit of improvement is warranted in the use of any expedients that will attain an end, perhaps otherwise unattainable. Despotism is a legitimate mode of government in dealing with barbarians, provided the end be their improvement, and the means justified by actually effecting that end' (CW XVIII, p. 224). Here he is alluding to certain social conditions which make progress very difficult, and which might require despotism, rather than liberty, to bring it about. 'Barbarism' would then be a reference to such a state of society, and 'barbarians' a reference to all those, whatever their different individual capacities might be, who live in such a society.

However, it is true that Mill does not always confine the use of 'barbarous' and 'barbarian' to this sense. As we shall see, he sometimes refers to highly undesirable practices, such as female infanticide, human sacrifices, and slavery, as barbarous. There is thus a sense in which those who engage in such practices are barbarians. But the central sense of barbarism relevant to our discussion is its application to a state of society, and a failure to see this is likely to lead to serious misunderstandings of Mill.

As D.G. Brown (1999, p. 83) has rightly noted, for Mill, 'Barbarism is a state of society, however pernicious its effect on the character of individuals, and no one who has lived in our century can deny that a society of mature, responsible, cultivated individuals can be barbarous.' Brown also points out that Mill is not talking about the personal qualities of, for example, the people in India or other non-European societies, but of 'the intractability of a political and social condition.' Brown (1999, p. 84) notes that, for Mill, 'Barbarous and semi-barbarous societies are those marked by oppression, injustice, and violence.'

We will get a more detailed account of the relevant political and social conditions which leave societies in barbarous or semibarbarous states when we consider Mill's discussion of related issues, beginning with his views in *Representative Government* on 'the government of dependencies by a free state' (CW XIX, pp. 562–77). These dependencies are acquired either through conquest or by colonization. Mill distinguishes those dependencies, like America and Australia, which are at the same level of civilization as the ruling country, and those, like India, which, according to him, are not. In the former cases, there should be 'the fullest measure of internal self-government' (CW XIX, p. 563). However, in the latter cases, the dependencies are not yet ready for representative government, and have to be governed by the ruling country, or by persons delegated by the ruling country. Such an arrangement is acceptable if it facilitates the transition of the subject people from their current stage of development to a higher stage (CW XIX, p. 567).

Under certain conditions, despotism might be the best arrangement for the improvement of society. But a native despotism is unlikely to succeed. On the other hand, a despot from a more civilized and free people might be able to produce the beneficial effect. The choice of government for a dependency may well be one between different despotisms. The despotism of those who lack knowledge of their subjects is likely to be worse than that of those with such knowledge. It is difficult for foreigners to govern a country well. They 'do not feel with the people,' and lack much relevant knowledge available to natives (CW XIX, p. 568).

Mill was particularly sensitive to foreigners imposing their religion or way of life on the natives. In the case of English rule in India, he observes that the English are most likely to interfere with the work of their delegates in two areas. The first is 'to force English ideas down the throats of the natives' (CW XIX, p. 570). He includes among such undesirable activities 'measures of proselytism, or acts intentionally or unintentionally offensive to the religious feelings of the people' (CW XIX, p. 570). He relates these activities to the general demand in England to have the Bible taught in Government schools if students or their parents request it. The demand might seem just and fair from a European perspective, but it would be viewed differently through 'Asiatic eyes' (CW XIX, p. 570). Asians attribute improper motivations to governments that license their officials to do certain things. Even if Government schools taught Christianity only to those who willingly sought it, Hindu parents in India would believe that their children were being unjustly converted to Christianity. Only a total failure on the part of the schools to convert any child would convince them to the contrary.

A second area in which the policies in English colonies are likely to be influenced by the opinions of those in England is when the interests of English settlers are affected. English settlers in India, who have friends at home with whom they share a common language and common ideas, have 'the ear of the public at home' (CW XIX, p. 571). But the Government at home is often more enlightened than the settlers, who seek to promote their own interests at the expense of the natives, whom they treat with 'the scornful overbearingness of the conquering nation,' and as 'mere dirt under their feet' (CW , XIX, p. 571).

Even when the attention of the English public is focused on being just and philanthropic to the subject community, it is the interests of the powerful individuals or groups which are the objects of focus, rather than the plight of the weak and oppressed. Thus it is that privileged landlords have no difficulty in getting their interests advanced as against those of the people from whom they extort.

Given the limitations of rule by foreigners, Mill puts a case for indirect rule of a country like India. Direct rule of a dissimilar people by a branch of the home country's executive will almost certainly fail. It is best to govern through a comparatively permanent delegated body. This, of course, was how India was ruled through the East India Company, for whom Mill worked for many years until its dissolution in

1858. *Representative Government* was published in 1861, and no doubt drew heavily from Mill's experiences in the Company, whose abolition he regarded as a 'shortsighted policy' for which 'both India and England will pay a severe penalty' (CW XIX, p. 573).

But Mill does not believe that indirect rule of a dependency by a delegated body will necessarily ensure good government. Indeed, in the prevailing circumstances, good government, which requires an identity of interests between the rulers and the governed, is not possible. What we have is only 'a choice of imperfections' (CW XIX, p. 573). A delegated administration has the advantage of concentrating on the promotion of the interests of the governed. It is insulated from the pressures and influences to which the home government and Parliament at home are subjected. Except for the appointment to the highest office in the dependency, the Viceroy of British India, all the delegated administrators should be experienced professionals who have learned their business in the dependency by working through the lower ranks, with promotion obtained through competence rather than by seniority.

In 'A Few Words on Non-Intervention,' Mill also discusses the conditions under which one country is justified in interfering with the affairs of another country. The scope of the discussion is broader than foreign rule of a dependency. It also includes intervention in quarrels between two foreign states, or in civil wars, or in order to procure mild treatment for the vanquished, or to stop some major harm like the slave trade. Mill argues that, while interference in self-defense is justified, it is unacceptable to interfere simply to promote our own country's commercial and other interests. This means that it would be wrong for one nation to prevent all other nations from receiving some great advantage, even at its own expense. But such a conflict between the interests of one nation and the interests of the rest of humanity is, in practice, unlikely.

Of interest is Mill's view of whether a nation is justified in going to war 'for an idea.' He is strongly opposed to it. 'To go to war for an idea, if the war is aggressive, not defensive, is as criminal as to go to war for territory or revenue; for it is as little justifiable to force our ideas on other people, as to compel them to submit to our will in any other respect' (CW XIX, p. 118).

Mill distinguishes between the rules of international morality, which applies between two civilized nations, and the different rules which apply between civilized nations and barbarians. Among the most important differences is the inability of barbarians to reciprocate, and thereby to conform to a fundamental rule of international morality. It is also the case that barbarous nations will have their development impeded by the independence and nationality which are essential conditions for the growth and development of already civilized nations. Barbarous nations would benefit from being subjected to foreigners from civilized nations. Mill goes on to assert: 'barbarians have no rights as a *nation*, except a right to such treatment as may, at the earliest possible period, fit them for becoming one. The only moral laws for the relation between a civilized and barbarous government are the rules between man and man' (CW XXI, p. 119).

Mill makes an important point here about how barbarous societies are to be treated. In denying them any right as a nation, he is presumably claiming that they do not have the right to rule themselves, and that appropriate foreign rule would be justified. But Mill sometimes refers to individuals as barbarians. As noted earlier, this is in the derivative sense that they are members of barbarous nations. We would therefore expect barbarians individually to be at different levels of intellectual and moral development, just as different members of the same civilized society vary in their levels of development. For example, in his campaign to be elected a Member of Parliament, Mill was challenged as to whether he had said that 'the lower classes, though mostly habitual liars, are ashamed of lying.' Mill's affirmative answer was applauded by the largely working-class audience. This confirmed Mill in his view that, even though members of the working class were not then at a high level of intellectual or moral development, they had the capacity to improve themselves (Ten, 1998, p. 372).

Mill was worried that Parliament in his (civilized) country would be dominated by 'a low grade of intelligence,' and that the 'instructed minority' with 'superior intellects and character' would be completely swamped (Ten, 1998, pp. 379–80). He advocated a system of plural votes in order to increase the influence of the superior intellects. They would be given two or more votes, while others would receive only one. This proposal gives the superior intellects an influence greater than their numerical strength, but Mill also wants to ensure that their voting strength is not so great as to be capable of outvoting the numerically larger group of people with only one vote each. Mill also suggested other measures, especially a form of proportional representation, that would not only increase the influence of cultivated minds, but also increase the range and diversity of views to be discussed in Parliament (Ten, 1998, pp. 381–2).

Cultivated minds are not for Mill the monopoly of civilized nations, any more than people of 'a low grade of intelligence' are the monopoly of barbarous or semibarbarous nations. Lynn Zastoupil has drawn attention to a remark Mill made in a letter to Charles W. Dilke of February 9, 1869, in which he chided Dilke for referring to the Bengalis as 'mere savages,' pointing out that some of them 'are the most cultivated of all the Hindoos' (Zastoupil, 1994, p. 164; CW XVII, pp. 1,560–2). Again, in a letter to Mrs Charlotte Spier Manning of January 14, 1870, Mill responded to her request for information about 'the administrative capacity shown by so many ladies of ruling families in India & especially whether these ladies are Hindoos or Mohomedans' (CW XVII, p. 1687). He explained why they were almost all 'Hindoos,' but pointed out that one of 'the most remarkable of these ladies,' Sekunder Begum of Bhopal, was a Mahomedan (CW XVII, p. 1,687). She was the only child of the ruler of the country, and, on his death, custom prevented her from inheriting the position of ruler, but allowed her to transfer it to her husband. However, she was so much 'the stronger mind,' and very popular, that the people obeyed her instead of her husband. After his death, she was allowed to govern the country. Mill adds, 'She was a most energetic, prudent, and just ruler, and her daughter who has now succeeded her, and who has been carefully trained by her to public business, is expected to tread in her footsteps. Her own mother too was a remarkable woman' (CW XVII, p. 1,687).

So nations, whether civilized or barbarian, have individuals with different mental capacities and characteristics. But, even so, one would expect that, from Mill's perspective, individuals belonging to the same nation at a particular stage of its development would tend to share some similar characteristics, different from those of the members of another nation at a different stage of development. In fact, Mill refers to national characters and national cultures which form the basis of some generalizations he makes. Thus he writes: 'an essentially *subjective* people like the Germans, and an essentially *objective* people like those of Northern and Central Italy, the one affectionate and dreamy, and the other passionate and worldly, the one trustful and loyal, and the other calculating and suspicious, the one not practical enough, the other overmuch; the one wanting individuality, the other fellow-feeling, the one failing for want of exacting enough for itself, the other for want of conceding enough to others' (CW X, p. 105; Robson, 1998, p. 354).

However, such differences in national character and culture are not the products of 'inherent natural differences:' 'Of all the vulgar modes of escaping from the effect of social and moral influences on the human mind, the most vulgar is that of attributing the diversities of conduct and character to inherent natural differences. What race would not be indolent and insouciant when things are so arranged, that they derive no advantage from forethought and exertion?' (CW II, p. 319; Robson, 1998, p. 358).

So, if one nation is to be justified in ruling another nation, it is not in virtue of the former being inherently superior. Mill argues consistently and passionately against the idea that some races were inherently and naturally superior to others. Thus, in 'The Negro Question,' he responded to Carlyle's racist comments published the previous year in *Fraser's Magazine*. Carlyle's derogatory remarks were directed at black ex-slaves in the West Indies, many of whom had abandoned the British-owned sugar plantations for their own farms which Carlyle called 'pumpkin farms.' Carlyle believed that Negroes should be servants of the whites, who were born wiser than they. Mill responds by interpreting him as claiming that whites are 'born more capable of wisdom' than Negroes (CW XXI, p. 92). Mill calls this proposition 'the vulgar error of imputing every difference which he finds among human beings to an original difference of Nature' (CW XXI, p. 93). He likens Carlyle's claim to the view that two trees coming from the same stock must be of the same height unless there is some difference in the original seedling. But differences can be the product of differences in the soil, the climate, and various other external influences. 'Human beings are subject to an infinitely greater variety of accidents and external influences than trees, and have infinitely more operation in impairing the growth of one another; since those who begin strongest, have almost always hitherto used their strength to keep others weak' (CW XXI, p. 93).

Mill further argues that spontaneous improvement 'beyond a very low grade,' from internal sources, and without help from others, is a very rare phenomenon. It is the result of 'an extraordinary combination of advantages' and 'many accidents.' The fact that Negroes are not one of these rare cases of improvement does not show that they lack the capacity for improvement. Indeed, the earliest known civilization seem to be a Negro civilization. From the evidence of their sculptures, we can infer that the original Egyptians were a Negro race. So it was from Negroes that 'the Greeks learned their first lessons in civilization; and to the records and traditions of these Negroes did the Greek philosophers to the very end of their careers resort (I do not say with much fruit) as a treasury of mysterious wisdom' (CW XXI, p. 93).

But Mill maintains that, even if the facts were otherwise, and the whites were in fact born superior in intelligence to the blacks, this would not justify the former subduing the latter by force and making them work for the benefit of the whites. Slave emancipation is a great victory which should not be reversed.

In the letter to Dilke of February 9, 1869, Mill gently criticizes him for writing as if race and climate were the only sources of national character. Mill continues: 'But as you show, in many parts of your book, a strong sense of the good and bad influences of education, legislation, and social circumstances, the only inference I draw is that you do not, perhaps, go so far as I do myself in believing these last causes to be of prodigiously greater efficacy than either race or climate or the two combined' (CW XVII, p. 1,563).

Mill's antiracism and his concern that blacks be treated justly were again shown in his reaction to the conduct of Governor Eyre of Jamaica in suppressing an uprising in Morant Bay in October 1865. About 400 blacks marched on the courthouse, beating to death a magistrate and a few of his associates. Governor Eyre declared martial law, and, although the uprising was suppressed in about a week, martial law remained in force for several more weeks. During this period 439 Jamaicans were killed, 600 flogged, and a thousand dwellings burnt, while the government troops suffered no casualties. Those executed included a popular mulatto politician, George William Gordon, who was an outspoken critic of Governor Eyre. Gordon was convicted of high treason, and sentenced to be hanged by 'a dubiously constituted and managed court' (Kinzer et al., 1992, p. 185).

When news of the events in Jamaica reached London, a Jamaica Committee was formed to seek justice. Mill, who had been elected a Liberal Member of Parliament in 1865, was away at Avignon, and he joined the Committee from there. Subsequently, the Jamaica Committee discussed the possibility of pressing for the prosecution of Eyre for the murder of Gordon. The Chairman of the Committee was against the prosecution, and relinquished the chairmanship when he could not persuade the majority of the executive committee to adopt his position. At a subsequent meeting, Mill was elected the new Chairman.

Both in Parliament and through the relentless activities of the Jamaica Committee outside Parliament, Mill pursued the matter of seeking legal proceedings against those who had committed unlawful acts in Jamaica. But the Jamaica Committee's campaign against Eyre provoked his supporters to form The Eyre Defense and Aid Fund Committee in 1866 (Kinzer et al., 1992, p. 206). Among the members of the Eyre Committee was Thomas Carlyle. The Jamaica Committee was unsuccessful in its actions against Eyre, and it dissolved in July 1868. In a 'Statement of the Jamaica Committee' issued at the time and signed by Mill and two others, the Committee stated its three aims in rather broad terms, and claimed success for two of them (Kinzer et al., 1992, pp. 211–12).

The aims were 'to obtain a judicial inquiry into the conduct of Mr Eyre and his subordinates; to settle the law in the interest of justice, liberty and humanity; and to arouse public morality against oppression generally, and particularly against the oppression of subject and dependent races' (Kinzer et al., 1992, p. 211). The Committee conceded that it failed to achieve its first aim.

The formulation of the third aim in terms of a fight against 'the oppression of subject and dependent races' brings it close to one of Mill's deepest and most enduring interests, and it explains the intensity and relentless dedication with which he tried to bring Eyre to justice. He was aware that he had taken up an unpopular cause. In his *Autobiography*, he mentions his receipt of 'abusive letters' which 'graduated from coarse jokes, verbal and pictorial, up to threats of assassination' (CW I, p. 282). His campaign against Eyre probably cost him the loss of his parliamentary seat when he stood for reelection in 1868. He was made fun of, and a magazine referred to him as 'Mill who's such nuts upon niggers' (Reeves, 2007, p. 381).

Kinzer et al. observe that it was Mill's commitment to the rule of law which is the nucleus of his case against Eyre. They refer to a letter Mill wrote to Urquhart on October 4, 1866, in which he said: 'you see that I am not on this occasion standing up for the Negroes, or for liberty, deeply as both are interested in the subject – but for the first necessity of human society, law' (Kinzer et al., 1992, p. 214; CW XVI, p. 1205).

They also point out how Mill was reminded by the events in Jamaica of the Indian Mutiny. In the same letter, Mill notes, 'my eyes were first opened to the moral condition of the English nation (I except in these matters the working classes) by the atrocities perpetrated in the Indian Mutiny and the feelings which supported them at home' (Kinzer et al., 1992, p. 216, CW XVI, p. 216). The Indian Mutiny took place in northern India in May 1857, when Mill held the top position of Examiner in the East India Company, to which he had been promoted only a year ago. The Mutiny was triggered off by the Sepoys of the Bengal Army refusing to use cartridges for their new rifles because the cartridges had been greased with fat from animals forbidden by their religious dietary laws (Wilson, 2003, pp. 201–2). Each cartridge had to be bitten off before it was loaded into the gun. The Hindus were alarmed by beef fat in their mouths, and the Muslims by pork fat. False rumors had been spread that the British were trying to make Hindus eat beef fat in order to make them Christians. In fact, the use of forbidden fats was a mistake, which the East India Company corrected as soon as it was noticed, with strict orders that the grease used should be a mixture of sheep fat and beeswax (Wilson, 2003, p. 202). The revolt spread, although large parts of the country remained unaffected. Fighting continued for over a year, until the revolt was finally crushed, sometimes ruthlessly.

Mill was disturbed by the negative attitudes towards Indians which developed as a reaction to the Mutiny. We have seen his reference to the feelings of those in the home country who supported the atrocities committed by the British in India. A.N. Wilson refers to a leader-article in *The Illustrated London News* that sums up the reactions of most of the British to the suppression of the Mutiny: 'At home the same feeling is prevalent.... men the most peaceful... burn with an irrepressible desire to punish the murderers of women and children and wreak avenging justice upon the traitors and cowards who have done us this wrong' (Wilson, 2003, p. 218).

Wilson also drew attention to the cruel and violent racism of some of the British officers and soldiers in India during the Mutiny: 'Sewing Muslims into pigskins, or smearing them with pork fat before execution, was another torture favored by the British.... Officers boasted that they had "spared no one", or that "peppering away at niggers" was a pastime which they "enjoyed amazingly"' (Wilson, 2003, p. 214). Lynn Zastoupil comments: 'Also noticeable in British India after 1858 was an upsurge in violent passions and racist sentiments among British officials and soldiers, who saw in the bloodshed of 1857-58 evidence of ungrateful barbarism in the Indian population' (Zastoupil, 1994, p. 163).

Zastoupil notes that Mill was worried about 'the growing racism and general lack of respect for India in post-Mutiny British administrators' (Zastoupil, 1994, p. 163). Mill addresses these issues in his private letters, including a letter to Charlotte Speir Manning of January 14, 1870, in which he commends her purpose in writing her book, 'that of inspiring greater respect for the people of India in the minds of those who are appointed to govern them' (CW XVII, p. 1686). He also praises her for 'putting within reach of the English public' specimens of 'the thoughts and intellectual productions of the Hindoos,' adding that 'Opinions will differ as to the merits of these productions, & of the state of civilization which they indicate; but they are authentic & interesting product of the human mind; and they deserve to be known' (CW XVII, p. 1,687).

The Indian Mutiny hastened the abolition of the East India Company in 1858, and its replacement by direct rule of India from Westminster, 'by the second and third class of English parliamentary politician,' as Mill puts it in his *Autobiography* (CW I, p. 249). Mill retired. He had fought hard but unsuccessfully for the Company's continuance. He wrote 'The Petition of the East-India Company,' which was presented to

Parliament. This defended the Company's administration of India. He mentions specifically the Company's abstaining 'from all interferences with any of the religious practices of the people of India, except such as are abhorrent to humanity' (CW XXX, p. 81). He observes that the success of this policy was demonstrated by the fact that in the Mutiny, 'said to have been caused by unfounded apprehensions of danger to religion, the heads of the native states, and the masses of the population, have remained faithful to the British Government' (CW XXX, p. 81). He also refers to 'the demonstrations of indiscriminate animosity towards the natives of India, on the part of our country men in India and at home, which have grown up since the late unhappy events' (CW XXX, pp. 81–2). These sentiments are 'fundamentally unjust,' and there would be a loss of confidence by the Indians in the intentions of their rulers if it were thought that the changes in the administration of India were influenced by these sentiments.

Mill also attacks the view that India is to be administered for the special benefit of the English settlers there. This view, though widely held, goes against the practice that acknowledges 'no such distinction as that of a dominant and a subject race; but has held that its first duty was to the people of India' (CW XXX, p. 82).

In 'Memorandum of the Improvements in the Administration of India during the Last Thirty Years,' Mill lists the improvements the Company had made in India. These include improvements in revenue and judicial administration. He also refers to actions taken against 'barbarous usages' or practices of the natives. Among these practices are female infanticide, human sacrifices, and slavery. He also refers to 'the disorder and confusion' in most of the native states before their connection with the British Government (CW XXX, p. 151). States with military strength attacked their weaker neighbors, and 'hordes of undisciplined adventurers' invaded various parts of India. But now the native states are as safe as the British dominions. Disputes are adjudicated in an impartial and fair manner. Offenses against the general peace of the country are tried in criminal courts, which Mill regards as 'a powerful agent of civilization' (CW XXX, p. 152). Mill also gives details of some of the measures 'for raising and civilizing the oppressed races' (CW XXX, p. 153). The reference is to certain hill tribes that Mill claims were treated like 'wild beasts' by the native Governments. The tribes had become robbers, destroying the security of the neighboring plains. The Company's officers managed to enter their ranks and gain their confidence. Through explanation and persuasion, the robber tribes were induced to become peaceful cultivators. They received land, tools, and money to enable them to become successful cultivators. In one case, irrigation works were also carried out to help them. Some of the robbers became peacekeepers under British officers.

We have tracked Mill's views on barbarian societies in the different contexts in which he expressed them: theoretical, practical, and personal. There is now a clearer and fuller basis for what he regarded as legitimate foreign interference with what is going on in such societies. We are considering cases in which the issue is not one of self-defense against aggressive conduct. Despotic arbitrariness and the absence of the rule of law are features of barbarian societies. There is uncontrollable violence and robbery, as well as various harmful and unjust practices inflicted particularly on weak and vulnerable groups. Moreover, the societies are unable to change from within, and so external intervention has to be considered. The justification for external intervention is not any inherent incapacity on the part of the natives to change. Rather, it is because the prevailing local circumstances are such as to rule out internal change, whereas foreigners, who are not inherently superior, come from societies with more propitious conditions. But foreign intervention must be directed at the removal of harm, and to bringing about changes that will lift the society to a higher stage of development. It is the interests of the natives that should drive policy. As Tunick has argued, 'The imperialism Mill defends is not self-aggrandizing but reluctant. Intervention in the affairs of others is done not for commercial advantage, but for moral purposes, such as to end slavery, reconcile belligerents, end civil wars, or intercede for mild treatment of the vanquished' (Tunick, 2006, pp. 591–2).

There is no scope for the kind of missionary work involving the suppression of nonharmful native ways of life, and their conversion to what are regarded as superior ways of life, whether these be religious or more broadly cultural. To force barbarian natives to accept an alien way of life may not, in Mill's terms, affect their rights as a nation. But it certainly violates 'the universal rules of morality between man and man.' In some cases, the natives' way of life could be part of a widely shared culture. Where there is no harm to others, Mill is particularly sensitive to allowing people, civilized or barbarian, to lead lives of their own choices without interference from others. Indeed, even when the foreign power is legitimately seeking to eliminate or decrease violence and harmful native practices, due regard should be paid to established customs, not least because this would affect both the human cost and the effectiveness of the necessary and desirable changes.

Similarly, when Mill says that 'Despotism is a legitimate mode of government for dealing with barbarians,' this should not be taken to mean *any* form of despotism. As we have seen, arbitrary despotism is precisely one of the undesirable and static features of a barbarian society. To replace one form of despotism with another similar form is to entrench the society in its current and undesirable form of barbarism, when the justification for intervention is to move the society forward. So the legitimate mode of despotism should be one that introduces into the society, perhaps in an incremental manner, elements of the rule of law, and prepares the way for its own eventual demise when the society becomes civilized. Tunick makes the perceptive point that 'The despotism Mill defends imposes a regime of legal rights that enforces toleration; it does not deny subjects their rights, or support their enslavement or arbitrary punishment, or require their assimilation' (Tunick, 2006, p. 599). Reforms in social and economic arrangements are also, for Mill, important sources of improvement. For example, people who own the agricultural land on which they work are likely to have greater incentives to produce more than those who work for landlords.

The theoretical foundations of Mill's attitude to barbarian societies are quite coherent, and he applied his views honestly and in light of the facts as he saw them. Indeed, he fought bravely to remain faithful his own high ideals of helping the weak and vulnerable, without regard to his own self-interest. This is an ideal both for individuals and for governments when they intervene in the affairs of other countries. He fought against the deep and growing racial prejudices of his compatriots, which were unleashed or heightened by any conflict, or perceived conflict, between their own interests and those of natives.

But did he get it right about the actual situations in societies he regarded as barbarous? Was he right in thinking that his own high-minded motivations for seeking the improvement and advancement of barbarian societies were, or could be, shared by enough of his compatriots? Was he also right in thinking that imperial rule would be more just, and more successful in advancing barbarian societies, than the possible alternative of slow internal change? He absorbed at a very early age his father's negative views about India. No doubt, as he worked in the East India Company, some of these views changed in the light of new knowledge, experiences, and intellectual perspectives. But he never visited India. In his factual assessments of conditions in the country, did he remain to a significant extent the prisoner of some of his father's convictions? These issues can be debated. But, in his own time, he was widely regarded, and derided, as a friend and champion of the blacks.

Certainly, compared with many of his contemporaries, he stood out as a moral and intellectual giant.

References

Brown, D.G. (1999) 'Millian Liberalism and Colonial Oppression,' in *Civilization and Oppression*, C. Wilson (ed.) (Calgary: University of Calgary Press).

Kinzer, B., Robson, A.P., and Robson, J. (1992) *A Moralist In and Out of Parliament: John Stuart Mill at Westminster, 1865–1868* (Toronto: Toronto University Press).

Metcalf, T.R. (1994) *The New Cambridge History of India, Part III.4: Ideologies of the Raj* (Cambridge: Cambridge University Press).

Mineka, F.E. and Lindley, D.N. (1972) *The Collected Works of John Stuart Mill: The Later Letters of John Stuart Mill, 1849–1873 Part 4*, Vol. XVII (Toronto: University of Toronto Press).

Reeves, R. (2007) *John Stuart Mill: Victorian Firebrand* (London: Atlantic Books).

Robson, J.M. (ed.) (1969) *The Collected Works of John Stuart Mill: Essays on Ethics, Religion, and Society*, Vol. X (Toronto: University of Toronto Press).

Robson, J.M. (ed.) (1977a) *The Collected Works of John Stuart Mill: Essays on Politics and Society Part 1*, Vol. XVIII (Toronto: University of Toronto Press).

Robson, J.M. (ed.) (1977b) *The Collected Works of John Stuart Mill: Essays on Politics and Society Part 2*, Vol. XIX (Toronto: University of Toronto Press).

Robson, J.M. (ed.) (1984) *The Collected Works of John Stuart Mill: Essays on Equality, Law, and Education*, Vol. XXI (Toronto: University of Toronto Press).

Robson, J.M. (ed.) (1990) *The Collected Works of John Stuart Mill: Writings on India*, Vol. XXX (Toronto: University of Toronto Press).

Robson, J.M. (1998) 'Civilization and Culture as Moral Concepts,' in *The Cambridge Companion to Mill*, J. Skorupski (ed.) (Cambridge: Cambridge University Press).

Robson, J.M. and Stillinger, J. (eds.) (1981) *The Collected Works of John Stuart Mill: Autobiography and Literary Essays*, Vol. I (Toronto: University of Toronto Press).

Schultz, B. and Varouxakis, G. (eds) (2005) *Utilitarianism and Empire* (Lanham: Lexington Books).

Ten, C.L. (1998) 'Democracy, Socialism, and the Working Classes,' in *The Cambridge Companion to Mill*, J. Skorupski (ed.) (Cambridge: Cambridge University Press).

Tunick, M. (2006) 'Tolerant Imperialism: John Stuart Mill's Defense of British Rule in India,' *The Review of Politics*, 68(4), 586–611.

Varouxakis, G. (2005) 'Empire, Race, Euro-centrism: John Stuart Mill and His Critics,' in *Utilitarianism and Empire*, B. Schultz and G. Varouxakis (eds) (Lanham: Lexington Books).

Wilson, A.N. (2003) *The Victorians* (London: Arrow Books).

Zastoupil, L. (1994) *John Stuart Mill in India* (Stanford: Stanford University Press).

9
The Objection from Justice and the Conceptual/Substantive Distinction

Leonard Kahn

1 Introduction

I begin this chapter by outlining Mill's thinking about why justice is a problem for utilitarians. Next, I turn to Mill's own account of justice and explain its connection with rights, perfect duties, and harms. I then examine David Lyons's answer to the question of how Mill's account is meant to answer the Weak Objection from Justice. Lyons maintains that Mill's account of justice has both a conceptual side and a substantive side. The former provides an analysis of such concepts as 'justice' and 'rights.' The latter, based on the Principle of Utility, provides an explanation of when these concepts apply. As a result, utilitarians can allow for circumstances in which actions are wrong because they are unjust, while also claiming that the standards of right and wrong (as well as justice and injustice) are determined by the Principle of Utility.

However, the main thesis of this chapter is that Lyons's interpretation is flawed. The distinction between the conceptual and the substantive levels of Mill's thinking does not hold up to scrutiny, and, even if it did, it would not support Lyons's reading of Mill. It would, instead, support a debunking interpretation of justice, an interpretation recently explored by Roger Crisp. Such a debunking interpretation suggests a very different response to the Weak Objection from Justice, one that many, but not all, utilitarians will find unwelcome.

2 Why justice?

Chapter V of John Stuart Mill's *Utilitarianism* is largely given over to a discussion of justice. It is worth asking at the outset *why* Mill wanted to say anything at all about this topic. This question might strike one as odd. Mill was, after all, a philosopher, and philosophers have been debating the nature of justice since the time of Socrates. More to the point, Mill wrote extensively on moral, political, and legal philosophy as well as on what we would now think of as epistemology, metaphysics, the philosophy of mind, the philosophy of language, the philosophy of science, and the philosophy of logic. And this astounding body of work was only one facet of Mill's career. He was also an economist, and his *Principles of Political Economy* went through seven editions during his lifetime and thirty-two editions in all. Mill's *Principles* has, quite reasonably, been called 'the standard economics work of the century' (Reeves, 2007, p. 212). Furthermore, Mill was a journalist, editor, and publisher. He wrote popular works on almost every political and social question of his day, and he founded the *London Review* in 1834, merged it with *Westminster Review* two years later, and ran it until 1851 as a forum for reformist and radical ideas. Again, Mill was a high-ranking public administrator. He spent a professional lifetime working for the British East India Company and rising to the second-highest position within the company. Yet further, Mill was both a politician and an activist. He served for three years as a Member of Parliament and for decades as a champion of women's rights at a time when this cause was regularly dismissed as a fantasy – or worse. Given this background, one might ask: why *wouldn't* someone who was a philosopher, an economist, a journalist, a civil servant, an elected politician, and a social activist write about justice? Indeed, the right question to ask might be: 'Why didn't Mill write *more* about the topic?' All that said, Mill had a quite specific aim in mind in Chapter V. Mill tells us that he means to remove what he sometimes calls 'one of the strongest obstacles' (CW X, p. 240) to utilitarianism and at other times goes so far as to label 'the only real difficulty in the utilitarian theory of morals' (CW X, p. 259).

In order to see why justice is supposed to be problematic for utilitarianism, a bit of background is in order. To begin with, let me distinguish, quite roughly, between what I shall call 'minimal' and 'maximal' understandings of utilitarianism. A minimal understanding of utilitarianism denotes the theory in a form that all and only utilitarians would accept; a maximal understanding picks out the theory in a more specific way that many, but never all, utilitarians would, at least in part, reject. Mill's usual statements of utilitarianism are decidedly minimal in nature. For example, Mill calls utilitarianism 'The creed which accepts as the foundation of morals, Utility, or the Greatest Happiness Principle' (CW X, p. 210), and he defines this principle (usually called the 'Principle of Utility') as follows: 'actions are right in proportion as they tend to promote happiness, wrong as they tend to produce the reverse of happiness' (CW X, p. 210). It will be useful to have a slightly more formal statement of this principle:

> The Principle of Utility: Whether or not it is right for agent A to do action F in circumstances C is solely a function of the happiness produced by A's doing F in C.

Mill sometimes refers to this as 'the general principle to which all rules of practice ought to conform' (CW VIII, p. 951). While the minimal understanding of utilitarianism has its uses, it leaves many important questions unanswered. Perhaps the most pressing of these is: 'In precisely what manner is rightness and wrongness a function of happiness?' What is needed in order to answer this question is a maximal understanding of the theory. Now, the most widely discussed maximal understandings of utilitarianism in recent times are:

> Act Utilitarianism – It is right for A to do F in C if and only if A's doing F produces at least as much good as an alternative action which A could have done in F.

and

> Rule Utilitarianism – It is right for A to do F in C if and only if A's doing F is in accordance with a set of rules which would, if internalized by all, produce more happiness than any other.[1]

A great deal of ink has been spilled over the question of whether act utilitarianism, rule utilitarianism, or something else altogether is the maximal understanding of utilitarianism that Mill accepted (or *should* have accepted). Despite the scholarly acumen and ingenuity exercised on all sides of this debate, I do not believe that we yet have an entirely convincing answer to this question. Even after more than fifty years of debate, it is still possible for two authors in the same volume to disagree deeply about the matter. For example, in one such volume Alan Fuchs maintains that Mill 'generally regards morally right actions as those specified by the rules of the rule utilitarian ideal code' (2006, p. 156), while Wayne Sumner claims that 'Mill had some other role for rules in mind' – namely 'to act as an indirect guide to action in lieu of the Principle of Utility itself' (2006, p. 194). Another such volume is this one.[2] So we can be thankful that a minimal understanding of utilitarianism is sufficient for seeing why justice is, or is supposed to be, problematic for the theory in general, as I shall explain in a moment. For this reason, I shall get past still contentious questions about Mill's maximal understanding utilitarianism here in the simplest manner possible: by ignoring them. Instead, I shall attribute nothing more specific to Mill's version of utilitarianism than the Principle of Utility as stated above.[3]

It is worth puzzling for a moment over Mill's comment that justice has raised problems for utilitarians, not only in Mill's time but in 'all ages of speculation' (CW X, p. 240). For it seems natural to think of utilitarianism as a thoroughly modern doctrine. Of course, this is not to say that the Principle of Utility does not predate Mill. Jeremy Bentham, for example, described himself, in *The Rationale of Judicial Evidence: Especially Applied to English Practice*, as holding the view that 'the only sources and tests of right and wrong [are] human suffering and enjoyment, pain and pleasure' ([1827] 2010, p. 120). But Bentham was only a generation older than Mill. How much farther back can utilitarianism be said to go? In answering this question, it is fair to note that the Principle of Utility has its antecedents as well. Bentham might have encountered an earlier formulation of it in Cesare Beccaria's *Essay on Crimes and Punishments* (first published in English translation in 1767) or Joseph Priestly's *The First Principles of Government and the Nature of Political, Civil and Religious Liberty* (first published in 1768). It was Karl Marx ([1867] 1995, p. 488), no friend of utilitarianism, who traced the Principle of Utility, in one form or another, back to Claude Adrien Helvétius, whose *De l'esprit* (originally published in 1758) Bentham read in 1768. Moreover, Bentham certainly took over the term 'utility' from Helvétius as well as David Hume (1739/1740), though he later came to regret it, since Bentham used the term more narrowly than his predecessors (Dinwiddy, 1989, p. 26). Nevertheless, even if we suppose that Mill was claiming all of these earlier thinkers as utilitarians when writing this passage, it hardly warrants confidence in his talk of the theory as existing in '*all* ages of speculation' (italics added).

In order to try to solve this puzzle, let me suggest that in this passage Mill is running together utilitarianism and hedonism. Why might he do so? We should recall that, at the time that Mill wrote *Utilitarianism*, almost everyone who considered him- or herself a utilitarian also considered him- or herself a hedonist.[4] So, from a dialectical point of view, making a distinction between utilitarianism and hedonism would not seem to be especially important to Mill, especially in this context. Indeed, Mill appears to blur the differences between utilitarianism and hedonism elsewhere as well. For example, when Mill presents the

Principle of Utility in Chapter II of *Utilitarianism* he immediately follows it with a commitment to hedonism, telling us that 'By happiness is intended pleasure, and the absence of pain; by unhappiness, pain, and the privation of pleasure' (CW X, p. 210). Mill also speaks casually of a range of writers 'from Epicurus to Bentham' as holding 'the theory of utility,' when it is clear that he has hedonism, not utilitarianism, in mind (CW X, p. 209).[5] So it is quite plausible that Mill conflates utilitarianism and hedonism at the beginning of Chapter V as well. Of course, it would be a serious mistake for one of our contemporaries to run these theories together in this way. For it has become clear since Mill's day that one can be a utilitarian about right and wrong action without being a hedonist about happiness and value, and, by the same token, one can be a hedonist without being a utilitarian.[6] Nevertheless, we can put aside this matter for now, since the objection from justice I shall discuss raises no special problems for hedonism and does not in any way depend on understanding utilitarianism in hedonistic terms.[7]

3 The objection(s) from justice

Let us return to the main theme of this chapter. Why did Mill think of justice as 'one of the strongest obstacles' (CW X, p. 240) to utilitarianism? Certainly, many since Mill have thought he was right, most influentially, perhaps, John Rawls ([1971] 1999, especially pp. 19–24). John Skorupski puts it this way: 'the question of justice ... presents the acutest challenge to aggregate utilitarianism. It is here that the coherence of Mill's ethical and political outlook faces its severest, and most significant, test' (1989, p. 328). Similarly, David Lyons claims that 'most critics of utilitarianism see justice as its Achilles' heel. Indeed, we tend to think of utilitarians as having no appreciable account of social justice, and thus as neglecting the most important aspect of morality' (1994, p. 68).[8]

But what exactly is this problem (which I shall hereafter call the 'objection from justice' or simply 'OJ')? Michael Sandel's answer is that utilitarianism 'makes justice and rights a matter of calculation, not principle' (2009, p. 260).[9] The answer which Sandel offers is essentially correct, though it is the victim of somewhat ambiguous phraseology. The worry is not that utilitarianism denies that justice is a matter of principle in the technical sense of 'principle.' For, as we just saw, utilitarians *do* hold that, one way or another, everything, including justice, is answerable to the Principle of Utility. Rather, the real worry is that utilitarianism denies that justice is a matter of principle in a sense of the term more familiar in ordinary language. The idea here is that justice is a matter of reliable rules which are not contingent upon the exigencies of the circumstances. In Mill's own language, OJ holds that justice is not simply a matter of 'General Expediency' (CW X, p. 240).

Now, we must recall that Mill addresses the matter of expediency earlier in *Utilitarianism*. However, when Mill took up the matter in Chapter II, he was concerned not with the confusion of expediency and justice but rather with the confusion between expediency and right action more generally. Opponents of utilitarianism, Mill explains there, try to score a quick victory by moving [i] from the Principle of Utility to expediency and [ii] from expediency to wrong action and, therefore, [iii] from the Principle of Utility to wrong action. As Mill hints in Chapter II and explains more fully in Chapter V, there is indeed an important relation between the Principle of Utility and expediency, even though the relation is not identity. However, what is vital to note, Mill thinks, is that the sense of 'expediency' in [i] is not synonymous with the sense of 'expediency' in [ii], so the inference to [iii] is invalid. In [i], 'expediency' is what Lyons calls 'Mill's general term for the evaluation of actions in general' (1994, p. 51). So it is no surprise to learn that Mill thinks that what is in conformity with the Principle of Utility is what is expedient in this sense of the term. However, Mill thinks that there is another sense of 'expediency' which 'is opposed to the Right' (CW X, p. 223). It is this latter sense that is at stake in [ii]. Mill tells us that 'expediency' in this context 'generally means that which is expedient for the particular interest of the agent himself; as when a minister sacrifices the interests of his country to keep himself in place.' As we might put it today, the expedient in this sense is what has agent-relative instrumental value. That which is expedient provides (or tends to provide) that which is beneficial to the agent – even if it harms others. However, no utilitarian holds that the Principle of Utility permits (much less requires) that one seek such agent-relative instrumental value at the cost of overall utility and, therefore, of right action. Quite the contrary! So it is no surprise to learn that Mill thinks that what is expedient in this sense need not be in conformity with the Principle of Utility. Indeed, Mill tells us, 'if the principle of utility is good for anything, it must be good for weighing these conflicting utilities against one another, and marking out the region within which one or the other preponderates' (CW X, p. 223). In short, the argument against utilitarianism in Chapter II is guilty of equivocation.

In Chapter V, Mill has a very different kind of challenge in mind. More specifically, he is thinking of

> The Objection from Justice, Strong Version (Strong OJ): According to utilitarianism, the ultimate criterion of right and wrong is the Principle of Utility. But justice is the ultimate criterion of right and wrong. So utilitarianism is incorrect.

Strong OJ is in many ways a familiar-looking criticism to contemporary readers. Consider the following two thought experiments:

> Switch – A trolley is out of control and will run over and kill five innocent people if you do nothing. However, you are standing next to a trolley track switch. If you throw the switch, then you will divert the trolley onto a secondary set of tracks and, as a result, save these five people. But there is another innocent person on the secondary set of tracks, and if you flip the switch, then he will be run over and killed.
>
> Bridge – A trolley is out of control and will run over and kill five innocent people if you do nothing. However, you are standing next to a very large man, and both of you are on a bridge above the tracks. If you push the large man onto the tracks, then you will thereby stop the trolley and save these five people. But the large man will be run over and killed.[10]

The thought here is that in Switch the right thing to do is to throw the trolley-track switch and save the five innocent people, but in Bridge the right thing is to leave the large man alone, even though five innocent people will die if you do not. Why? It is at this point that the criticism that Mill is engaged with diverges from the kind of criticism which attracts the attention of *some* contemporary critics. For, according to the criticism Mill worries about, it would be *unjust* to push the large man on to the tracks. However, utilitarianism, the objection has it, is committed to saying that, on the contrary, it would be unjust not to save the five innocent people in both Switch and Bridge. Since this response is incorrect, utilitarianism is not the correct moral theory.[11]

Nevertheless, it is hard not to notice a simple but devastating reply to Strong OJ. Its second premise is that justice is *the* criterion of right and wrong. Mill clearly conceives of the premise in this way, characterizing it as holding that 'justice [is] totally independent of utility, and [is] a standard *per se*, which the mind can recognise by simple introspection of itself' (CW X, p. 251). Hence, anyone who accepts Strong OJ must also accept that any action is right if and only if it is just and wrong if and only if it is unjust. But surely it is a mistake to accept this result. For it simply blurs the line between, say, justice and virtues such as charity and mercy. So goes the reply.

Now, Mill certainly gives serious thought in Chapter V of *Utilitarianism* to the distinction between moral duties involving justice and moral duties which are independent of justice. Nevertheless, this is not his response to Strong OJ. And that is probably just as well, since there is a less problematic version of the objection which avoids this response while still offering support for criticisms such as those based on Switch and Bridge.

> The Objection from Justice, Weak Version (Weak OJ): According to utilitarianism, the ultimate criterion of right and wrong is the Principle of Utility. But in at least some cases, actions are right or wrong because they are just, not because of their relation to the Principle of Utility. So utilitarianism is incorrect.

Those who accept Weak OJ are not committed to the claim that any action is right if and only if it is just, and wrong if and only if it is unjust. They are only committed to the weaker and more reasonable claim that at least some actions are both right because they are just, and some other actions are both wrong because they are unjust.

4 Lyons's interpretation of Mill's response

How should we understand Mill's response to Weak OJ? As is so often the case, controversy lurks in every shadow, but this much is *not* disputed: Mill provides an account, from the ground up, of what justice is. In particular, he attempts 'to ascertain what is the distinguishing character of justice, or of injustice: what is the quality, or whether there is any quality, attributed in common to all modes of conduct designated as unjust (for justice, like many other moral attributes, is best defined by its opposite), and distinguishing them from such modes of conduct as are disapproved, but without having that particular epithet of disapprobation applied to them' (CW X, p. 241). Here, Mill attempts to determine what all and only just things have in common and what all and only unjust things have in common. I say 'things' as something of a hedge. Mill is not finicky about what kind of entity can or cannot properly be called just or unjust. He somewhat sweepingly classifies these entities as 'the various modes of action, and arrangements of human affairs'

(CW X, p. 241) and appears, as he often does, to be leaving his options open when it comes to using an important predicate. Furthermore, Mill appears to see no relationship of priority between these actions and arrangements. He does not seem to think that actions are called just or unjust only because of their relationship with institutional arrangements or vice versa. In general, I shall follow Mill in speaking loosely about the proper subject of the terms 'just' and 'unjust,' since it does not lead to any significant mischief.

Yet we still need to know *why* Mill's story about justice is supposed to vindicate utilitarianism from Weak OJ. And here Mill's approach is open to rival interpretations. Lyons provides one ingenious and influential interpretation, an interpretation which has two main steps. First, Lyons argues that there is 'a division in Mill's philosophy between analysis and justification' (1994, p. 78). According to Lyons, Mill provides, on the one hand, an account of justice, rights, and morality generally that is purely 'conceptual,' and, on the other hand, an account of how the Principle of Utility determines the application of these concepts that is 'substantive' rather than conceptual (1994, pp. 19, 51, 57, 64–5, 71, 79, 82, 131–2, and 137). So 'Mill's basic theory of morality and justice do not assume utilitarianism,' Lyons tells us (1994, p. 51). In fact, 'This analysis makes no reference to utility;' rather, 'To *use* such analyses ... one must appeal to substantive values' (1994, p. 78, italics added). So, according to Mill, the Principle of Utility applies indirectly, not directly, to actions. As Lyons puts it,

> [Mill] is committed to the end of happiness, and to evaluating all other things that may serve as means to it accordingly. From this it does not follow that he requires each person always to maximize utility. What he wishes is for us to choose our means most wisely to serve the end of happiness. (1994, p. 64)

Lyons's second step is to argue that, because the Principle of Utility applies indirectly, not directly, to our actions, Weak OJ fails. Justice is not, according to the utilitarian, simply a matter of calculation. It is a matter of principle, despite what Sandel and company say. However, these principles are not free-floating or grounded in something nonutilitarian. They themselves are determined, ultimately, by the Principle of Utility.

In Section 5 of this chapter, I turn a critical eye on this interpretation. But for now, let us consider how Mill attempts to determine what is essential to justice and injustice, since this is central to both the case for and the case against Lyons's interpretation. Begin, however, with the *genus* into which the class of all just and unjust actions falls, the class of morally right and wrong actions. How should one try to determine matters such as these? 'To find the common attributes of a variety of objects, it is necessary to begin by surveying the objects themselves in the concrete' (CW X, p. 241). In particular, Mill tells us that

> If in everything which men are accustomed to characterise as just or unjust, some one common attribute or collection of attributes is always present, we may judge whether this particular attribute or combination of attributes would be capable of gathering round it a sentiment of that peculiar character and intensity by virtue of the general laws of our emotional constitution, or whether the sentiment is inexplicable, and requires to be regarded as a special provision of Nature. If we find the former to be the case, we shall, in resolving this question, have resolved also the main problem: if the latter, we shall have to seek for some other mode of investigating it. (CW X, p. 241)

Turning to the matter of right and wrong, Mill tells us that

> [W]e call any conduct wrong, or employ, instead, some other term of dislike or disparagement, according as we think that the person ought, or ought not, to be punished for it; and we say, it would be right, to do so and so, or merely that it would be desirable or laudable, according as we would wish to see the person whom it concerns, compelled, or only persuaded and exhorted, to act in that manner. (CW X, p. 246)

It is this which is 'at the bottom of the notions of right and wrong.' A little more specifically,

[1] It is wrong (i.e., impermissible) for A to F in C if and only if A ought to be punished in some way for doing F in C.
[2] It is right (i.e., permissible) for A to F in C if and only if it is not wrong for A to F in C.

However, this criterion is 'the characteristic difference which marks off, not justice, but morality in general' (CW X, pp. 241–2). So we need to go deeper to find, as it were, not only the *genus* but also the *differentia* of justice on Mill's account.

Mill's thinking on this matter is compressed and requires considerable unpacking. He begins with the simple idea that an action is just if and only if it violates someone's legal right, that is, with violations of a person's 'personal liberty, his property, or any other thing which belongs to him by law' (CW X, p. 241). It is worth noting that this is an understanding of injustice that applies much more comfortably to individual actions and individuals more generally than it does to state actions and states. An individual cannot, generally speaking, avoid violating the legal rights of another by nullifying a law that protects that person, by invalidating a contract that guarantees the receipt of some good, and so on. But, at least in principle, a state could act this way. Perhaps Mill can make room for the possibility of a state violating elements of a system of customary law, such as the English common law. It would seem that a state lacks the right sort of authority to void the laws of such a system arbitrarily, at least under ordinary conditions. Still, this understanding of justice does provide far less protection against a state than it would against an individual and a substate group, particularly where such customary law does not exist.

Nevertheless, Mill almost immediately rejects the idea that an action is unjust if and only if it violates only a *legal* right. For

> the legal rights of which he is deprived, may be rights which ought not to have belonged to him; in other words, the law which confers on him these rights, may be a bad law. (CW X, p. 242)

If it is, then 'opinions will differ as to the justice or injustice of infringing' legal rights. That is to say, judgments about the injustice of violating a legal right depend in part on whether the law that confers this right is a 'bad law.' If such a law is bad, then the violation will not constitute an injustice. Yet this point prompts the following response. On the one hand, Mill asserts that an act does not count as unjust if the prohibition against it is supported only by a bad law. On the other hand, he (at least initially) omits the claim that a bad law *failing* to provide a prohibition of an action appears to have no relevance to whether an action is just or unjust. For example, if you assault me, and the law fails to prohibit assault against me simply because I am Irish, your action does not count as unjust. Such a conception of justice appears not to have moved far enough away from the law and unfairly privileges what merely happens to be in the legal code. However, it seems likely that Mill is only being slightly careless when he first moves from talk of legal rights to talk of moral rights. Later in *Utilitarianism*, he writes, 'it seems to be universally admitted that there may be unjust laws, and that law, consequently, is not the ultimate criterion of justice, but may give to one person a benefit, or impose on another an evil, which justice condemns' (CW X p. 242). And, again, he claims that injustice is 'taking or withholding from any person that to which he has a moral right' (CW X, p. 242). So, despite some careless formulations, Mill is not open to the objection that his conception of moral rights does not fully escape the orbit of his conception of legal rights.

But, if Mill's concern is with moral rights, why does he even bother to talk about legal rights? Would not it have been more economical and less confusing to cut out a consideration of legal rights? I think that there are two related motives behind Mill's detour through legal rights. The first of these centers on the relationship between utilitarianism and moral rights. As we have already seen, Mill is, ultimately, defending a moral theory according to which happiness is what determines the rightness and wrongness, as well as the justice and injustice, of actions. The notion of a moral right does not immediately fall out of this tradition, to say the very least. Indeed, though Bentham was not hostile to legal rights, he was a harsh critic of any kind of talk about rights over and above those conferred by law and enforceable by an authority. He famously called them 'pestilential nonsense' and 'nonsense on stilts' (Bentham [1843] 1987, p. 53). So, even though Mill rejected Bentham's parsimony about extralegal rights, it is natural for him to want to trace a path through them in his discussion of justice. Mill's second motive for a discussion of legal rights here concerns a deep source of doubt about the notion of moral rights, a source of doubt that is far more general than the utilitarian tradition. The origin of moral rights is often seen as mysterious at best. It is not only unclear what they are and what they require; it is also a murky matter what provides their foundation. But legal rights and their source are not nearly so obscure. Legal rights are conferred by law. In some cases, this conferral is immediate, as when a law specifies that others cannot, for instance, enter my house without my permission. In other cases, this conferral is mediate, as when a law (or a system of law) allows me to contract with others and puts them under an obligation, for example, to supply me with payment after I have delivered some goods to them. By stressing the connection between moral rights and legal rights, Mill makes the former appear at least a little less mysterious.

What, then, are the necessary and sufficient conditions that separate that which is just from that which is unjust? Mill's answer is more complex than it might first appear. Mill maintains that the 'one common attribute or collection of attributes [which] is always present' in the case of injustice is the violation of someone's moral right (CW X, p. 241). Moreover, he is at pains to explain what such a moral right is. 'When we call anything a person's right,' Mill tells us, 'we mean that he has a valid claim on society to protect him in the possession of it, either by the force of law, or by that of education and opinion. If he has what we consider a sufficient claim, on whatever account, to have something guaranteed to him by society, we say that he has a right to it' (CW X, p. 250).[12] In saying this, Mill seems to commit himself to the following three biconditionals:

[3] A acts unjustly with regard to B if and only if A violates at least one of B's moral rights.
[4] A violates at least one of B's moral rights if and only if A violates a valid claim that B has on society to protect him in possession of X.

Therefore,

[5] A acts unjustly with regard to B if and only if A violates a valid claim that B has on society to protect him in possession of X.

But this leaves us to ask: 'What determines whether one has a valid claim of this sort on society?' I shall return to this point in a moment.

For now I want to touch on the fact that, in giving us necessary and sufficient conditions for justice, Mill relies on several notions *in addition to* that of a moral right. Two more closely aligned ideas are those of duty and obligation. Mill tells us that 'duties of perfect obligation are those duties in virtue of which a correlative right resides in some person or persons; duties of imperfect obligation are those moral obligations which do not give birth to any right' (CW X, p. 246). So Mill seems to embrace several further biconditionals:

[6] A violates at least one of B's moral rights if and only if A violates a perfect duty to B.

We can deduce from [4] and [6] the further claim that

[7] A acts unjustly with regard to B if and only if A violates a perfect duty to B.

Some of Mill's contemporary critics have looked askance at [6] and [7]. Lyons (1994, pp. 136–8) is quite clear that he thinks that rights do not line up with perfect duties. For example, he thinks that, if I am the only person who can save a drowning swimmer, then I have a perfect duty to do so, even though the swimmer does not have a right to be saved by me. However, it is worth noting that Mill is ambivalent about the use of the terms perfect and imperfect duties and calls them 'ill-chosen expressions' (CW X, p. 246). Indeed, Mill seems to accept two different readings of these terms. On the strong reading, Mill thinks of imperfect duties as being such that 'the particular occasions of performing it are left to our choice, as in the case of charity or beneficence, which we are indeed bound to practise, but not towards any definite person, nor at any prescribed time' and perfect duties as being such that we do not have this choice with regard to person and place (CW X, p. 246). On the weak reading, Mill says merely that 'duties of perfect obligation are those duties in virtue of which a correlative right resides in some person or persons; duties of imperfect obligation are those moral obligations which do not give birth to any right' (CW X, p. 246). The problems to which Lyons points follow only if we accept the stronger, rather than the weaker, reading of perfect and imperfect duties, and not much is lost by accepting the weaker.

Mill links yet another of our basic ideas to justice. In each of the cases we call unjust, Mill claims, two things are present: 'a wrong done, and some assignable person who is wronged' (CW X, p. 246). Again, justice involves 'the conception of some definite person who suffers by the infringement; whose rights (to use the expression appropriated to the case) are violated by it' (CW X, p. 250). So

[8] A acts unjustly with regard to B if and only if [i] A acts wrongly and [ii] A wrongs B.

[9] A violates at least one of B's moral rights if and only if [i] A acts wrongly and [ii] A wrongs B.

Here, too, Mill appears to be open to attack. Consider the possibility of free riding, in which one or more individuals help themselves to some social benefit without contributing their fair share to the production and maintenance of whatever brings this benefit into being. Mill himself was clearly aware of this problem (CW III). Plausibly, free riding is unjust, but it is far from clear that it wrongs any one particular person or persons. Moreover, it does not obviously violate anyone's rights. In order to determine whether Mill can avoid this attack, it is useful to move on to a further connection Mill makes.

Mill links a handful of very closely related matters with justice. These are the 'rules,' 'maxims,' 'precepts,' and even 'dictates' of justice. These rules are what 'protect every individual from being harmed by others, either directly or by being hindered in his freedom of pursuing his own good, are at once those which he himself has most at heart' (CW X p. 255). So

[10] A acts unjustly with regard to B if and only if A violates a rule (maxim, etc.) R that protects individuals from harming each other.

Therefore, from [8], [9], and [10]

[11] A violates a rule (maxim, etc.) R that protects individuals from harming each other if and only if [i] A acts wrongly and [ii] A wrongs B.

Furthermore,

[12] A violates at least one of B's moral rights if and only if A violates a rule (maxim, etc.) R that protects individuals from harming each other.

Once we see the connection that Mill makes between harming and wronging, worries about phenomena such as free riding become less urgent. For Mill was also working with a rather liberal conception of harm. 'Injustice,' Mill tells us, 'may also be done by treating a person better than others; but the wrong in this case is to his competitors, who are also assignable persons' (CW X, p. 247). Moreover, 'wrongful interference with each other's freedom' also constitutes harms or 'hurts' (CW X, p. 255). If we read 'wrong' in the same broad way that we seem meant to read 'harm,' then it seems reasonable to conclude that everyone who contributes to a public benefit is wronged by free riders, and everyone's rights are thereby violated by them. Mill was not thinking of free riders when he wrote the following, but it can easily be extended to them:

> He who accepts benefits, and denies a return of them when needed, inflicts a real hurt, by disappointing one of the most natural and reasonable of expectations, and one which he must at least tacitly have encouraged, otherwise the benefits would seldom have been conferred. (CW X, p. 256)

Of course, free riders do not, generally speaking, raise reasonable obligations *directly*, as one might do in a transaction. However, they can be said to do so by accepting the benefit in question. To be sure, this reading of the relevant terms is much broader than that employed by most people today, but it appears to be coherent.

Let me return now to the question of how we should interpret Mill's story about justice as a reply to Weak OJ. Recall that, according to Lyons,

> Mill's division of morality has two aspects. One is a conceptual distinction between justice and other moral obligations. This concerns the idea of justice and, by implication, the rest of morality, but does not tell us much about the substance of justice and non-justice obligations. (1994, p. 110)

Clearly, Lyons thinks that we should understand propositions [1] through [12] as being conceptual, not substantive, in nature. As he puts it, 'The characterization of this sort of argument does not require commitment or even reference to utilitarianism' (1994, p. 80). More generally, 'the analysis itself does not identify or limit the values that might be used in arguing for such protections and thus, in Mill's view, rights' (1994, p. 80). Now, return to the question we put off a moment ago: 'What determines whether one has a valid claim of this sort on society?' Mill's own answer is that, if asked this question, he 'can give him no other reason than general utility' (CW X, p. 250). As Lyons reads this passage, it is only at this point that the Principle of Utility comes into play. Hence, the second aspect of Mill's division of morality is composed of 'the substantive doctrines' which tell us how to apply the concepts analyzed in the first aspect (1994, p. 110). That is to say, 'the moral concepts provide schemas for evaluating conduct *from a moral point of view*' (1994, p, 79, italics in the original).

Earlier we saw the outline of Mill's reply to Weak OJ, at least on Lyons's reading of him. We can now fill out that outline. One of the premises of Weak OJ is that, in at least some cases, actions are right or wrong because they are just, not because of their relation to the Principle of Utility. Given the distinction between conceptual and substantive accounts, this premise is false – indeed, confused. For it is simply untrue that, if an action is wrong because it is unjust, then it is not wrong because of its relation to the Principle of Utility. Quite the opposite. For the very meaning of the terms 'justice' and 'rights' as analyzed above shows us that an action is unjust if and only if it violates someone's moral rights, and it violates someone's moral rights if and only if it transgresses against something for which someone has a valid claim to society's protection. Furthermore, the meaning of the term 'wrong' shows us that, since this protection comes in the form of punishment (and, prior to the act, the threat of punishment), an action is wrong if it violates someone's moral rights and, thereby, is unjust. A utilitarian such as Mill need not deny any of this in order to respond to Weak OJ. Rather, Mill can accept all of this but also, turning to substantive rather than conceptual matters, argue that it is the Principle of Utility which determines what moral rights individuals have. As a result, Mill need not maintain that 'the difference between the just and the Expedient' is 'a merely imaginary distinction' (CW X, p. 254). On the contrary, 'no one of those who profess the most sublime contempt for the consequences of actions as an element in their morality, attaches more importance to the distinction than I do' (CW X, p. 254), Mill tells us.

5 Against Lyons's interpretation

While Lyons's interpretation of Mill 's reply to Weak OJ is inventive and powerful, I think there are some reasons to doubt that it is the best that Mill can do. Let me begin with Lyons's distinction between the conceptual and the substantive. Lyons does not offer a detailed account of either of these categories, though, in fairness to him, doing so in a fully satisfactory manner is more than we could expect in work dedicated to another topic. Nevertheless, it is not immediately obvious what Lyons could mean by claiming that an account of terms such as 'justice' and 'wrong' is conceptual but not substantive. To be sure, one might claim that these terms are not normatively substantive at all. For example, one might argue that they denote certain patterns of behavior that agents, as a matter of fact, observe. But that is certainly not how Mill understands the terms. As we have already seen, Mill understands 'wrong' in terms of what *ought* to be punished, not simply what is punished. Likewise, he understands 'right' in terms of what society *ought* to protect, not simply what it does protect. Lyons even helps himself to this fact on occasion, noting, for example, that 'evaluating conduct from a moral point of view *does not leave it optional* whether to take rights seriously' (1994, p. 79, italics in the original). So, even if one concedes to Lyons that there are concepts that are thoroughly lacking in normative substance, the concepts which Mill discusses do not seem to be among them. In fact, seeing Mill's response to Weak OJ as depending on something like conceptual analysis seems against the spirit of his work as a whole. Mill sets his face against the claim that 'the principles of morals are evident *a priori*, requiring nothing to command assent, except that the meaning of the terms be understood' (CW X, p. 206). Instead, Mill holds that 'right and wrong, as well as truth and falsehood, are questions of observation and experience' (CW X, p. 206).

It is also somewhat confusing what it would mean to assert that Mill's invocation of the Principle of Utility is substantive but not conceptual in any important way. Granted, Mill does not attempt to *define* the Principle in his discussion of justice and related issues. Furthermore, he is quite clear that the Principle cannot be derived from anything more basic:

> It has already been remarked, that questions of ultimate ends do not admit of proof, in the ordinary acceptation of the term. To be incapable of proof by reasoning is common to all first principles; to the first premises of our knowledge, as well as to those of our conduct. (CW X, p. 235)

Granted all of this, Mill appears to draw a number of deep connections between justice, right, and the application of the Principle of Utility. Justice, Mill claims,

> is a name for certain classes of moral rules, which concern the essentials of human well-being more nearly, and are therefore of more absolute obligation, than any other rules for the guidance of life; and the notion which we have found to be of the essence of the idea of justice, that of a right residing in an individual implies and testifies to this more binding obligation (CW X, p. 254).

By calling 'justice' a 'name' he is not thereby falling back into what he disavows: *a priori* analysis. Rather, on Mill's way of thinking, a name is simply that which denotes an object. In particular, Mill sees 'justice' as the nominalization of the adjective 'just' and the adverb 'justly' and, therefore, an abstract singular name. Though 'justice' lacks its own connotation, it does have a meaning by way of the associated connotative terms 'just' and 'justly.' And Mill insists that such connotations have informative content, not merely semantic content. Mill did think that names come to have such connotations by convention, but that is not to say that these conventions are knowable *a priori*. Indeed, that is surely why Mill provides such a long and detailed story about the origins of our thinking about justice in Chapter V. So Mill's account of justice, rights, duties, and the like is not conceptual in the narrow sense of the term familiar from contemporary work on analyticity. But, according to Mill, nothing informative ever is (CW II and III).

However, the account is conceptual in a broader sense, a sense tied up with the questions 'What is justice?' and 'What is virtue?' that have been a deep concern to philosophers since the time of Socrates, as noted in Section 2. So it is no wonder that, speaking of Chapter V, Paragraph 15 of *Utilitarianism*, Lyons notes that 'Mill's way of putting the point in this passage quoted tends to run the conceptual and substantive levels of his division of morality together' (1994, p. 114). Mill was not running these things together; he never divided them to begin with, and he had good reason not to, as we shall see.

Suppose that Lyons were able to offer a distinction between the conceptual and the substantive that was sufficiently sharp to avoid the problems I have just raised. Doing so would, I think, make matters worse. For such a sharp distinction would make problematic the move from the conceptual to the substantive that Mill would ultimately have to make. If justice, rights, and the like have no normative content, then there is no reason why they should, as it were, mediate between the Principle of Utility and our actions. It might be true that the term 'justice' has this or that origin, that it has this or that current use. But why should we care about this matter, except as a matter of idle curiosity? Such purely conceptual truths can tell us nothing about how we ought to act.

In fact, if we understand Mill's account of justice and the like as being purely conceptual we are driven toward a rather different interpretation of his response to Weak OJ. This interpretation is, in Roger Crisp's words, 'debunking' (1997, p. 158). Like Lyons's interpretation, this debunking interpretation also denies the second premise of Weak OJ. But, unlike Lyons's interpretation, it does not assert that this premise contains a false dichotomy. Instead, it simply maintains that it is false because no actions are right or wrong in virtue of the fact that they are just or unjust. Since justice and injustice are conceptual rather than substantive, they cannot determine the substantive question of what is right or wrong to do. If concepts such as justice and injustice are sufficiently entrenched within a society, then one may well be required by the Principle of Utility to take them into consideration. But that no more rehabilitates justice than would the fact that other concepts which are racist or sexist are so entrenched.

In recent work, Crisp has pushed this debunking interpretation to its logical conclusion, though as his own proposal, not as a reading of what Mill himself would have accepted. According to Crisp, we ought to embrace 'the avoidance of moral concepts.'

> Which concepts do I have in mind? At the most general level there are ... the concepts 'right' and 'wrong', where wrongness may be

> understood in terms of what is 'required', 'demanded', or 'forbidden', and rightness in terms of what is 'permitted'. (2006, p. 25)

Furthermore,

> 'Duty' should not be used, nor notions related to supererogation, such as 'going beyond the call of duty' or 'morally praiseworthy'. The concept of moral 'must' is also to be avoided, as are the notions of what is 'morally good' or 'morally bad'. More specific, thicker moral concepts include that of 'moral value', and alleged moral values such as 'fairness', and the concepts of 'virtue' and 'vice' and of individual virtues such as 'justice' and 'generosity'. (2006, p. 25)

This is not the right place to evaluate Crisp's proposal, of course. My point in mentioning it here is simply to show that, even if Lyons's distinction between the evaluative and the substantive is correct, it supports a very different conclusion from Lyons's. The question of how to interpret Mill's response to Weak OJ remains, and we will have to look elsewhere if we hope to answer it.

Notes

1. On the distinction between act utilitarianism and rule utilitarianism, see, for example, Harrod (1936), Toulmin (1950), Harrison (1953), Mabbott (1953), Urmson (1953), Smart (1956), Brandt (1959, 1979, and the essays in 1992), Lyons (1965, 1994), Hare (1981), Parfit (1984), Railton (1984), Brink (1989), Kagan (1989), Riley (1998), Hooker (2000), and Shaw (2000).
2. See the chapters in this book by Brink, Miller, Shaw, and West. Elsewhere, see especially Lyons (1994, pp. 26, 47–65, 75–6, 77, 79, and 82) as well as Urmson (1953), Brown (1974), Berger (1984), Crisp (1997), and Donner (1998).
3. On this point, compare the approaches of both Sumner (1979, p. 100) and Skorupski (1989, pp. 310–15).
4. See, for example, Donner (1998, p. 256).
5. Mill could have traced the line back farther than Epicurus, of course. For example, Vlastos (1975, pp. 386–94) considers the possibility that Democritus was a sort of hedonist. Indeed, Mill would almost certainly have to go this far back if he wanted to make good on this claim about 'all ages of speculation.'
6. The discussion of this point by Parfit (1984, pp. 493–502) is now canonical, though there is a massive literature on the topic that I can only gesture at in this footnote.
7. There is an irony here. For some of Mill's early respondents, including Henry Sidgwick (1907, p. 94 and p. 121) and G.E. Moore (1903, pp. 71–81), believe that his theory of happiness strays so far from his Benthamite origins that it cannot properly be called 'hedonist' at all. At the very least, his thinking on

this subject might, as Roger Crisp puts it, be thought 'to point in a direction away from hedonism' (1997, p. 43). That issue is, however, beyond the scope of this paper.

8. Also see Lyons (1994, pp. 70–1 and 75).
9. Sandel also complains that utilitarianism tries to 'translate all human goods into a single, uniform measure of value, it flattens them, and takes no account of the qualitative differences among them' (2009, p. 260). Though Sandel seems to offer this as a criticism of the utilitarian account of justice, it is probably better to see it as something closer to an attack on the utilitarian account of the good. But, even as such, Sandel's complaint does not seem plausible when it is applied to a sophisticated version of hedonism such as Mill's, as Donner (1993) persuasively argues.
10. See Foot (1967) and Thomson (1976). The literature that has grown up around the so-called 'trolley problem' is far too large to cite here.
11. See especially Kagan (1989) and Unger (1996). Crisp (1997) illustrates OJ using another thought experiment familiar from contemporary ethical theory: the sheriff in the Old West. There are a number of other possibilities as well, of course. There is not much to be said by way of choice among them.
12. This was no slip of the pen on Mill's part. He also avers that no one has a right to F if 'society ought not to take measures for securing it to him, but should leave him to chance, or to his own exertions. Thus, a person is said to have a right to what he can earn in fair professional competition' (CW X, p. 250). Furthermore, if someone has a right to F, then 'society has come under an obligation to provide' him or her with F. Again, 'To have a right, then, is, I conceive, to have something which society ought to defend me in the possession of' (CW X, p. 250).

References

Beccaria, Cesare ([1764] 2010) *Essay on Crimes and Punishments* (New York: Nabu).

Bentham, Jeremy ([1827] 2010) *The Rationale of Judicial Evidence: Especially Applied to English Practice* (New York: Nabu).

Bentham, Jeremy ([1843] 1987) 'Anarchical Fallacies,' in *Nonsense upon Stilts: Bentham, Burke, and Marx on the Rights of Man*, Jeremy Waldron (ed.) (London: Methuen).

Berger, Fred (1984) *Happiness, Justice, and Freedom: The Moral and Political Philosophy of John Stuart Mill* (Los Angeles: University of California Press).

Brandt, R.B. (1959) *Ethical Theory* (Englewood Cliffs, NJ: Prentice-Hall).

Brandt, R.B. (1979) *A Theory of the Good and the Right* (Oxford: Oxford University Press).

Brandt, R.B. (1992) *Morality, Utilitarianism, and Rights* (Cambridge, UK: Cambridge University Press).

Brink, David (1989) *Moral Realism and the Foundations of Ethics* (Cambridge, UK: Cambridge University Press).

Brown, D.G. (1974) 'Mill's Act-Utilitarianism,' *Philosophical Quarterly* 24, 1–12.

Crisp, Roger (1997) *Mill on Utilitarianism* (London: Routledge).

Crisp, Roger (2006) *Reasons and the Good* (Oxford: Oxford University Press).
Dinwiddy, John (1989) *Bentham* (Oxford: Oxford University Press).
Donner, Wendy (1993) *The Liberal Self: John Stuart Mill's Moral and Political Philosophy* (Ithaca: Cornell University Press).
Donner, Wendy (1998) 'Mill's Utilitarianism,' in *The Cambridge Companion to Mill*, John Skorupski (ed.) (Cambridge, UK: Cambridge University Press), pp. 255–92.
Foot, Philippa (1967) 'Abortion and the Doctrine of Double Effect,' *Oxford Review* 5, 28–41.
Fuchs, Alan (2006) 'Mill's Theory of Morally Correct Action,' in *The Blackwell Guide to Mill's Utilitarianism*, Henry West (ed.) (Oxford: Blackwell), pp. 139–58.
Hare (1981) *Moral Thinking: Its Levels, Meaning, and Point* (Oxford: Oxford University Press).
Harrison, J. (1953) 'Utilitarianism, Universalisation, and Our Duty To Be Just,' *Proceedings of the Aristotelian Society* 53, 105–34.
Harrod, R.M. (1936) 'Utilitarianism Revised,' *Mind* 45, 137–56.
Helvétius, Claude Adrien ([1758] 1970) *De l'esprit* (New York: Burt Franklin).
Hooker, Brad (2000) *Ideal Code, Real World* (Oxford: Oxford University Press).
Hume, David ([1739/1740] 2000) *A Treatise of Human Nature*, David Fate Norton and Mary Norton (eds) (Oxford: Oxford University Press).
Kagan, Shelly (1989) *The Limits of Morality* (Oxford: Oxford University Press).
Lyons, David (1965) *Forms and Limits of Utilitarianism* (Oxford: Oxford University Press).
Lyons, David (1994) *Rights, Welfare and Mill's Moral Theory* (Oxford: Oxford University Press).
Mabbott, J.D. (1953) 'Moral Rules,' *Proceedings of the British Academy* 37, 97–117.
Marx, Karl ([1867] 1995) *Capital: An Abridged Edition*, David McLellan (ed.) (Oxford: Oxford World Classics).
Moore, G.E. (1903) *Principia Ethica* (Cambridge, UK: Cambridge University Press).
Parfit, Derek (1984) *Reasons and Persons* (Oxford: Oxford University Press).
Priestley, Joseph ([1768] 2005) *The First Principles of Government and the Nature of Political, Civil and Religious Liberty* (New York: Adamant).
Railton, Peter (1984) 'Alienation, Consequentialism, and the Demands of Morality,' *Philosophy and Public Affairs* 13, 134–71.
Rawls, John ([1971] 1999) *A Theory of Justice*, revised ed. (Cambridge, MA: Harvard University Press).
Reeves, Richard (2007) *John Stuart Mill: Victorian Firebrand* (London: Atlantic).
Riley, Jonathan (1998) *Liberal Utilitarianism: Social Choice Theory and J.S. Mill's Philosophy* (Cambridge, UK: Cambridge University Press).
Robson, J.M. (ed.) (1965) *The Collected Works of John Stuart Mill: Principles of Political Economy Part 2*, Volume III (Toronto: University of Toronto Press).
Robson, J.M. (ed.) (1969) *The Collected Works of John Stuart Mill: Essays on Ethics, Religion, and Society*, Vol. X (Toronto: University of Toronto Press).
Robson, J.M. (ed.) (1974a) *The Collected Works of John Stuart Mill: A System of Logic Ratiocinative and Inductive Part 1*, Vol. VII (Toronto: University of Toronto Press).

Robson, J.M. (ed.) (1974b) *The Collected Works of John Stuart Mill: A System of Logic Ratiocinative and Inductive Part 2*, Vol. VIII (Toronto: University of Toronto Press).

Robson, J.M. (ed.) (1977) *The Collected Works of John Stuart Mill: Essays on Politics and Society* (1977) Vol. XVIII (Toronto: University of Toronto Press).

Sandel, Michael (2009) *Justice: What's the Right Thing to Do?* (New York: Farrar, Straus and Giroux).

Shaw, William (2000) *Contemporary Ethics: Taking Account of Utilitarianism* (Oxford: Blackwell).

Sidgwick, Henry (1907) *The Methods of Ethics*, 7th ed. (London: Macmillan).

Skorupski, John (1989) *John Stuart Mill* (London: Routledge).

Smart, J.J.C. (1956) 'Extreme and Restricted Utilitarianism,' *Philosophical Quarterly* 6, 344–54.

Sumner, Wayne (1979) 'The Good and the Right,' in *New Essays on John Stuart Mill and Utilitarianism*, W.E. Cooper, Kai Nielson, and S.C. Patten (eds) (Guelph: Canadian Philosophical Association), pp. 99–114.

Sumner, Wayne (2006) 'Mill's Theory of Rights,' in *The Blackwell Guide to Mill's Utilitarianism*, Henry West (ed.) (Oxford: Blackwell), pp. 184–98.

Thomson, J.J. (1976) 'Killing, Letting Die, and the Trolley Problem,' *The Monist* 59, 204–17.

Toulmin, S. (1950) *The Place of Reason in Ethics* (Cambridge, UK: Cambridge University Press).

Unger, Peter (1996) *Living High and Letting Die* (Oxford: Oxford University Press).

Urmson, J.O. (1953) 'The Interpretation of the Moral Philosophy of J. S. Mill,' *Philosophical Quarterly* 10, 33–9.

Vlastos, G. (1975) 'Ethics and Physics in Democritus,' in *Studies in Presocratic Philosophy*, Vol. 2, D.J. Furley and R.E. Allen (eds) (Routledge: London), pp. 381–408.

Index

GPSR Compliance
The European Union's (EU) General Product Safety Regulation (GPSR) is a set of rules that requires consumer products to be safe and our obligations to ensure this.

If you have any concerns about our products, you can contact us on

ProductSafety@springernature.com

In case Publisher is established outside the EU, the EU authorized representative is:

Springer Nature Customer Service Center GmbH
Europaplatz 3
69115 Heidelberg, Germany

www.ingramcontent.com/pod-product-compliance
Ingram Content Group UK Ltd.
Pitfield, Milton Keynes, MK11 3LW, UK
UKHW020043040925
462575UK00013B/512
* 9 7 8 1 3 4 9 3 6 6 8 1 1 *